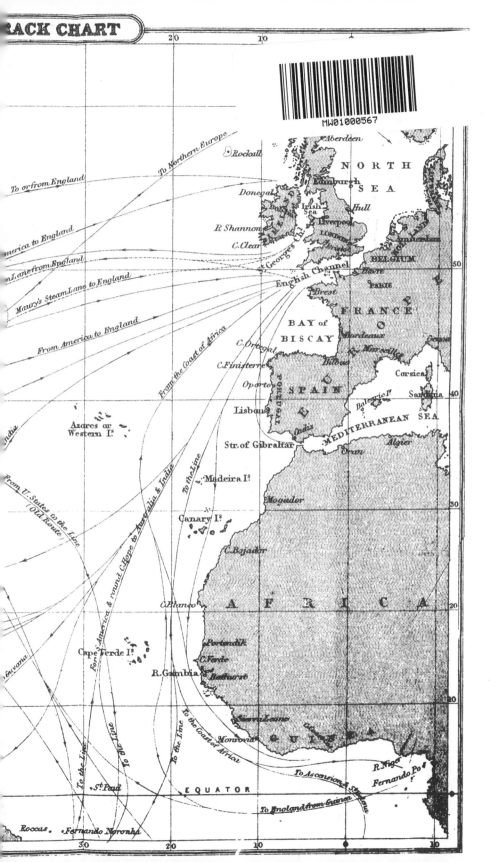

RACK CHART

20 10

Aberdeen

N O R T H
S E A

Rockall

To Northern Europe

To or from England

Donegal

Edinburgh

Hull

America to England

Irish
Sea

Liverpool

R.Shannon

C.Clear

Lane from England

BELGIUM

50

Maury's Steam Lane to England

St.Georges Ch!

English Channel

PARIS

From America to England

Brest

F R A N C E

BAY of
BISCAY

Bordeaux

C.Ortegal

Bilbao

C.Finisterre

Corsica

Oporto

SPAIN

Sardinia

40

Azores or
Western I!

Lisbon

MEDITERRANEAN SEA

Str.of Gibraltar

Oran

Algier

From the Coast of Africa

To the Line

Madeira I!

From U. States to the Line
(Old Route)

Mogador

30

Canary I!

For America & round C.Hope to Australia & India

C.Bojador

Cape Verde I!

C.Blanco

A F R I C A

20

Portadick

C.Verde

R.Gambia

Bathurst

Guyana

10

Sierra Leone

To the Coast of Africa

To the Line

To the Line

Monrovia

G U I N E A

R.Niger

To Ascension & St Helena

Fernando Po

EQUATOR

St Paul

To England from Guinea

Roccas

Fernando Noronha

30 20 10 10

THE AMERICAN MARITIME LIBRARY: VOLUME XII

Captain Blaisdell commissioned artist Richard Faxon
to paint this portrait of his 547-ton, 143-foot ship
Mount Washington at Bordeaux in 1848.
(Courtesy Brick Store Museum)

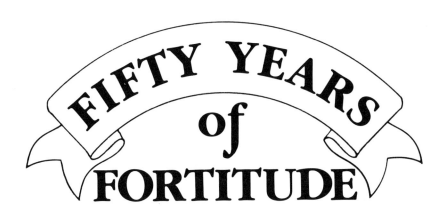

FIFTY YEARS of FORTITUDE

The Maritime Career of
Captain Jotham Blaisdell
of Kennebunk, Maine,
1810-1860

KENDRICK PRICE DAGGETT

1988
Mystic Seaport Museum, Inc.
Mystic, Connecticut

COPYRIGHT © 1988 BY MYSTIC SEAPORT MUSEUM, INC.

Cataloging in Publication Data

Daggett, Kendrick Price, 1951 –

   Fifty years of fortitude: the maritime career of captain Jotham Blaisdell of
   Kennebunk, Maine, 1810–1860.
   Mystic, Conn., Mystic Seaport Museum, Inc., 1988
   xvi, 173 p. illus. 23 cm. (American Maritime Library Series; v.12)
      1. Blaisdell, Jotham, *ca.* 1793–1874. 2. Trade Routes—19th Century.
3. U.S. Commerce—History. 4. Kennebunk, Maine.
HF3023.B5
ISBN 0-913372-43-9

Manufactured in the United States of America

This twelfth volume in The American Maritime Library

Fifty Years of Fortitude

has been composed by Commercial Typographers
and produced by the Anthoensen Press.

To the memory of Abigail Price Daggett

Table of Contents

List of Illustrations

ix

Foreword

THE PURPOSE of the historian should always be to pare away from a subject the natural encrustation of nostalgia and romance laid upon it by the passing of time. In few areas of American history is this distortion more pronounced than in nineteenth-century maritime endeavor. The undenied beauty of the wooden sailing vessel and the romantic appeal of its foreign ports and exotic cargoes have taken precedence in the modern mind over the harsh realities of the business world that spawned the ships and provided employment for generations of mariners.

In *Fifty Years of Fortitude: The Maritime Career of Captain Jotham Blaisdell of Kennebunk, Maine, 1810–1860* Kendrick Daggett has provided a rare and welcome look at the demanding and less-than-romantic life of the men who sailed America's merchant ships during her Golden Age of sail. From the vantage point of Jotham Blaisdell, who went to sea at the age of twelve and eventually became a master employed by William Lord, one of Kennebunk's foremost merchant-shipowners, Daggett has traced a meticulous—in many instances day to day—account of the difficulties and stress inherent in the life of the nineteenth-century mariner. Working with the extensive papers of William Lord at Kennebunk's Brick Store Museum, and the shipmasters' guides that would have been used by Blaisdell himself, Daggett has succeeded in presenting an honest view of the career of the typical master.

The average shipmaster did not follow the lucrative trade routes of the Far East, although it is upon this early trade and the turn-of-the-century masters who pursued it that the romance of the Yankee sea captain and his gleaming white mansion filled with exotic treasures rests. Jotham Blaisdell and others like him sailed the "tramps" and common carriers of the regular trader class. Their cargoes were the raw materials of America, particularly the cotton of the southern states, and Europe's manufactured goods. Such men made a living wage, and the homes they built in New England coastal villages were modest.

Jotham Blaisdell's story is told largely in his own words, indeed in the vernacular and unique orthography of the undereducated man. Daggett quotes liberally from Captain Blaisdell's letters, which are preserved with William Lord's papers. Here is Blaisdell writing to his employers, "Gentlemen, I take this opertunity to Inform you of my arival at leangth, after a teagous Passage of 58 days from Trinidad, of all the Passages that Ever I made this is the Crowner I have ben tempted more then once like old Mr. J Gooch to say almost God." In such letters the nature of the man comes through clearly: his mind, his personality, even his voice. This is not a stereotypical sea captain, but a real man who, with little education, no financial resources, and no marketable skills, chose a career that offered him a chance to make a decent living.

But more important than this portrait of a nineteenth-century mariner is Daggett's presentation of the business world in which he functioned. A shipmaster faced more than the danger and uncertainty of wind and wave. The financial success of a voyage depended on his ability to analyze market values, on his choice of the right cargo and port of destination, and, should disaster strike, on his understanding of maritime law. The vessel's owners and agents could provide him with only general guidance because of limited mail service to distant ports. While native intelligence and experience might help a master deal with the many responsibilities that were his, chance and luck played a large role in the ultimate success or failure of each voyage.

Fifty Years of Fortitude will be of particular importance to the people of the Kennebunks and others who are interested in the business dealings of shipping merchants and shipbuilders in a small New England town. No other book of the many that have been published about the Kennebunks' rich maritime history has presented so graphic a picture of its business side. But this is not a parochial story. Daggett breaks new ground in the study of America's maritime endeavor. Moreover, he points the way to other historians who, working with sets of unified documents like the Lord papers, are wise enough to understand that by presenting the unromantic realities of Jotham Blaisdell's world they will not diminish the glory of the sailing ship but reinforce its enduring appeal.

JOYCE BUTLER
Manuscript Curator
The Brick Store Museum

Preface

THREE DAYS after Christmas in 1805 a twelve-year-old boy named Jotham Blaisdell presented himself in Kennebunk's custom office to be officially entered into the district's registry of seamen. From that day commenced a maritime career which spanned the next fifty-odd years. They were years that saw the boy rise from apprentice seaman to master mariner, growing from a callow youth to a respected graybeard; years that, by the time of his retirement in 1860, had tested him in both body and spirit. However, for the common man the length and richness of a life provide no sure defense against obscurity, and so in the years following his death in 1874 the traits of Jotham's character, the events of his life, and finally his existence itself all faded from the collective memory.

By the time of my first encounter with him, Jotham had receded into a shadowy, obscure figure surviving in a bit of family tradition. The tradition centered on a fine old colonial house which still stands in the Lower Village section of Kennebunk. During my childhood, my mother would occasionally point out the house to me, observing that it had been built by one of our ancestors. While this individual was never given a name or any additional embodiment beyond his role as builder, I never forgot the tradition, and years later it became the catalyst for my research.

As is so often the case when dealing with family tradition, a careful search of the land and probate records housed in the county courthouse revealed our story to be apocryphal. No illustrious ancestor had built the fine old home. However, if the records did not support the tradition they did at least show the basis for it. The house had, for over forty years in the last century, belonged to one Jotham Blaisdell who proved to be a forebear some five generations removed. I now had a name; other facts of Jotham's life were to follow.

Concurrent searches in a local cemetery had located Jotham's toppled and faded gravestone, upon which was engraved in abbreviated form the word that led directly to the writing of this book: Capt. Captain Jotham Blaisdell—the title captain caught both my eye and imagination, calling up romantic images of maritime glory, of an era when vessels launched on her small river carried Kennebunk's name around the world. But beyond the vague embodiment given him by his rank, I still knew as little of Captain Jotham Blaisdell as I had of the legendary builder.

xiii

Further research uncovered the fact that Captain Blaisdell had commanded vessels owned by William Lord. The Lord connection in turn led
me to Kennebunk's Brick Store Museum where I discovered, preserved in the
museum's collection, William Lord's papers. Among them were letters
written by Captain Blaisdell over a span of twenty-two years.

It is regrettable that no portrait or likeness of Jotham has been discovered.
In existing records he is described as having been a strong and active man.
Standing five feet eleven inches, he was taller than many of his contemporaries. His eyes were gray, his hair brown, and as an adult the fair complexion of his youth had become weathered and darkened from his time at sea.
However, while the physical record of the man is inexact, the character
portrait delineated in the letters written to William Lord is very clear. As I
read through them, a narrative evolved that completely laid to rest any half-
formed ideas about nineteenth-century sea captains crossing the oceans on
glorified pleasure cruises with attendant romance and adventure. What did
emerge was the fact that the command of a vessel was an often difficult
position of unending responsibility and ever-present concern.

This story is Captain Blaisdell's, and to the greatest extent possible I have
allowed him to tell it in his own words. I have attempted on my part to
round out the story, filling in gaps and placing the events of his life in the
context of the time. It is my hope that the setting down of the gathered facts
may add a few more pieces to the intricate mosaic that is the past.

As is always the case in an undertaking of this sort, many people and
organizations deserve acknowledgment. I give my sincere thanks to the
following: the Brick Store Museum and its director, Sandy Hubka, for allowing me access to the collection and permission to publish material from it;
Joyce Butler, both in her capacity at the museum and for her generosity in
sharing her research; Mrs. Marion Dutch for helping on the many Saturday
mornings I worked at transcribing the captain's letters; the Kennebunk Free
Library for the use of the Walker Diaries and permission to publish the
photograph from the Kenneth Joy Collection; Mr. Richard Wells for help
with the *Swiss Boy*; Charles Morgan for permission to publish photographs
from his collection; Mystic Seaport, for permission to publish Jotham Blaisdell's letters to Daniel Lord; the Mariners' Museum and the Peabody Museum of Salem for the use of illustrations; Andrew German, for all the advice
and help; and finally my wife Victoria for all her assistance and enthusiasm.

FIFTY YEARS OF FORTITUDE

The small house at right was the boyhood home of Jotham
Blaisdell, from which he ventured forth to sea in 1805.
(Courtesy Kennebunk Free Library, Kenneth Joy Collection)

ONE

Beginnings
1793–1826

SATURDAY, May 16, 1874—Capt. Jotham Blaisdell who lived near the village at the Port, died on the 12th inst. aged 84 [sic] years. He began to go to sea when he was about 12 years of age. Those who know say he was master of a vessel at least 50 years ago and continued to follow the sea until the last 13 years. He was a healthy, strong, and active man admiring to be on the ocean. Although in comfortable circumstances, except in cold weather, he was in the habit of going a fishing alone in a small boat, unless the weather was stormy. He was the son of Jacob Blaisdell of this village who worked in the Iron Works on the Mousam River.[1]

With that laconic entry the town clerk of Kennebunk, Maine, noted the passing of a long and eventful life; a life, however, which neither the writer nor his contemporaries would have viewed as having been extraordinary. For Captain Jotham Blaisdell was but one individual among the now largely forgotten host of men who commanded vessels during the age of sail. Yet his being one of many does not condemn him as a mere cipher. The American essayist Ralph Waldo Emerson made the observation that "there is properly no history; only biography."[2] Not only the great and powerful but also men of humbler destiny must be embraced by Emerson's maxim. The specific events of Captain Blaisdell's personal experience reflect the general conditions of the merchant marine in his time and do much to illustrate the workings of trade and the duties and responsibilities of a master mariner during the first half of the nineteenth century.

One of seven children, Jotham was born in Kennebunk about 1793, the son of Jacob and Susannah (Wakefield) Blaisdell. His father, Jacob, had come to Kennebunk from Kingston, New Hampshire, some twenty years earlier as an organizer of an iron manufacturing scheme. By the time of Jotham's birth the poor quality of the local ore and the raging waters of a spring flood had caused the enterprise to fail, and his father, Jacob Blaisdell, forgeman, had become simply Jacob Blaisdell, laborer. In the reduced circumstances of his family and surroundings, young Jotham's prospects were meager at best.

During the first years of the nineteenth century, as had been the practice in earlier times, boys who had attained the age of twelve or thirteen were often

1

apprenticed in some trade for which they had shown an inclination or apti-
tude. In 1805, when Jotham reached the age of such consideration, he was
sent to sea. In many parts of coastal Maine at that time, a voyage or two to the
islands of the West Indies was seen as an integral part of any youth's upbring-
ing, regardless of what his future occupation might be.[3] In Jotham's case a
career at sea had some real advantages. It was a profession that required little
capital outlay or skill to enter, and a man with some native ability could rise to
the top through hard work and determination. In reality, a life at sea held
more opportunity than did one ashore. Considering the monotony, discomfort, and peril that were often the lot of a seaman, it was a hard reality indeed.

The name and master of the first vessel on which Jotham served are not
known, but there was ample opportunity for a "likely" boy to find a position
on one of the several schooners and brigs that called the Kennebunk River
home. From the closing years of the eighteenth century, the villages of Kennebunk and Kennebunkport had an active and growing maritime industry. Like
other enterprising people along the Maine coast, who under the impetus of
profit managed to build and launch vessels in seemingly difficult and unlikely
places, the citizens of the two communities had turned the Kennebunk River,
their small outlet to the sea, into a doorway that opened on all the world.

The Kennebunk is a shallow tidal river rising about twenty miles inland
from the coast. From its source it snakes its way through a varied landscape of
field and forest. Along its lower reaches it cuts through a meadowland. In
colonial times, lumber cut in the interior woodlands was sent down the river
and landed at the meadows to await shipment to the West Indies. It was at the
Kennebunk Landing, as the area around the meadows came to be called, that
several shipyards sprang up. Using the rise of the tidal waters, and later a lock,
these yards launched a steady stream of vessels into the river. Later, as the size
of the vessels continued to increase, the operations were moved downstream to
yards in Kennebunkport and the Kennebunk Lower Village.

As with their counterparts in countless other large and small New England
ports, the lure of the West Indies inspired the men of the Kennebunks to
construct their small, stout vessels on the unpromising river. The first vessel of
record slid down the ways in 1755,[4] and by 1799 the small port could boast a
fleet of thirty-six craft engaged in trade with the islands of the Caribbean.[5] In
the two decades between 1800 and 1820 their contribution to the region's
merchant marine included thirty ships, ninety-seven brigs, and twenty-seven
schooners, as well as a number of snows, barks, and boats.[6] Sailing from their
home port laden with farm produce, dried fish, and especially local lumber,
these vessels made landfall at such places as St. Thomas, Grenada, and St.
Vincent, returning with cargoes of rum, coffee, molasses, and brown sugar.
The twenty-five arrivals recorded in the Kennebunk customs records for the six
months from July to December 1800 brought into port 82,613 gallons of rum,
24,499 gallons of molasses, 110,092 pounds of brown sugar, 7,576 pounds of
coffee, and 5,651 bushels of salt, on which duties totaling a little more than

$27,000 were collected. By 1812, rates and volume had increased to the point where the amount collected reached $119,850.[7]

The era was a turbulent one, and in 1812 young Blaisdell's career, the growing prosperity of the Kennebunks, and the entire maritime industry of the nation were dealt a severe setback. The blow had been some time in coming. England and France were at war. Both sides wreaked havoc on American shipping, the French seizing ships and cargoes and the British impressing seamen. Attempting to remain completely neutral, the United States retaliated as best it could. First, overseas trade was prohibited by the Embargo Act of 1807, which lasted fourteen months. A policy of non-intercourse replaced the act in 1809. In 1810, Macon's Bill No. 2 lifted the policy of non-intercourse but promised to reinstate it against one power if the other would ease its restrictions on neutral shipping. France saw the opportunity and used the act to her advantage, getting non-intercourse renewed against the British. By 1812, relations between the United States and Great Britain had deteriorated to a state of war.[8]

Starting with the Embargo of 1807, the actions taken by the national government were very unpopular in maritime New England. Even though the interference of the French and English was troublesome, and overseas trade was interrupted at times, it still continued to be a profitable undertaking in the years just before the war.[9] Trade was carried on with the Spanish islands in the Caribbean. Ports on the Baltic Sea were visited more frequently, and trade with Russia became a specialty in the port of Boston.[10] Any curtailment of trade had devastating effects not only on the shipping business, but also on all associated trades, and it cut off the markets for lumber, farm produce, and fish.

With the declaration of war in 1812 virtually all activity in American ports came to a standstill. The reaction in New England was predictable. Although ostensibly the war was to protect and avenge maritime interests, many saw it as only an excuse for the war hawks of the western interior to make a grab for Canada. In the town of Wells, of which Kennebunk was then a part, a poll or vote was taken on the advisability of the United States entering into a war with England. The results—four in favor of war and 246 opposed—reflect the sentiment of New England as a whole.[11]

In the hundreds of coastal communities like the Kennebunks, where prosperity was based upon shipping and its allied trades, the impact of the war was keenly felt. In 1811 fifteen vessels, mostly brigs, were built and launched from the banks of the Kennebunk, but in 1812 only a brig and a sloop were registered at the customhouse.[12] As more and more British ships were seen patrolling the coast, local vessels were moved further up the river for protection, and a fort was erected on the eastern shore near its mouth.[13] For the duration of the war the vessels remained there, partially dismasted and rotting, an outward symbol of the region's economic malady. Unable to follow their customary trades, men turned to other occupations in an attempt to survive.

Shipwrights became housewrights. Sailors who had seldom been long ashore joined the "horse marine" and guided horse or oxen drawn "vessels," loaded with goods that had been smuggled into eastern Maine, over the roads to Boston.[14]   After unsuccessful attempts to send out vessels under the Danish flag, local men turned their energies to privateering. The short and disastrous careers of their two ventures, the *Gleaner* and the *Macdonough*, which were quickly seized and their crews sent to Halifax and Dartmoor, discouraged much further action in that direction.[15] As the war dragged on depression set in, and people got by as best they could while awaiting with stubborn optimism the inevitable better times that the future must always hold.

The Treaty of Ghent, ending the War of 1812, was signed in December of 1814. News of the war's end reached Boston on 13 February 1815 and was carried to Kennebunk the following day. All New England rejoiced at the news, and the reaction of the citizens of the Kennebunks was typical. People gathered and paraded from Kennebunk village to the village at the Port. Bells were rung, flags displayed, cannon fired, and buildings illuminated. The culminating event was a "Grand Peace Ball" at which there were "free libations of rum, gin, brandy, and wine in which male and female indulged to their heart's content."[16]

In 1815 began an era of fifty years now considered the "Golden Age" of the American merchant marine. Maritime New England underwent a renaissance, reaching an apex of activity and prosperity. All along the coast, ports large and small flourished initially. In proof of this was the dramatic revival in the yards on the Kennebunk River. In 1814 only two sloops and two schooners totaling 178 tons were launched; by the end of 1815 twenty-four new vessels with an aggregate capacity of 4,281 tons had been built.[17]

The West India business, freighting, and shipbuilding quickly regained their pre-war momentum, and undoubtedly young Jotham was soon able to resume his interrupted career.[18] At first the West India trade assumed its former place of preeminence, with vessels generally making two or three trips each year. Traditionally, sailing in late December, a master could reach the islands in mid-January and be back in his home port by the last of February to reload and leave again, returning in late April. During the summer months, when yellow fever and hurricanes were a concern, master, crew, and vessel remained in port. In October many owners sent their vessels out on a coasting run or a third voyage to the Caribbean.[19]

However, as the era progressed, the place of importance long held by the West Indies was slowly eroded. In 1820 shipments to the West Indies accounted for 20 percent of America's exports, but just prior to the Civil War the volume had dwindled to a mere 7 percent.[20] In the Kennebunks, as in other areas of Maine and New England, the local stands of timber were showing the effects of over-cutting, reducing both the quality of the lumber and the demand for it in the islands. Just ten years after the Treaty of Ghent the port of Kennebunk had only a few remaining West India trading vessels, and by

1840 only one firm continued in the trade, employing three brigs that made the customary three annual voyages to Puerto Rico and landed their cargoes at Philadelphia, New York, or Boston, returning to Kennebunk in ballast.[21] Eventually, the majority of the vessels registered in Kennebunk were engaged in the freighting business and rarely, if ever, returned to the river on which they were built.

Boston, New York, and Philadelphia were the main ports of entry on the Atlantic Coast, and, for New England, Boston and New York predominated. During the Embargo and the early part of the War of 1812, when foreign trade was almost nonexistent, the coasting trade had continued and was extremely profitable, due to the risk involved. A glimmer of the region's former activity was thus kept alive at Boston, and men with maritime interests were drawn there from their untenable situations in the smaller ports along the coast. It was during the war years that the importance of Boston as a regional maritime center was demonstrated, and after the war her trade grew at the expense of outlying ports.[22] The owners of vessels registered in the myriad smaller ports found in Boston the best market to discharge and sell their cargoes. Many of these smaller satellite ports survived only as shipbuilding centers or through a specialty trade. In terms of imports, Boston was second only to New York, and some satisfaction could be, and was, taken in the fact that New York's merchant and shipping interests were dominated by a great number of transplanted Yankees.

By 1819 Jotham was in Boston, one of the many men drawn by the burgeoning commercial activity of the city's waterfront. At some point during this period he attained the rank of first mate. The mate's berth was often the proving ground for potential masters, building a man's knowledge and character for the eventuality of assuming command. Ideally, the mate was seen by those interested in a vessel as a safe and competent successor to the captain should the need arise in the course of a voyage. On a vessel the mate was the active superintending officer. When working the ship, he commanded the forward part of the vessel from the forecastle, and to the extent practicable the captain when on the quarterdeck would issue any orders to the crew through him. At sea the mate had charge of the larboard watch; the starboard or captain's watch usually falling to the second mate. Navigational skills were of the utmost importance, and the mate honed these when working with the master in the taking of observations and the plotting of courses. The officers of each watch made hourly notations on the log slate concerning such details of the voyage as the vessel's course, her speed, the sail she was under, and the direction of the wind. Once every twenty-four hours the mate copied the information into the logbook. In addition to his sea duties the mate was expected to take care of the ship while in port. He had to keep an account of all cargo received and to supervise its safe stowage.[23] It was a difficult and demanding job. The safety of vessel and crew depended upon the proper execution of orders. Friendship with a master was rare and with the crew unwise, as the mate had to command the respect and often the fear of those under him. Yet, the job did have small rewards in the privileges of somewhat better food and a cabin aft near the captain's, and the ultimate reward for a job well done—the command of a vessel.

While still declaring Boston as his place of residence, the year 1821 found Jotham serving as first mate aboard the Kennebunk brig *Augustus*.[24] The 143-ton *Augustus* had been built in the David Little yard by master carpenter Nathaniel Gilpatrick and registered in November 1820.[25] Her owner, Michael Wise, was a local merchant who had come to Kennebunk shortly after the Revolution, opening a store that dealt in West India goods.[26] As a natural extension of his business interests he expanded into the shipping of goods to and from the West Indies.[27]

Although the *Augustus* was primarily a West Indiaman, trading local commodities such as boards, staves, fish, or leather for the goods Wise needed in his store, changes in routes and ports of call were already in evidence. Instead of the usual direct trip between Maine and the islands, Captain Joseph Wise had the brig and her crew of six at New Orleans in June of 1821.[28] From New Orleans she made her way to Matanzas, Cuba, and then on to Kennebunk with a cargo of thirty-eight hogsheads of molasses.[29]

Upon his return to Kennebunk, Jotham left the *Augustus* to take the mate's berth on a new brig nearing completion at the Landing. Christened the *Florida*, she was built by William Bourne for Hugh McCulloch and his son Adam.[30]

It was said of this period that almost every man with a few thousand dollars or a respectable farm held some interest in shipping. These small investors usually looked to some local entrepreneur to take the lead in organizing ventures. One such man was Hugh McCulloch. Locally known as the most spirited and courageous man of his generation, he had become Kennebunk's wealthiest citizen prior to the War of 1812 on account of his West Indies trade.[31] His comfortable home and position of prominence in the community had mirrored those of the merchant princes of Newburyport, Salem, and Boston, and the same forces that toppled many of them during the war brought ruin to him as well.

In 1811 his capital was invested in two large ships that were roughly twice the size of vessels usually built on the river. One, the 407-ton *Rubicon*, he owned in concert with William Gray of Salem. Not long after her launch she was idled by the British blockade and became a financial loss. The other, a vessel of 479 tons, never left the river and by the war's end had rotted beyond repair.[32]

As principal owner of four new vessels launched in 1815, McCulloch began to rebuild his fortune, but by 1820 his age and ill health brought his son Adam to the forefront. The brig *Florida* was Adam's first principal venture. Carefully groomed by his father, he soon headed a group of investors known as Adam McCulloch and Company.[33] One member of this group was young

Adam McCulloch, Sr., (1794–1869) was the Kennebunk merchant who gave Jotham Blaisdell his first command in 1826. Oil painting, artist unknown. *(Courtesy Brick Store Museum)*

The 258-ton brig *Herschel*, built at Kennebunk in 1822, is representative of the brig *Florida*, aboard which Blaisdell served as mate and master from 1821 to 1834. Watercolor by Ange-Joseph Antoine Roux, 1823. *(Courtesy Peabody Museum of Salem, Massachusetts)*

William Lord, who would waste little time in establishing himself as the district's leading shipping magnate.

The *Florida* was registered in Kennebunk on 8 November 1821. The 236-ton vessel was commanded by Captain Israel Durrell.[34] She carried a crew of six, including Jotham as first mate.[35] Her maiden voyage provided further evidence of the subordinate role the West Indies were assuming in the pattern of shipping, becoming one leg of the journey rather than the ultimate destination. Her owners intended to send the *Florida* south to take advantage of the growing cotton trade.

Maine vessels had carried cotton since 1802, but it was only after 1815 that the trade was pursued with any vigor.[36] In the decade from 1820 to 1830 cotton production in the United States doubled, and 80 percent of the crop was exported to Europe. Profits for cotton growers were high, as was the European demand that encouraged expansion. The freighting rates given made carrying cotton a lucrative business.[37] For a generation after 1815 cotton was the major expansive force in the American economy.[38]

While there was good cargo to be had in Southern ports, there was little demand for the produce the *Florida* might carry out of Kennebunk. Not willing to send the brig south in ballast, the McCullochs looked to the West Indies as a market of long tradition and habit. Sugar, molasses, or some other product of the islands could then be carried to New Orleans for domestic consumption or the re-export market. Following the pattern of old, the *Florida* sailed late in 1821 and arrived at Aux Cayes, Haiti, early in the new year; but instead of returning north she left Haiti for New Orleans, arriving there in early March. Unable to get enough cotton to fill her hold, Captain Durrell took the brig on to Savannah. There the hold was filled and she set sail for Liverpool, arriving in September.[39]

For the following two years, under the command of Captain Durrell, the movements of the *Florida* followed the same pattern. In December she would sail from Kennebunk for the West Indies, and from a port there she would sail on to New Orleans where cotton was loaded and carried to a European market. The practical knowledge Jotham gathered on such voyages would prove invaluable later in his career.

In October of 1824 the *Florida* returned to Kennebunk from Havana in ballast.[40] Captain Durrell had decided to leave her in order to take command of the new brig *Mexico* owned by James Titcomb.[41] Not unreasonably, Jotham may have looked for promotion, but if he did he was disappointed when Adam McCulloch named a Captain Bourne to the post. The change of masters did nothing to alter the routine of the *Florida*: June of 1825 found her in New Orleans loading cotton for Liverpool.[42]

The return passage of the *Florida* brought her back to Kennebunk in September.[43] While ashore during the brig's layover Jotham was married. On 29 September 1825, sixteen-year-old Elizabeth Towne became his wife in a ceremony performed by the Reverend Fletcher of the Second Congregational Church.[44]

Entrusting his bride of little more than a month to the care of his mother, Jotham rejoined the *Florida* and left Kennebunk on the evening of 19 November. The routine departure was marred by tragedy. Five local men had joined with the *Florida*'s crew to aid in clearing the narrow river and getting the brig to sea. For their return to shore a small boat was in tow alongside. Soon the brig was well underway, making six to eight knots. Their task completed, the five jumped from the brig into the waiting boat for the row home. But their weight, combined with a heavy sea and the velocity of the brig, promptly swamped the boat. Despite the frantic efforts of those onboard the *Florida*, one of the men, Charles Brown, slipped beneath the waves and disappeared. The other four men were rescued and returned to shore.[45] The brig continued on her passage despite any mutterings from superstitious seamen.

During 1826 the *Florida* did not make the usual stop in the Caribbean islands. In a passage of twenty-nine days she went from Kennebunk directly to New Orleans. Once in port on the Mississippi she took a coastwise cotton freight to Providence, Rhode Island. From Providence she returned to New Orleans and loaded cotton for Liverpool, which she reached on 14 June. Forty-seven days after concluding her business and leaving England with a cargo of salt and coal, she sailed into Boston Harbor. The month being August, the brig returned to Kennebunk as she did each year at about that season to be refitted and restocked in preparation for another year. Sometime during the fall, Captain Bourne resigned his command and Adam McCulloch decided to entrust the *Florida* to Blaisdell, whose nearly twenty years at sea and seven as mate qualified him well.[46] Jotham's gratitude apparently knew no bounds, as twenty-four years later he would still feel himself under an obligation to the McCulloch family for the promotion.

TWO

The Captain Takes Command
1826–1837

AT THE TIME Captain Blaisdell assumed his first command, vessels in the American merchant marine had become stratified into three general classifications. While a few maintained the traditional function of trading on their owners' accounts, most now found employment carrying cargo in exchange for freight money. Representing the extremes of the spectrum were the tramps and the packets. The tramps, more kindly known as transients, were the plebeians of trade. Sailing between a wide range of ports, without fixed routes or schedules, and prepared to carry any cargo, the only design of their masters was to seek out profitable business and freights wherever they were to be found. The aristocrats of sail, the packets, were the antithesis of the transients in virtually every respect. With their regular sailings on prescribed routes at fixed intervals, they offered dependable service for passengers, mail, and discriminating or demanding shippers. A bit more staid in their movements than the tramps, but of necessity more flexible than the packets, were the regular traders. From season to season these vessels maintained fairly predictable trading patterns between specific ports located on the major sea-lanes, allowing them to establish business contacts and reputations for carrying ability. However, unlike the packets, they might alter their routes in response to reports of a rising market or especially good freights, and sailing dates were always determined by business.[1]

The *Florida* and, with few exceptions, the subsequent vessels Captain Blaisdell would command were common carriers of the regular trader class. Generally the vessels would leave Kennebunk and sail either directly or via the Caribbean to Boston, New York, or more frequently New Orleans. New Orleans proved to be the port of preference. In the late 1820s, with the cotton and sugar of the deep South and the food products of the Ohio Valley coming down the Mississippi River, it became the number two exporting city in the United States. For a time during the late 1830s and early '40s it briefly surpassed New York to become the nation's major exporter.[2] Under optimum conditions, the large volume and variety of goods awaiting shipment would allow the captain greater selectivity in accepting a cargo that was both profit-

9

able to carry and destined for a port where a good return freight was apt to be found.

Following the protocol of time-honored tradition and practicality, Captain Blaisdell sailed from the Kennebunk in December of 1826. By 8 January 1827 the *Florida* was at anchor in the Haitian port of Jeremie. In all likelihood the brig sailed on to New Orleans for cotton, as in June she was spoken on a return passage from Liverpool. She called at Boston the first part of August and a few days later returned to her home port, ending Captain Blaisdell's first voyage as master.[3]

When the *Florida* set sail early in 1828 the captain took her to New Orleans via New York. From the Mississippi the brig was chartered to carry a cargo to the Hanse town of Bremen.[4]

Situated forty-five miles up the River Weser, Bremen lacked some of the geographic advantages of Hamburg, its rival on the Elbe, but the city offset nature's neglect with its reputation for reasonable rates in the handling and shipping of goods. Bremen, Hamburg, and the third Hanse city of Lubeck were the ports of entry through which sundry goods were channeled into the interior sections of Germany. By a treaty of 1827 the United States granted most favored nation privileges not only to vessels built in the Hanseatic Republics, as was customary, but extended the privileges to all vessels owned there. This arrangement would eventually cut most American vessels out of the German trade. During the five years from 1826 to 1830, vessels of United States registry made up fully 70 percent of the arrivals in the port of Bremen, but by 1840 they accounted for only 20 percent of the total.[5]

The Hanse merchants imported a wide variety of manufactured items and all types of West Indian and American produce. Exports included glass, hides, wines, and a broad selection of textiles.[6] For his return passage to the States Captain Blaisdell took on 25,000 bricks, which doubled as ballast and cargo, and then set a course for the Kennebunk.[7]

Returning to her home port in July, the *Florida* remained at anchor throughout the balance of the summer and into the fall. In September, Elizabeth Blaisdell gave birth to her first child, a son who was named Jotham. Assured that his wife and child were doing well, and entrusting them into the care of his mother, Captain Blaisdell boarded the *Florida* and on 20 October sailed for St. Thomas.[8]

For Elizabeth, 1829 was a year of worry and concern. As she waited for letters from her husband she followed his movements in the marine listings of the local paper. In March she read that the *Florida* had experienced very severe weather, losing her stern boat and suffering split sails. The brig had to put in to New York for repairs. In September news drifted back across the Atlantic that while in the English Channel in July, on her way to Hamburg, the *Florida* had collided with another vessel. Repairs were made in Calais. A month later Elizabeth learned that the brig had finally reached her destination.[9]

For the following two years matters carried on fairly routinely. The *Florida* continued to carry cargoes from New Orleans to Europe. Elizabeth continued to scan the paper and await word of her husband, and Jotham continued to write for news of the family he saw so seldom.

As he had done so often in the past, Captain Blaisdell sailed from the Kennebunk for New Orleans early in 1832.[10] He left behind his wife Elizabeth, his three-year-old-son Jotham, and his elderly mother, then seventy-four. During his absence in the following months personal tragedy would intrude on the family in an all-too-common manner. On 16 February young Jotham died. Four weeks later Susannah Blaisdell succumbed to age and infirmity, and her plain rectangular marker soon stood protectively beside the small stone of her grandson. Though the captain's presence at his wife's side would not have altered the course of events, the forfeited consolation of mutual support and the enforced solitary bereavement could only have added to the emotional and physical burdens each carried. It was not until October that the *Florida*, carrying salt and coal from Liverpool, brought Captain Blaisdell back to Kennebunk.[11]

The extent to which the premature death of their son and the passing of his grandmother had shaken the captain and his young wife is a matter of conjecture. He remained at home during November and December, but with the end of the year it was time to sail once more. During 1833, however, and again during 1834, Captain Blaisdell did not make any transatlantic voyages.

After sailing to Port-au-Prince, Haiti, in January of 1833, the *Florida* carried cotton from New Orleans to Providence. In May Captain Blaisdell had the brig back in New Orleans, and after a stop at Richmond she made Boston Harbor in July, ending her year in Kennebunk later that month. Early in the following year the brig sailed from Maine, bound for Jacmel in Haiti. From Jacmel she sailed on to St. Thomas and then to New Orleans. The *Florida* carried her Mississippi cargo to Portsmouth, New Hampshire, where she arrived in April, and after a return to New Orleans she was back at Portsmouth in July. Following a brief stop in Kennebunk at the time of his daughter's birth, Captain Blaisdell took the brig out to Trinidad, Cuba, where a cargo was loaded for Boston and delivered on 29 November. Arriving back in Kennebunk on 11 December 1834, Captain Blaisdell surrendered his command of the brig.[12] The *Florida* would continue to sail until April of 1837. Then being deemed obsolete, she was taken up the river, hauled ashore, and broken up. Her timbers were found to be generally sound after fifteen years, and some of them, along with her anchors, would go into another vessel commanded by Captain Blaisdell.[13]

Leaving the *Florida* and the docks behind him, Captain Blaisdell traveled the short distance to his new home in Kennebunk Lower Village. The house had been purchased that summer, when the captain had returned to be with his wife during her confinement. On 1 August 1834 he had paid $400 for a two-story house and a barn situated on five acres of land.[14] It was to be the

Blaisdells' home for the rest of their married life. It was in their new home that on 22 August the Blaisdell's second child, a girl, had been born and given the name Elizabeth.

Kennebunk Lower Village was part of the town of Kennebunk, but geographically it was more an extension of Kennebunkport, with which it was connected by a drawbridge across the Kennebunk River. A small village of neat clapboarded houses strung along a crossroads and bounded by the river, the little community could boast a school, a church, three stores, and even a saloon. Along the riverfront there were wharves and shipyards.[15]

The captain's stay ashore ended when he took command of the 100-ton coasting schooner *Packet* in February of 1835. Since her launch from the Landing shipyard of Jacob Perkins in 1830, she had worked in the coastwise trade carrying goods to and from Kennebunk, Boston, and ports south.[16]

Vessels employed in the coasting trade far outnumbered those making foreign voyages. In the absence of a rapid and economical overland transport system the coasting trade flourished. Countless smaller vessels, often schooners, carried regional produce to the larger trading centers, where it was sold or exchanged for the goods needed in the home port. Increasingly, coasting vessels were called upon to transport goods and produce between the agricultural West and South and the rapidly industrializing Northeast.

By 15 February 1835 the *Packet* had arrived in Boston and was advertised for Mobile. From Mobile the schooner sailed back up the coast, stopping first in Richmond and then going on to Portland, arriving in that Maine port in May. On 19 May Captain Blaisdell brought the schooner to anchor in the Kennebunk, which he had left four months earlier in the grip of winter and now found in the bloom of spring.[17]

There was little opportunity to enjoy the change of season, however, for in the first week of June the *Packet* was back in Boston. Five days after her arrival she cleared Boston, bound for Port-au-Prince, Haiti. Even a New England spring might pale in comparison with the tropical island of Haiti. Her purple mountains and lush green vegetation were a welcome sight after the weeks at sea. The *Packet* made Port-au-Prince in July. Captain Blaisdell secured a cargo of coffee and logwood and had it back in Boston Harbor on 14 August. Before the month of August was out he was making the short journey from the banks of the Kennebunk to his own front door.[18]

It is possible that Captain Blaisdell accepted command of the *Packet* in an attempt to mitigate the frequency and duration of his absences from home. After a year's service aboard the schooner he found that the amount of time he was able to spend with his family had not increased appreciably, and later evidence shows that the command of a coasting schooner could fulfill neither his professional nor his financial ambitions. For these reasons, and perhaps others, the captain soon left the *Packet* and some time during 1836 became master of the bark *Augusta*.

William Lord (1799–1873) became Kennebunk's most prosperous merchant and Blaisdell's greatest patron. Oil painting by Thomas Badger, 1835. *(Courtesy Brick Store Museum)*

Cadiz, on the Spanish coast northwest of the Strait of Gibraltar. Painted by Noel and printed by H. Schweizer, Paris. *(Courtesy Mariners' Museum, Newport News, Virginia)*

The *Augusta*, a vessel of 303.88 tons, had been built under the direction of Aaron Bourne at the Kennebunk Landing in 1833.[19] Though Captain Blaisdell may have looked upon his command of the bark as a beginning of sorts, it very nearly became his end.

Early in 1837 the *Augusta* sailed south to Baltimore, then on to New Orleans where she loaded cotton for England. Reaching Great Britain in May she discharged her cargo, but was unable to secure a return freight. Blaisdell then decided to sail on to Cadiz, Spain, where he could load salt. On 15 June the *Augusta*, with a crew of ten, sailed from the River Clyde bound for Spain.[20]

Cadiz was considered to be the finest port in Europe and was the leading commercial center of Spain, handling virtually the entire trade of the country. However, for vessels sailing under a foreign flag the discriminatory duties of Spain made it more advantageous to enter her ports in ballast. Since 1820 the Spanish government had levied additional duties ranging from 10 to 50 percent on the produce of other nations when not carried in vessels of Spanish registry. Foreign vessels were also subject to hefty tonnage fees that fluctuated unpredictably. The burden of these charges fell most heavily on American vessels, and in consequence these vessels called at Spanish ports only when no suitable return cargo could be found elsewhere, and when their empty holds insured that they would escape the discriminatory duties.[21]

After taking on salt at Cadiz the bark made ready to return to Boston, and on 15 July she set sail on what was to become her last voyage. Some time out of Cadiz the *Augusta* developed a leak requiring the use of her pumps. From that point on matters rapidly deteriorated. Captain Blaisdell described the disaster in a letter that was printed in the *Kennebunk Gazette*.

On the 5th inst. (August) about latitude 44.50, longitude 51.30 she had one pump going for a leak forward, which had existed for a few days: the wind still blowing fresh and a heavy head swell, making more water than usual, set both pumps going. At 4 P.M. found the leak still increased very much, both pumps going and just able to keep her free. The night was calm and foggy, and all hands were going at the pumps as hard as possible, the leak still gaining. At noon on the 6th, discovered another leak aft, on the larboard side. Cut away the ceiling and two timbers and saw the water pouring in a stream. Found it impossible to stop the leak or even get at it. The leak still increasing, the water rapidly gaining, and the salt fast dissolving. After having duly considered the matter among all hands, came to the resolution of abandoning her, still keeping at the pumps to try and save life. In the afternoon at 6:00 o'clock all hands still striving at the pumps, discovered the French brig Active at anchor fishing. Came to anchor in 45 fathoms of water: got out the boat and put the clothes of the ship's company on board, the crew of the French brig assisting. At 8 P.M. left her with 6 feet of water in her hold. At daylight on Monday the 7th went on board but found it dangerous to stay along side to save anything the Barque having settled on her starboard side nearly to her gunwhale. At 45 minutes past 10 A.M. saw the Augusta sink, her stern being completely blown out at the time.[22]

The scene of the *Augusta* slipping below the surface of the water, and the sight and sound of her stern blowing out, made a deep and lasting impression on Captain Blaisdell. But for the luck of the crippled bark reaching the Grand Banks and the fishing vessels there, a watery grave might well have claimed the crew of the bark.

From the brig *Active*, Captain Blaisdell and five of the crew were transferred to the schooner *Pamlico*. The remainder of the crew went on board the schooner *Harriet Newell*. The men were taken to Truro, Nova Scotia, where they boarded the schooner *Post Boy* and eventually made their way home.[23]

One can only speculate on the thoughts and emotions of the captain as he made the voyage home, not commanding from the deck of the *Augusta*, but as a passenger, having lost the vessel entrusted to his command and care. The *Augusta* had been insured for $15,000, but the cargo was a total loss to the owners.[24]

Whatever the captain's personal feelings respecting the catastrophe, the loss of the *Augusta* was not judged to have occurred through any negligence on his part. The local respect for his integrity and ability remained intact. In proof of this, upon his return he was given command of a new vessel being constructed for Adam McCulloch and his associate William Lord: the brig *Swiss Boy*.

Captain Blaisdell's acquaintance with Adam McCulloch was long standing. How well he knew William Lord is unclear, but from this time, if not sooner, began a friendship and business relationship that continued for the remainder of their lives.

In 1837 William Lord was well on his way to becoming Kennebunk's most prosperous and influential man. He had begun his career in Boston as a clerk in the firm of his brother-in-law. In 1820, at the age of twenty, he had gone into business for himself on Kennebunk's Main Street, and by 1825 he had built the "Brick Store," which is still a landmark today. In that early period he was in partnership with Henry Kingsbury, but in 1827 the partnership was dissolved and Kingsbury became a shipbuilder at the Kennebunk Landing.

After ending his partnership with Kingsbury, Lord gave up operation of the store and concentrated his efforts in creating a local hay trade. Lord bought up all the local hay available and then shipped it to markets where the demand was high. During this time he also began to buy shares in local vessels, many of which were used to transport his hay.

Lord reopened the store in 1830 and continued shipping hay. In 1831 he added banking to his other interests when he bought shares in a bank organized in the nearby town of Saco. In 1832 he also became a moving force in a local venture known as the Mousam Manufacturing Company.[25]

Since the inception of his hay trade in 1828, William Lord had owned shares in various vessels. It was not until 1832, however, that he appeared as a principal owner. In January of 1832 his ship *Neva* was launched from the yard of Bourne and Kingsbury. The *Neva* was followed in 1834 by the bark

Diantha, built in the yard of Robert Smith, Jr. The *Swiss Boy*, under construction in the yard of Bourne and Kingsbury in 1837, was the third vessel in which Lord owned the principal share.[26]

In September 1837 Captain Blaisdell was back in Kennebunk. On the day after Christmas the *Swiss Boy* was registered, and soon after her registration she left on her maiden voyage to New Orleans.

The harbor at Havana, a major port
in the Caribbean sugar trade.
Gleason's Pictorial, 17 December 1853.

Half model of the 258-ton brig *Swiss Boy*, built in
1837 and commanded by Blaisdell from 1837 to 1845.
(Courtesy Brick Store Museum)

THREE

The Brig *Swiss Boy*
1837–1839

BEARING A NAME borrowed from the title of a then popular song, the 258-ton *Swiss Boy* was said to have been built "with but little floor, and quite sharp." Her bowsprit and anchors had all seen previous service, as her owners, in the tradition of thrifty Yankees, had found them still serviceable after breaking up the *Florida* in the spring of the year. Evidently the brig was capable of some speed, as she would be remembered fifty years later for having "outsailed some of the vessels of her time 'as if they laid at anchor.' "[1]

The honor and implied confidence of being entrusted with the command of a vessel on her maiden voyage must have served as a balm to Captain Blaisdell's spirit following the loss of the *Augusta*. His pleasure on the occasion would have been compounded by the fact that his wife was to accompany him on the passage. The presence of a captain's wife on a sailing vessel in the nineteenth century was no novelty, but it was an occurrance that was viewed with varying degrees of approval by those closely involved in maritime pursuits. Daniel Cleaves, a relative and sometime business associate of William Lord, wrote to Lord in 1857 concerning a master's request for his wife to join him. Cleaves's tone indicated that the practice was not encouraged, though it was preferred to the conduct of such masters as Captain Brown, who apparently kept himself supplied with female companions, wife or no. "It seems to be the general custom for masters to either have their wives or 'Lady or Stewardess' a la Brown, one might as well consent at once as it gives a more respectable appearance."[2] In the Blaisdells' case there was only one other known occasion when Elizabeth joined her husband at sea. As with the *Swiss Boy*, it was on the vessel's maiden voyage, and occurred only with the approval of the other owners. The necessity of obtaining the owners' consent was not the main constraint that kept Elizabeth Blaisdell at home. During a very difficult time later in the captain's career William Lord offered to allow Mrs. Blaisdell to join him, but the captain reluctantly refused for the same reason that had prevented him taking her on earlier occasions: their family. By December of 1837 they had two daughters. In addition to Elizabeth, who was then four years old, there was Sarah Ann who had been born in 1835. The little girls remained behind in Kennebunk in the care of relatives.

There was a flurry of activity as Elizabeth supervised the closing-up of the house, the packing, and the settling in of her daughters with their aunt and uncle. At last all was ready. After a tearful farewell, Captain Blaisdell escorted his wife aboard the awaiting brig. The anchor was weighed and the *Swiss Boy* began to edge her way down the river toward the sea. For Captain Blaisdell it was surely a most satisfying time. He not only commanded a new vessel, but had the company of his wife as well. He would eagerly share with her the things that constituted such a large part of his world.

No time was lost in getting the vessel underway, and the *Swiss Boy* sailed on toward New Orleans, a passage that generally took about four weeks to complete. The brig was hailed by an inward bound vessel while off Cape Cod during the first week of January.[3] She made Abaco Light in the Bahamas within a few moments of the captain's reckoning and later nearly foundered in the Gulf of Mexico.[4] On 17 January the *Swiss Boy* made her way up the Mississippi and docked along the levees at New Orleans.[5]

While stevedores loaded the brig's hold with cotton, the Blaisdells could tour New Orleans, a city the captain knew well. Elizabeth would be able to experience firsthand things she had only heard about before, much of which must have seemed a world away from Kennebunk. From the Creole atmosphere of New Orleans the brig sailed to Liverpool, where once again a place long known vicariously to Elizabeth spread before her in reality.[6]

After unloading her cotton the *Swiss Boy* left the island of Britain for the island of Cuba in the Caribbean. During this period, trade with the West Indies as a whole showed a tendency to decline. In contrast to this general trend, American commerce with Cuba was undergoing rapid expansion.[7]

The protective policies of Spain were employed to maintain in Cuba a viable market for European, particularly Spanish, produce. The price of any goods imported into Cuba reflected the cost of transporting them. The greater the distance between the product's point of origin and its eventual market, the greater the amount added to its cost. In the cost of shipping, the United States held a real geographic advantage in relation to Spain, but the mother country countered by imposing stiff duties and charges that fell heavily on American shippers and artificially inflated the cost of their goods.

High import duties, tonnage dues, and port charges caused most American vessels actually to lose money on their outward bound cargoes to Cuba. Shippers often had to draw on homeward cargoes to make up the difference and meet their expenses. The resulting loss was passed along in the price of goods imported from the island. The only real profit to American capital was through the resale or re-export of Cuban raw materials processed in the United States, or the direct carrying of goods from the island to Europe.[8]

While American shipmasters could expect to pay duties up to 50 percent higher than Spaniards on goods whose official values, as fixed by the government, were already inflated, there were inducements for trade with Cuba. They were coffee and molasses. Until her coffee groves were destroyed by a hurricane in 1844, Cuba was one of the most important suppliers of coffee,[9] and from 1820 to 1850 America's demand for coffee more than doubled.[10] The American public was also developing a sweet tooth. The annual per capita consumption of sugar would rise from four pounds in 1821 to twenty-one pounds by 1860.[11] The islands produced great quantities of sugar, but enterprising merchants such as John Bundy Brown of Portland, Maine, developed processes to refine cheaper molasses into sugar.[12] There was an added incentive in the fact that American vessels entering with cargo were exempted from tonnage duties if they intended to carry away a cargo of molasses.[13]

Coming to anchor at Havana, the *Swiss Boy* was boarded by two customs officers. Captain Blaisdell had to present them with two copies of his manifest. These documents listed the name of the vessel, her master, and her port of origin, as well as a careful and detailed accounting of her cargo. The precise time when the mainfests were surrendered had to be noted and countersigned by the attending officers. From that point the captain had twelve hours during which he could call at the customhouse and make any amendments. Once the twelve hour grace period had passed, any goods found on board that were not listed on the manifest were seized. According to the value of these goods, fines were imposed that went up to, and included, confiscation of the vessel.[14] While the brig was discharging her cargo another revenue officer was stationed on board.[15] He was required to make a daily report at the customhouse, for which a fixed fee was charged to the master and owners of the *Swiss Boy*.

From Havana the brig sailed in ballast around to the port of Trinidad on the southern side of the island. There a cargo was loaded for Europe, where orders for its delivery awaited.

It had been nearly eight months since the *Swiss Boy* left the Kennebunk River, and Elizabeth, perhaps realizing she was pregnant, was anxious to return home. The brig's destination did not allow for a stopover in the United States, but an opportunity for her return did present itself off the Bahamas. The *Swiss Boy* hailed a vessel bound for America, and arrangements were quickly made to transfer the captain's wife from the brig.[16] Elizabeth eventually made her way to Kennebunk and her daughters while the captain continued his passage to Europe.

The brig stopped at Cowes on the Isle of Wight in September to pick up delivery orders from the owners, and Captain Blaisdell took the opportunity to send off letters to Kennebunk. On the twelfth he wrote to Adam McCulloch, describing his crossing of the Atlantic.

> I take this opertunity to Inform you of my arival at leangth, after a teagous Passage of 58 days from Trinidad, of all the Passages that Ever I made this is the Crowner I have ben tempted more then once like old Mr. J Gooch to say almost God. I commited a great Error in the first place by beeting up around the Island [Cuba] in stead of going round the South side in the gulf. the course that I took was much the shorter and had I been as fortunate in my winds as from Havanah to

Trinidad I should have shortened my Passage by it. but as it happened [page torn] it. I hapened to take a bad chance. I had strong trade winds to beet against untill I got out of the Passage and then I had it Calm for a long time with a curant against me. whereas if I had gone the other way I should have had the currant with me, but I done of course what I thought for the best. I found my Orders waiting for me at My arival for Antwerp and shall procead thence as soon as the wind permits. I have received no advices from you later then the 18th of may from Mr. Lord. I wish I knew your views respecting my destanation from Antwerp I dont Expect I shall git any return freight. if I dont here from you and dont succead in giting any return freight I think I shall Ether take coals or go to Cadiz for salt, it is verry Strange that I have received no letters from you I think you have written—

It has ben calm her for several days and still remains so I was three days in sight of the Isle of wight before I got in

thinking of nothing more of importance

I remain Gentlemen your Obt servent[17]

Although a captain might command his vessel, in many other respects he was quite helpless. He was at the mercy of the vagaries of wind and weather. The slow and undependable mail service often left the wishes of the owners in doubt. Time and again a shipmaster would have to draw on experience and native ability to make decisions, the results of which were not always desirable. But, as Captain Blaisdell said, "I done of course what I thought for the best."

On 13 September the *Swiss Boy* left Cowes bound for the River Schelde and the city of Antwerp. Before leaving Cowes, Captain Blaisdell had to arrange for the Belgian consul to inspect the vessel and make a notation on the *Swiss Boy*'s manifest that while in port the cargo had remained unbroken. Upon reaching the Schelde the brig stopped at the city of Flushing and took on two customs officers who were required to sail with her to Antwerp. A pilot also came aboard, for Belgian regulations stipulated that no vessel could move or navigate on the river or in its ports without a pilot.

Antwerp was the major commercial center of Belgium. Virtually all the trade of the provinces passed through the hands of her merchants. Her location on the Schelde allowed vessels of any burden to reach the city, and goods were easily transported to and from the interior through an excellent network of canals. Antwerp imported most kinds of West Indian goods, but especially coffee and sugar. After concluding his business the captain prepared the brig for departure. Before the *Swiss Boy* could sail, a certificate of seaworthiness had to be issued by Belgian authorities, but once that formality had been met the brig made her way down the Schelde to Flushing under the guidance of a pilot.[18]

The *Swiss Boy* had left Antwerp on 8 October, and 7 November found her still waiting at Flushing Roads for a favorable wind, a hostage of the weather. She was not alone in her predicament, and while Captain Blaisdell impatiently paced the brig's decks he wrote to Kennebunk describing the situation.

I wrote you from Antwarp previous to my leaving that Port informing you of my being ready for sea bound for the Canary Islands, from thence to New York. and advising you of my having remited £1100, to Messrs. Bearing Brothers & co. wich undoubtly you have used long before the receipt of this, You will no doubt be surprised to find me still at this port. I left Antwarp on the 8th and have ben detained Ever since by strong westerly gales, I am quite discouraged, after making Such a long passage here and then to be detained so long is most to bad but it may be all for the best, & it is useless and a great Sin to murmur I have ben fortunate notwithstanding my delays and it may all turn for the best. the time is not quite so preacious in the freighting business at this season as at any Other, and I hope to be in New York in good time, it greaves me however that I could not have ben there sooner On acount of coming home a few days to see my famaly, but I fear I shall now be deprived of that pleasure, there is a great number of Amarican vessels laying here wind bound the same as my self So[me] have ben here longer then me, amongst them is the ship Gardener Capt Jackson, ship Franklin, Burgess, Barque Tasso, Brig Chipola, Capt Davis, Brig Mars, Capt Bowen, and several others all outward bound & wind bound like my self, the weather has ben verry bad and some heavy gales, On the 30th of Octr it blew a tramendious Gale from the westward in wich I lost the best bower anchor parted the shackle in the ring of the anchor, and after rode out the gale with the old Floridas small anchor, but when it came up it was crooked as a pot hook. there was scarcely a vessel in Flushing Roads but lost anchors.

the sea was so heavy that the Swiss Boy piched her keel out forward all though drawing 10 1/2 ft. of Water, some of the deep vessels that did not part had to slip or founder at their anchors amongst the rest was a duch East Endiaman of a thousand tons deep loaded with sugar, the sea made a clear breach Over her in so much they had to slip two chains and run up the river, the only vessels that bound to the westward that left here since I have ben here was the Ship Madora off & for Charlestown, Brig Grand Turk for N. Orleans & Brig Commerce for Gibralter, they went to sea with the wind ssw and got as far as the downs when it came On a heavy gale & they have ben laying there Ever since, you may rest asured that I shall git to sea as soon as possable and leave this place I hope for the last time for I surely never desire to see it again

the Brig Commerce returned here a few days since after being to sea nine days blowing constant gales and it was with great dificulty he kept off Shore, the Brig Grand Turk that sailed in company with him went into the downs and lost both cables & anchors and went on shore but Expected to git off a great number of vessels have ben lost in the Late gales, two English brigs was seen on the sands by the steamer and it was suposed that all hands was lost, an Amarican brig was seen near the sands in the gales, I have defered writing thinking Every day there would be a chance to go to sea and intended to write you when I sailed but I am now completely discouraged and dispair of Ever gitting another fair wind, I thought possably I mite not be reported and you mite git uneasy about me So I thought I would write now and again when I sailed and I hope if it pleases God that will not be long I feel in hopes to find my anchor again, in case I dont I can git a good anchor for Eight cents per lb. wich is something cheaper then they would be in the downs, I hope if it pleases God to git clear of these confounded average scrapers, for there is seldom any thing gained by them, it is much cheaper to pay a

reasonable price for a chain or anchor then have an average scrape, I shall write
you When I sail, . . .[19]

Having lost his anchor, Blaisdell could have filed an average claim against the
cargo for the value of the anchor. But rather than delay himself further with a
protracted suit, he chose to avoid the "average scrapers" who lived off such
suits and either recover his anchor or purchase a new one. Five days after
having made his excuses, Captain Blaisdell was able to catch a favorable wind
and sail on his way to the Canary Islands. At Port de Cabras he obtained a full
cargo of barilla, an alkali produced by burning marine plants and used for
linen bleaching and hand soap and glass manufacturing. Clearing for New
York, the *Swiss Boy* finally arrived back in the United States on 11 February
1839.[20]

Unlike William Lord's other vessels, whose accounts were handled in Boston
by his agent George Callender, the *Swiss Boy*'s accounts were handled by
Adam McCulloch in Kennebunk. While she was in New York, however, Lord
had another agent for the brig in his older brother Tobias.

Tobias Lord had begun his career at sea. By the age of twenty he was the
commander of the brig *America* in the West India trade. At one time he was
imprisoned by the British for eight months, but managed to escape. Before
the War of 1812, he had built up a business in Kennebunk, which he later
moved to Boston. In Boston he was involved in the West India trade and the
general commission business.

From the end of the war until about 1828 he had been among the most
prominent shipping merchants in Boston. Working in his office at that time
was young George Callender, who went on to become a successful merchant in
his own right, and who would handle the accounts of many of William Lord's
vessels. Following business difficulties in 1830, Tobias Lord had moved on to
New York, where he continued in the commission business and where he
handled the *Swiss Boy* in 1839.[21]

Not long after her arrival, the *Swiss Boy* was ready to sail. Through the
efforts of Tobias Lord, she had taken on a cargo for Havana that included forty-
five drums of fish, 137 pounds of potatoes, and six tons of coal.[22] On 8 March
Captain Blaisdell put to sea; he had been in New York less than two weeks. It
had been a year and three months since he had left Kennebunk on that
December day in 1837.

Besides the overseeing, handling, and management of his vessel, Captain
Blaisdell had to exercise good business sense. Early in his career the owners of
his vessels gave him fairly specific instructions for conducting the business
aspects of each voyage, but as he gained in experience, and especially after he
had become part owner in the vessels he commanded, more of the decision
making was left up to him. In money matters he was very careful and could
never be accused of being a spendthrift.

After the *Swiss Boy* left New York, Tobias Lord complained to his brother William in Kennebunk that he had not received what he considered proper payment for his services. He wrote that Captain Blaisdell

> was well satisfied with my attention to the vessel etc. as he stated to me. Still as his owners were pretty close he feared they would not like it—to pay me the customary commission & objected to about 4/9 of the amount—& as I am situated I wish everyone to be satisfied & I made no further objections than to state that what I had charged was customary & what I always had received—as far as he was interested he said he should be perfectly willing to allow it—I can send you a copy of the accounts if you wish." . . .[23]

While William Lord smoothed his brother's ruffled feathers, the *Swiss Boy* was well on her way to Cuba. After discharging her cargo, Captain Blaisdell took her from Havana to Matanzas, where she took on cargo for England.

By July the brig was unloading in Liverpool. Through agents in that port the captain obtained a return cargo to New York, which he would have to load in London.[24] Finishing his business in Liverpool, he proceeded on to London and had his cargo completely loaded by the end of the month. Then he busied himself finding men to fill out his crew.

In the days of the West India trade a crew would consist of local men, but as the West India trade continued to decline and the transatlantic trades to increase, vessels launched at Kennebunk did not often return to their home port. They worked instead out of Boston, New York, or New Orleans, and service aboard them was no longer attractive to local men. The trend was the same all along the Atlantic seaboard. As opportunities in the nation increased, the demanding life of a seaman lost its appeal, and the quality of crews deteriorated.

As a result, a captain could not know and trust his crew as he once had. When the *Swiss Boy* left New York in March of 1839, she had a crew of nine besides her master. They ranged in age from twenty to thirty-nine and hailed from several different locations. The only Maine native among them was the mate, John Soule, but even he called New York home. The remainder of the crew considered themselves residents of either New York or Philadelphia. They had been born in Massachusetts, Delaware, Pennsylvania, and New York, and two of them were natives of Denmark.

Captain Blaisdell kept this crew intact while in Cuba, and in Liverpool, but at London in July seven of the nine deserted. Only the mate and one sailor remained. Six replacements were signed on at London, a collection of Americans and foreigners who sailed the brig across the Atlantic to New York in September.[25]

The *Swiss Boy* arrived at New York on 16 September with a very mixed cargo, including wine, raisins, white lead, gunpowder, acid, soap, spermaceti, dye stuffs, and 300 tons of chalk. Tobias Lord noted her safe arrival in a letter to his brother. For future reference in cargo decisions he noted that the large fish carried by the *Swiss Boy* to Havana had fetched a better price than did the small ones.[26]

Captain Blaisdell did not tarry long in New York. Leaving the brig in the care of his mate and under the watchful eye of Tobias Lord, he hurried up the coast to Kennebunk and his family. He had been away from home for almost two years. The happy reaction of his family on his arrival can be imagined. There was the joy of his wife Elizabeth and the shy skepticism of the children who now numbered three. Besides Elizabeth and Sarah the Blaisdells had a third daughter, Maria, who may have been conceived during Elizabeth's voyage aboard the *Swiss Boy*. The Captain's stay with is family lasted until November, when he had to rejoin the *Swiss Boy* in New York.

In his absence, the mate had seen to it that the brig was refitted and put in top sailing order. Tobias Lord had been diligently looking for cargo, and once the captain arrived the brig took on 200 tons of paving stones and 200 bales of hay, all bound for New Orleans. In a letter to his brother, Tobias lamented the fact that the rates on the stone had dropped while he waited for the arrival of the captain, but he went on to explain that he had not dared to act without consulting Captain Blaisdell in his capacity as master and part owner.[27]

Loading the brig proved to be a problem. For nine days the wind blew so hard that the lighter transporting the cargo from shore could not maneuver properly to load the brig. A rainy spell followed, which further delayed the loading of the hay.[28] Finally, in mid-December the *Swiss Boy* cleared New York Harbor.

In Boston, at almost the same time, George Callender had been negotiating the insurance policy for the *Swiss Boy* at the Atlantic Insurance Company, which was owned by William Lord's brother-in-law Francis Watts, a former resident of Kennebunkport. The policy that was drawn up seemed to cover all eventualities. Callender reported to William Lord:

> I have effected insurance on the Swiss Boy at Mr. Watts office $12,000 valued at same for one year from the 23d December at 7 1/4% to add 1% if in North Europe from October to 1 March & 2% if in West Indies except Cuba from 15 July to 15 October & to exclude her from the Nova Scotia Coal Trade. The latter clause I think of no consequence as I don't believe you would want to put her into that business. . . . I hope freights will be good enough to make up for the high rates of insurance. If after a few years the offices find they are getting rich by these premiums they will probably have to reduce them.[29]

FOUR

An Unfortunate
and Troublesome Business
1839–1845

MARINE INSURANCE in any age offered to owners and shippers a measure of financial security against the risks to both vessels and cargoes inherent in the prosecution of their voyages. The dangers that lurked were seemingly legion. Perils of the sea included "everything happening to a ship in the course of her voyage by the intermediate act of God without the intervention of human agency," as well as "men of war, fire, enemies, pirates, rovers, thieves, jettisons, letters of mart and countermart, suprisals, takings at sea, arrests, restraints, and detainments of all kings, princes, and people, of what nation, condition, or quality soever; barratry of master or mariners; and all other perils, losses, and misfortunes. . . ."[1] A vessel, the goods or merchandise she carried, and the freight or hire of the ship were all eligible to be insured against any or all of the above risks.

There were two kinds of policies: valued and open. In a valued policy the property was insured for a specific amount and the insurer was liable for no more nor less. In an open policy the property's value was not stated and in the event of a loss its owners had to prove its worth to gain their indemnity.[2]

The policy itself listed in strict detail the particulars: the names of the insured and the underwriters, the names of the vessel and her master, and in a valued policy the amount insured. The contract also had to state specifically what was being insured. If goods or merchandise, the place of their loading and their destination had to be named, as well as the exact times that liability would begin and end. When insuring a vessel where, when, and in what trades she could sail were all spelled out in advance. The perils and risks insured against were also explicitly stated. The amount of the premium and the date of execution rounded out the content of the typical document.[3]

Under the restrictions of her policy as negotiated by Callender in Boston, the *Swiss Boy* continued on her initial passage of the season to New Orleans. As day broke on 26 December the *Swiss Boy* was making her way toward the straits between Cuba and Florida that would bring her into the Gulf of Mexico. The sea grew increasingly restless as the day progressed, and the wind began to pick up, bringing with it intermittent rain. Aboard the *Swiss Boy* the daily round of duties continued as they had since the brig's departure from New York. The threatening weather would have given little cause for concern; Captain Blaisdell had made the passage to New Orleans countless times during the thirty-odd years he had been at sea.

Because of the cloud cover, darkness fell that evening without the benefit of moon or stars. With lanterns lit and watches posted, the *Swiss Boy* labored on her way in what was fast becoming a gale. Suddenly out of the dark loomed the rapidly approaching silhouette of another vessel. In one of those incredible occurrences that seem so unlikely on the wide waters of the sea, the vessel rushed onward, cutting into the bow of the *Swiss Boy*.

A sickening thud and sudden jar that sent all hands sprawling was accompanied by the loud splintering and cracking of breaking timbers. The sound of tearing canvas filled the air as masts and spars came crashing to the deck. For a brief instant time and events whirled in a disjointed blur as captain and crew scrambled to ascertain what had happened.

As it was reported in the Kennebunk newspaper,

> the Brig Swiss Boy, Blaisdell, of this port, from New York for New Orleans was run into on the night of the 28th ult., off and near Stirrup Key, by Ship Wm. Engs, of New Port, R.I.—the night being dark and squally, and the wind blowing a gale from the westward. The Brig had her bow cut near the fore-rigging to the water's edge, beams and deck planks broken, fore and main top mast, top gallant mast and fore-topsail yard carried away, and all the sails attached to them split,—and was completely disabled. The ship remained by the brig 24 hours, when, the gale increasing and the brig being in a sinking condition and near a lee shore, the captain of the ship thought it advisable not to lay by her longer, as he feared for the safety of his own vessel. The crew of the brig refused to remain any longer on board and she was abandoned—Capt. B. and the crew were taken on board the Wm. Engs and landed at Havana.[4]

The reported end of the *Swiss Boy* proved to be premature; although the owners, and Captain Blaisdell in particular, would have ample cause to wish she had sunk. A week after reporting her loss, the paper printed the news that she had been salvaged at sea by another vessel.

The letter quoted in the paper's article was undoubtedly written by Captain Blaisdell from Havana. Although the *William Engs* had not remained to see the *Swiss Boy* actually sink, the captain was sure that in her condition, with a cargo of stone, she inevitably would. Later he would learn that two days after her abandonment the *Swiss Boy* had been sighted by the ship *Junior*, out of Boston. The brig was drifting in a northeasterly direction about eighteen miles off the Bahamian island of Abaco. The captain of the *Junior* put his mate and four of his crew on board the abandoned vessel with orders to take her to Nassau, and with that the trouble began.[5]

Soon after Captain Blaisdell's letter reached Kennebunk another arrived for William Lord that gave a very different accounting of the *Swiss Boy*. A Mr. Wainwright of New York City wrote:

> I have received information from Captain H. W. Young of the ship Junior that on 28 Dec. last he fell in with the brig Swiss Boy. . . . Capt. Young says—'the brig was not leaking much, her bows was stove in in a small place, but no damage below her bend, her sails were torn to pieces considerable, her top masts gone— but the mate soon had her under her canvas and double reefed mizzen topsail & trysail, fore top mast stay sail & Gib'—
>
> From the Marine reports this morning I observe that the brig has arrived at Nassau—that the American Consul took charge of her but was divested of her as derelict [i.e., unclaimed property]
>
> It will therefore be necessary for you to put in your claim or if you have abandoned to the underwriters—to inform them—no time should be lost in this. . . .[6]

At Francis Watts's Atlantic Insurance Company in Boston no time was being lost. If an insured cargo was damaged to more than half its value, or when a vessel was forcefully detained, sunk, or injured to the extent that it was deemed not to be worth repairing, it could be considered a total loss.[7] When an owner was notified that such a calamity had happened through one of the perils insured against, he had the option of abandoning to the underwriters and claiming his indemnity. The owner was required to notify the insurers of his intentions within a reasonable time, usually five days, and they in turn had to accept or reject his claim in a timely fashion. The owner's right of abandonment depended on the probability, not the certainty, of a total loss. Once an owner had abandoned to the underwriters he gave up all rights of property to the vessel, its cargo, and its freight to them.[8]

The case of the *Swiss Boy* was complicated by the fact that she had been picked up at sea as a derelict. A derelict vessel was one whose captain and crew had abandoned her with no hope or intention of returning. However, in the eyes of the law such an action on the part of captain and crew did nothing to alter her owner's right of property, and anyone who subsequently found and took possession of such a vessel was legally bound to consider the original owner's interests. At the same time, by the act of saving the vessel the salvor gained a right of possession, which he could press in the form of a salvage fee.[9]

Since William Lord had abandoned the *Swiss Boy* to the Atlantic Insurance Company, all rights of property devolved to them. Learning of the brig's arrival in Nassau, they quickly sent out an agent, Captain Cotting, with instructions to gain control of the brig to the company's advantage.

About the same time, Captain Blaisdell arrived in Boston on his way from Havana to Kennebunk. After an interview with Mr. Watts, during which he learned the full extent of Watts's displeasure, he called on William Lord's

Boston agent, George Callender. Evidently fearing the reactions of Lord and McCulloch, Captain Blaisdell asked Callender to write an explanatory letter, which Callender gladly did.

It was with a deep feeling of chagrin that Captain Blaisdell, under a cloud of controversy, returned to his home town following his second disaster at sea in three years. His discomfort must have been great as he stood before William Lord, while Lord opened and read George Callender's letter.

Boston, Feb. 6, 1840.

This will be handed you by Capt. Blaisdell who has had an interview with Mr. Watts & will tell you the amount of their conversation. Mr. Watts says that Mr. Tyler's brother is out at Nassau & has written by his brother that the Swiss Boy is there & is very little injured & that she leaks scarcely any & he thinks it would not cost much over $500- to repair her & the captain of the Junior writes that she did not leak much. Mr. Watts takes the ground that under these circumstances the abandonment will not hold & that if he can get possession of the vessel by paying the salvage & repair her he can turn her upon the hands of the owners. He is about sending an agent out with ample funds to redeem her & repair her & he has given the captain formal notice to that effect & demands of him to go on & assist by his presence in recovering her from the court of admiralty & also to take possession of her for the owners after his, Mr. Watts' agent has had her repaired. And tells the captain it is his duty as master to do so. Mr. Watts applied to Mr. Tyler for his opinion & this is the result of his opinion—he says the abadoment cannot be sustained—If she should be sold before their agent gets out, I should think that would settle it. but if not and they get possession I do no know what would be the result. I have not consulted anyone nor taken any legal advice as I don't see that I have any more to do about it without your instruction—Capt. B- wished me to write to you & I thought it well to state to you the views of Mr. Watts—He & his directors seem to feel very much dissatisfied with the proceedings of the captain—if they can get possession of her they will not pay a total loss, I suppose without a lawsuit, I do not give my opinion because you know as much about it as I do, but I think it might be well for you to come up & hear what Mr. W- has to say & then you could take legal advice if you thought best—However Capt. B- can tell you the whole story & you will do what you think best. I shall not move in the business without instructions from you.[10]

"The whole story" is exactly what Captain Blaisdell had to tell. All evidence pointed to the fact that he had behaved badly in the crisis on the *Swiss Boy*. In the eyes of the insurers, the captain of the *Junior*, and others the brig was not as severely damaged as first reported, and should not have been abandoned. But whatever the captain had to say concerning his actions satisfied Lord, who adopted a wait and see attitude toward the insurer's attempts to gain possession of the brig. Lord continued to keep himself well informed of the proceedings through his agent George Callender.

On 17 February, eleven days after he had sent word by the captain, George Callender wrote again concerning the *Swiss Boy*.

Mr. Watts' agent to look after the Swiss Boy sailed some days since. He told me on Saturday that Mr. Tyler had got home & represented the Brig as but very little injured etc. said there was to be a hearing before the court about 1st February— did not know what would be the result but seemed to think they might wait to hear from this quarter before doing anything. Mr. W. complained that the Capt. represented to the Junior that the brig had 6 feet of water in her & would sink in an hour etc., etc., . . . I think so far as the damage to the vessel goes it is strong for you. It seems to me the survey makes her out quite as damaged as the Captain said she was—. . . [Mr. Sprague] will know whether the mate & any of the men were where they could be found if wanted. Said it would be well to keep the run of them as the Captain's testimony in case of a trial could not be taken he being part owner—it would be necessary to have other evidence. I think we must hear soon what course has been pursued at Nasau & we must wait for further intelligence.

This Swiss Boy business is unfortunate and troublesome but I don't see anything more can be done at present—I should be glad to hear she was sold.[11]

Meanwhile, the insurer's agent, Captain Cotting, was on his way to Nassau. He arrived on 21 February, and went to see the *Swiss Boy*; the condition of which he reported as "similar to your representation to me, but not near so bad." His final verdict would be that "the brig is perfectly tight and ought not to have come in here."[12]

The following day he went to see the salvor, Mr. Griffin, former mate on the *Junior*. They agreed on a salvage fee of $400. Captain Cotting explained, "I probably should have compromised for less but he had consulted an attorney, expense of which he bore—as the judge of the Admiralty Court, John C. Lees, Esq. had made an appointment to leave the Island 25 inst. to be absent six weeks, obliged me to compromise with Mr. Griffin at once or await the return of the judge."[13]

The salvage fee was the compensation due Mr. Griffin for his role in the rescue of the *Swiss Boy*. Under the law the amount due a salvor was not fixed, but was left to the judgement of the court of admiralty. The rate generally applied fluctuated between one half and one quarter of the value of the property saved.[14]

On 24 February, Captain Cotting and a lawyer he had engaged went to the judge's chambers. After presenting his credentials Captain Cotting was quickly awarded possession of the *Swiss Boy*, and as further compensation Mr. Griffin received one half the total value of the brig's cargo of hay.

Once the brig was in his control, Captain Cotting wasted no time in getting her hull repaired. The cost was $380, which he thought much too high a price: "were I in Boston I am confident she could be repaired for much less than half this expense—were I bound home with her I should secure some rough boards over the broken part & then secure a tarpaulin over the whole which would make her safe for the passage."[15]

New Orleans, not Boston, was the brig's destination, as she was still loaded with the paving stone bound for that city. After repairing the brig Cotting signed on a crew. Mr. Griffin consented to go as first mate. The other men were from the schooner *Andrew Adams* of Bristol, Maine, which had been wrecked on the island of Abaco. The captain had found passage to Boston, and his crew returned to the States by shipping on the *Swiss Boy*.[16]

Contrary to the express wishes and emphatic demands of Mr. Watts, Captain Blaisdell had remained in Kennebunk during the transactions in Nassau that brought the *Swiss Boy* back into the hands of her owners, but once she was secured and ready to sail he left for New Orleans to take up his command again. It is not clear whether he achieved his objective. The *Swiss Boy* was in New Orleans loading for Boston on 11 April.[17] On 28 April George Callender wrote to William Lord that "it is about time to hear of Captain Blaisdell's arrival. He will probably get there just in time to take charge of the brig."[18] Either Captain Blaisdell arrived after the brig had sailed or Captain Cotting refused to surrender his command until they reached Boston, for when the *Swiss Boy* entered Boston Harbor on 19 May Cotting was her master.[19]

After her arrival in Boston the brig underwent some refurbishing. Adam McCulloch wrote to William Lord as part owner: "the last I heard she was high and dry upon the railway. I hope you will not be at much expense about her copper unless the underwriters come in for a good share. I hope you will succeed in setting all up without much difficulty so that we can take a new start."[20]

Her overhaul completed, the *Swiss Boy* sailed on to Kennebunk. On the advice of Callender, William Lord had obtained a load of lumber to be carried to Havana.[21] Captain Blaisdell had orders that should the market prove dull at Havana he was to sail on to New Orleans.

Arriving at Havana early in July of 1840 Captain Blaisdell quickly disposed of the lumber and secured a cargo of sugar or molasses bound for Hamburg, Germany. On 12 July he set sail, planning to make a stop at Cowes on the Isle of Wight.[22]

While in Hamburg the Captain allowed himself to become involved in some dealings that caused a stir back in Boston. In New York, Tobias Lord received some documents from Germany. He quickly took them up to Boston to George Callender, who in turn relayed the particulars on to William Lord in Kennebunk.

> Mr. Lord is here from New York & has handed me a package of average papers sent him from Hamburg by direction of Captain Blaisdell. The papers are in a foreign language & I cannot make out anything except that it appears to be the expense of coppering and other repairs amounting to over $2,000—I have never heard of the Swiss Boy meeting with any accident & don't know on what grounds this claim against the offices is made. Mr. Lord and myself thought it was best to wait 'til I hear from you before presenting Mr. Watts the papers. I am afraid it will be very difficult to make the offices consent to pay for coppering unless she

met with some serious accident, particularly as they knew the copper was in a bad state when she was here. I shall therefore wait your instructions before doing anything.[23]

Callender's caution was understandable. All the details in the matter of the *Swiss Boy*'s adandonment were not yet taken care of, and would not be until 1841. Mr. Watts and his board of directors had had their fill of the *Swiss Boy*, and did not need to be further aggravated by flimsy claims less than a year after that episode.

William Lord certainly saw the difficulty, and quickly wrote to Callender that the papers were not to be presented. Callender responded that "of course I shall not present the papers nor make any claim for coppering the Swiss Boy. I presume the Capt. was put up to making the claim by his broker. He had a fine passage . . . to Cuba."[24]

And indeed by the time the papers had reached Boston Captain Blaisdell was in Cuba. He had left Cuxhaven, at the mouth of the Elbe below Hamburg, on 21 October. Unable to find a return freight in Germany he went on to Cadiz for salt. From Cadiz he took the brig on to the Spanish port of Malaga. Fully loaded, the brig left Spain in December, bound for Cuba.[25]

Late in January of 1841 the *Swiss Boy* made the port of Matanzas. By the middle of February she was loading for Boston. Her return passage was anything but easy. For ten days she remained caught between Block Island and the South Shoal off Nantucket in constant northeasterly and northwesterly gales. At last, on 19 March, Captain Blaisdell set foot on the streets of Boston.[26]

The physical damage to the *Swiss Boy* had been repaired, but the resulting financial damage to the owners, and the tarnished reputation of the captain, real or imagined, remained unremedied. As both doctor and patient, Captain Blaisdell exerted every effort to effect a cure, and make up for lost time and profits. In a scramble that left no opportunity for a return to Kennebunk, he discharged the Cuban cargo, procured an outward-bound one of hoops and casks, signed on a new crew, and saw to it that the brig was properly fitted for sea. Ten days after making port the *Swiss Boy* cleared Boston for Havana.[27]

Three weeks later the brig lay at anchor in Havana Harbor awaiting a new cargo. The hoops and casks, in great demand at the sugar warehouses, had been quickly sold at a good price. It was another matter, however, to engage a new cargo, especially as the captain was determined to show a profit, and was very particular as to what arrangements he would accept.

A week after the brig's arrival Captain Blaisdell had been offered a charter to the North Sea, which he had refused in the hope of a better opportunity.[28] The month of May passed, and still he had not secured a freight. The waiting was very tiresome, and with the coming of the hot and humid summer season, unhealthy. Jacob Emery, a member of the *Swiss Boy*'s crew, was stricken with yellow fever and died. Finally during the first week of June an agreement was reached to carry a cargo of sugar to St. Petersburg in Russia.

The freight was insured for $3,500, and within the policy was the allowance for one stop-over in an American port.[29] Sailing from Havana in the last week of June, the *Swiss Boy* headed for Boston, arriving there on 10 July 1842.[30] The stop was a brief one, and within a few days the captain, crew, and brig were ready to sail. However, nature did not cooperate, and there was a further delay while waiting for a fair wind. After a day and a half the wind changed, the captain shouted his orders, and slowly, with billowing sails, the *Swiss Boy* was on her way toward the Baltic.[31]

In a passage marked by favorable winds and calm seas the *Swiss Boy* made good time, calling at the Danish port of Elsinore in mid-August.[32] The brig's stop there was obligatory. Denmark controlled access to the Baltic Sea, with her islands of Funen and Zealand dividing the passage between the Danish peninsula of Jutland and Sweden into three channels known as the Little Belt, the Great Belt, and the Sound. All vessels bound for ports on the Baltic were required to stop to pay the toll exacted by the Danish government. Despite the complaints of other nations, including the United States, that the dues were burdensome and arbitrary, the right of collecting was a prerogative traceable to the Middle Ages, guaranteed by treaty, and jealously guarded by the Danes.

So after entering the Sound and coming to Elsinore the *Swiss Boy* lowered her sails in a salute to Kronborg Castle, and Captain Blaisdell perpared to deal with the collector of customs.[33] Since the stop at Elsinore could be planned upon, the captain used it to his advantage. There at a pre-arranged address he would receive his mail: business correspondence from William Lord giving news or advice to guide his business transactions at his destination, and the eagerly looked for letters from his family.

From Elsinore the *Swiss Boy* crossed the Baltic to the Russian port of Cronstadt, the port of Russia's entry for St. Petersburg. Principal imports included sugar, coffee, spices, and cotton, which were often carried in American vessels, but Russian crop failures in 1839 and 1840, coupled with the longstanding exclusion of American capital from Russian commerce, had contributed to a general decline in direct trade between the United States and Russia. Most of the sugar brought into St. Petersburg on American vessels such as the *Swiss Boy* was on freight for foreign account.[34]

Captain Blaisdell's prospects for a direct freight back to the United States were poor, as Russian produce was considered to be highly priced and consequently demand for it in the States was low.[35] However he was able to secure cargo bound from Cronstadt to LeHavre, France, and sailed in October. He called at Havre on 24 October and remained there into the middle of November. Still not fully loaded, he left Havre for the old stand-by of Cadiz and salt. It was not until February of 1842 that Elizabeth, waiting in Kennebunk, could read that the *Swiss Boy* had been sighted off Matanzas on 29 January and was bound in.[36]

Once back in Boston the captain hurridly concluded his business and traveled to Kennebunk. He had been absent from his family for more than a year. The last chance he had had to spend any significant time with them had been in the spring of 1840, following the abandonment of the *Swiss Boy*. Jotham was forty-nine years old in 1842 and Elizabeth was thirty-three. They both must have cherished the infrequent times they could spend together as a family. There were now three children. The oldest, Elizabeth, was nine years old, Sarah Ann was seven, and Maria, the baby, was nearly three. It would have taken a major effort on their mother's part to keep their long absent father from becoming a total stranger to them.

As heartwarming and gratifying as the visit was, it had to end, but happily with the knowledge that the separation would not be of such long duration as the previous had been. The *Swiss Boy* was then five years old, and except for the work done in 1840 following the collision with the *William Engs* she had had no major repair work done. The owners William Lord, Adam McCulloch, and Captain Blaisdell decided to bring her to Kennebunk in the fall for an overhaul.

Following a voyage that took her to Europe, the *Swiss Boy* returned to Boston on 3 September, loaded with coal from Newcastle, England. Since unloading her would take a great deal of time, Captain Blaisdell left her under the watchful eye of George Callender and went to Kennebunk to see his family and make the necessary arrangements for the arrival of the brig.[37]

When all was ready the captain returned to Boston and brought the *Swiss Boy* up the coast. During October and November local shipwrights and laborers worked on her. Daniel Curtis oversaw many repairs to her hull. The firm of Goodwin & Pope overhauled her rigging, and several others saw to her needs.

While the brig was being refitted a cargo of local lumber was gathered for her. Eben Webber charged $80 to carry and load the 180,000 board feet. With the work completed and the lumber loaded Captain Blaisdell said his goodbyes and boarded the brig. A pilot provided by shipbuilders D. and S. Ward guided the *Swiss Boy* down the river and out to sea in December 1842.

After carrying the lumber to Cuba and taking sugar to Europe, the *Swiss Boy* returned to Boston with a cargo of hemp from Riga in September 1843. Captain Blaisdell brought her back to Kennebunk, when further caulking was done to her hull, along with some additional general refurbishing.[38] It was during his stay at home in 1843 that the Blaisdell's fifth child, another daughter, was born. She was named Eunice for one of Elizabeth's sisters.

With the arrival of the new year it was time once more for the *Swiss Boy* to depart for Cuba. In Cuba the brig took on a cargo bound for Marseilles in southern France, a port with a ready market for West Indian produce. After crossing from the Caribbean to the Mediterranean Sea, landfall must have looked inviting indeed, but Captain Blaisdell would have prudently avoided any unnecessary stop at the free port of Gibralter. The quarantine regulations at Marseilles were strict and scrupulously enforced. In order to avoid the delay of a long quarantine at the end of the voyage any vessel that found it necessary to stop off Gibralter had to forgo most contact with shore; only papers and letters that had been dipped in vinegar as a health precaution could be taken on board. If the situation required that the captain actually make port he had to obtain a declaration from the French consul stating that no cargo had been either loaded or landed and that no commercial business of any kind had been transacted. Failure to take such measures would result in heavy duties for which the vessel and not the cargo was liable.

Upon approaching Marseilles the *Swiss Boy* would have taken on a pilot from one of the pilot boats stationed between Capes Cruzet and Couronne with their blue flags flying. When the brig reached the port proper Captain Blaisdell found himself beset by a flotilla of tow boats whose occupants were clamoring for the business of guiding the *Swiss Boy* to her mooring place. The usual fee for towing ranged between fifteen and thirty francs, but unless a master had the knowledge or foresight to strike a bargain at the outset he could find himself being charged at the rate of three francs per boat as well as three francs for every man they carried.

Captain Blaisdell's first order of business after docking was to file a report with the health office. All customhouse activity in France was done through the medium of brokers so he then had to engage a reputable individual to act on the vessel's behalf. The broker would enter and clear the vessel, pay the pilotage both in and out, and take care of customhouse, quarantine, and excise fees. A broker would also undertake to procure a return freight for the vessel.[39]

After completing his business in Marseilles, Captain Blaisdell sent off a letter informing the *Swiss Boy*'s other owners of his plans. In addition to the freighting charge of six dollars per ton he was to receive a sum equal to 10 percent of the total freight as primage. Primage was a payment made by shippers to the master of a vessel for his special care of their goods. Also known as "hat money," the payment was considered to be the captain's alone unless a previous agreement with his owners stated otherwise.[40] The fact that Captain Blaisdell mentioned it with the freight charge suggests that, as an owner of the *Swiss Boy*, he put his primage toward the general profit.

Blaisdell usually bought bills of exchange on London, which were negotiable notes drawn by one person on a second requiring them to pay a stated amount of money by a certain date to a third individual who held the note. These securities allowed for the safe and easy transfer of funds between nations or over long distances.[41] In this case he chose rather to purchase gold doubloons at one rate in Marseilles with the intention of turning a profit when they fetched a higher rate in America.

Marseilles Augt 12, 1844
I wrote you On my arival By a Bark for Boston, Informing you that I had some Idea of taking a freight from Parlarmo to New York but on reflection I gave it up I found I could not make Over a thousand dollars and having two Expensive ports to go to there would be nothing left at the End of the voyage. I am now laying On for Boston, I have got about 140 tons ingaged @ $6 per ton & 10% primage and I am in hopes to be able to git 200. or 250. tons, and although my detention is long still I think it better than going after salt, there has a great number of ships gone for salt, consiquently I Expect salt will be high in Cadiz & low in the States I have discharged four of my crew, so that My Expenses laying here is not verry high. I shall probably lay til the last of Augt I have settled my freight with Out any dificulty a considerable of the Cargo was damaged but there was no fault found, and the consignee has promised to ship some goods by me, in stead of buying Bills on London I have bought doubloons wich I consider more to your interest. I paid fr. 84.30—$15.70, they will probably be worth in the states $16.50, the Exchange On London about fr 25.30—

I received a letter from you On my arrival and on two days after I have hove the brig down here and cleaned the Bottom, the corral was six Inches long on the Copper & as hard as a bone I never saw the like of it in all my life time Every One that saw it was astonished I found the Copper better then I Expected I found Only a few places that was started a litte. I put On two or three sheets. I found some leaks above the Copper the Bill heaving down both sides and calking from the Copper up to the bends was fr 200. $28 about there is five amarican vessels here at present, two of wich is ready for sea bound to cadiz. One for N Orleans & One for New York. the Brig Trio arived yesterday from Havana By the way of Boston and is in quarinteen, a swedish bark of 350 tons was chartered yesterday for New York to lay 45 days—for $1400, that is the way they cut us up.[42]

By October the *Swiss Boy* had made her way back to Boston with a fragrant cargo containing lemons, almonds, licorice, castile soap, merchandise, and dye and drug stuffs.

Following a month at home the captain got an early start, leaving Kennebunk on 10 December 1844, bound for Matanzas with a cargo of several thousand board feet of lumber and bunches of cask hoops.[43] From Matanzas he intended to carry sugar or molasses to Europe and if possible find a return freight to Havana where he could pick up more sugar and make another run across the Atlantic. However, on reaching England the captain found nothing offering for Cuba and took a mixed cargo of scrap iron, iron bars, steel, tin, wine and brandy, figs, salmon, hemp, and chemicals from London to Boston instead. George Callender expressed the owners' reaction: "I think Capt. Blaisdell did about as well to take the freight to Boston as to return to Havana in ballast & probably better."[44]

Another factor that may have weighed in Captain Blaisdell's decision to return to Boston was his health, as he noted in a letter to McCulloch and Lord in Kennebunk.

Boston June 15, 1845

I take this Oppertunity to inform you of my safe arrival at last, after a teagous Passage of 48 days from the Downs, my ancsiaty has ben beyond discreption On this long passage thinking I mite possably loose a good summers work but had I have known the prospect I should not have fretted quite so much for I fear Our years work is finished, you will please write me at the receipt of this and direct me what to do, should you think of sending the Brig away again I think [I will] have to leave for my health is not verry good, in the mean time I shall git the Brig discharged as soon as Posable, I think if we could git any thing like a decent Charter for some part of the medatraenan it would be better for the vessel to run then to lay up in the sun all summer in the hot sun. she is in good Order and can be fitted Out with verry little Expense—I hope this will find Mr. McCullock quite recouvered his health.[45]

Ill health was to plague the captain throughout the remainder of his career. Blaisdell also spoke in his letter of the brig being in good order. Just before her arrival George Callender had noted to William Lord that, "I find the Swiss Boy stands A-2 on the books but that does not prevent their insuring her cargo as low as in any other vessel & in fact I got the freight insured as low as I could have got it in any A-1 vessel."[46] When a vessel was reclassified a boring was taken to check for rotting timbers. If a vessel passed the five year mark without rotting then in the conventional wisdom of the day she would have a long career. The *Swiss Boy*, true to form, would sail the seas until 1859.

Even though he planned to leave the vessel Captain Blaisdell continued to ready her for sea. At first prospects for a freight were not encouraging, as George Callender related: "The Swiss Boy commenced discharging yesterday. Nothing offers yet for future employment for her. The chance for a freight to Havana is not so good as it was owing to two or three vessels being put up for that port & not a great deal of shipping. I shall try all I can to get a charter of some kind. It rains & have stopped work on Swiss Boy."

But later the same day events took a turn for the better and he added, "Bark Flora, change of destination. Mr. Dow turned over to the Swiss Boy 1200 Qlts. Fish at 50 cts. & some lard etc. and could no doubt make $1000- and perhaps $1200- I consulted Captain Blaisdell & he thinks it the best thing that can be done & we have agreed to let Mr. Dow advertise her for Havana."[47]

Upon receiving Captain Blaisdell's request to leave the brig, Adam McCulloch traveled down to Boston to confer with him. He supported the captain's decision and notified William Lord to send on another master.

Boston June 24th 1845

Sir you will percive by the Paper the Swiss Boy is up for Havannah. She will probably make about $1000 freight, this is the best, and in fact almost the only thing we can do, we are to have immediate dispatch, and hope to be ready by the last of next week, Capt Blaisdell does not incline to go, and I suppose if we can get no one better we must take Capt Perkins, with the understanding that Capt B should take her again on her return if desirable, It would be necessary to have a Master here the first of the week, the Brig is (in) fine order and can be fitted out at a small expense, the prospect for freights in Cuba is better some think they will be £3, I wish she was ready to start now I think I shall come home tomorrow, the Brig will not be discharged before tomorrow night, She has a large quantity of Scrap Iron which comes out very slow.[48]

The bustling harbor of Marseilles, France's
major port on the Mediterranean. Aquatint,
drawn by Jacques-Raymond Brascassat, ca. 1830.
(Courtesy Mariners' Museum, Newport News, Virginia)

Matanzas, Cuba, which specialized in production of
muscovado sugar. Lithograph drawn by Pierre Toussant
Frederic Mialhe and printed by L. Marquier, ca. 1840.
(Courtesy Mariners' Museum, Newport News, Virginia)

FIVE

Another Venture
1845-1847

IT WAS NOT UNTIL the first of July that Captain John H. Perkins arrived in Boston to relieve Captain Blaisdell of his command. After remaining in Boston long enough to see the *Swiss Boy* off, Captain Blaisdell returned to Kennebunk and his family for a period of convalescence.

At some point during the summer the captain felt sufficiently recovered to begin casting about for employment. Although William Lord did not have a ship for him to command, before the season passed his search had met with success. In September he traveled from Kennebunk to Boston to take up the command of the bark *Abbot Lord*.

The *Abbot Lord* had been built in Biddeford, Maine, in 1840, and was registered at Saco on 6 November of that year. On 25 October 1841 she had been permanently registered at Boston. At 437 tons she was 121 feet long. Her owners were scattered geographically. Daniel W. Lord of Boston was her managing owner.[1] He was William Lord's nephew, though they were contemporaries in age. He had been born in Kennebunkport and had entered the West India trade there at the age of nineteen.[2] Two other Kennebunkport men, Captain Acter Patterson and Robert Towne, also held shares in the bark, along with James Thornton of Saco.[3]

Under Captain Blaisdell, the *Abbot Lord* departed Boston in September bound for New Orleans. By November the cargo had been discharged, and the bark was prepared for a Liverpool passage, loaded with 1,485 bales of cotton, 362 barrels of corn meal, and 585 hides.[4] Her hold was full, and some of the cotton was to be carried on deck.

Under the general terms of the policy insuring the cargo, the deck load would not have been covered. In the letter he wrote on 26 November, after being towed the hundred miles to the mouth of the Mississippi at Southwest Pass, the captain left the question of insuring them to Daniel Lord's discretion. He also mentioned the ships *Hartley* and *Ashland*. The *Ashland* hailed from Kennebunk and was owned by George Lord, William's older brother. The *Hartley* was on her maiden voyage. She belonged to William Lord and was commanded by, and named for, his son Hartley.

I wrote you dated the 24th informing you of my being ready for sea but I got disapointed by the tow Boat so I did not leave the Citty til the 25th and arrived here today and shall probably git to sea this Evening at high water, I forgot to mention in my last that I have twelve Bales of cotton left Out, six of Wich is On deck and six in the house. I did not git them Insured here—there is nearly 30 ships on the river bound up and at the Bar. the Ashland arrived up the day that I left the citty and I Expect the Hartley is on the River—I hope that I shall be fortunate anough to git back in time for a good freight Please to write me to Liverpool.[5]

Arriving in Liverpool on 9 January 1846, Blaisdell discharged the cotton cargo and took on a cargo of salt. Departing promptly, he set out for Cuba, arriving early in April after a very slow passage. He wrote Daniel Lord from Matanzas on 13 April to inform him of the situation.

Sir, I arrived here on the 10th Inst. after a tromendious passage of 64 days from Liverpool. I wrote you from Liverpool that I thought I should touch here and in fact I was obliged to put in some wheres to git water being nearly Out. I was in hopes to have found business here for the Bark but they Object to her being too large   I wrote to Havana On my arrival to Messrs Burnham and Tyng the Broker and got an answer to day with a New Orleans Price Currant of the 25th of march, which is the latest from there at preasant, so I shall clear tomorrow and Wich is as soon as I can On account of the Holy days wich has ben from the 10th and procead to New Orleans or some port in the Bay where I hope to meet with better Success then here   Freight here for vessels of 200 [sugar] Boxes is from £3.0 (Cowes) to £2.17.6 to (direct)—I think as it is so late in the season now that my best Chance is in New Orleans as there is a good deal of Provitions shipping there at a higher rate then cotton and in the Other ports there is nothing but cotton— this has ben the most teagous passage that I Ever had   the first part nothing but gales and the latter part calms   after I got into the vicinity of the trade winds I had nothing but calms and westerly winds.   I supplied the ship Monmouth with provitions on the Bahama bank that had ben Out 84 days from Liverpool.   the swiss Boy had 90 days from London, and there is a duch ship here that had 130 days from Europe.   I realy hope I shall find good business for the Bark in New Orleans   If I miss a good freight in Consiquence of my long passage I Shall be interly discouraged.   I have not much patience left now but I shall probably know my doom in a few days   If I could have got a freight here I could have sold the salt to have paid something Over the first cost.   the fine salt pays the best, the holy days has put things back here, if I have the wind favorable so I can touch at Apalach[icola]—or Mobile I shall   Otherwais make the best of my way to New Orleans Where I hope to be able to give you more favorable accounts then from here.[6]

Captain Blaisdell might well bemoan the length of his passage.   And while unpredictable winds and weather could prolong a voyage, the equally capri- cious workings of the marketplace could just as effectively alter the most careful of plans.   The captain's own plans to leave Cuba were abruptly laid to rest by unfavorable reports from New Orleans. Despite his initial gloomy evaluation of the situation in Matanzas, he instead found himself chartering the *Abbot Lord* to carry sugar.

The cargo the bark took on was not highly refined white sugar, which at that time was sold in loaves or cones and looked upon as a real luxury. Rather it was raw brown sugar of two varieties. Muscovado was obtained by draining molasses after the process of crystallization had begun, and it was shipped in hogsheads weighing about half a ton. Clayed sugar arrived alongside in long wooden boxes and received its name from the fact that the containers were sealed with moist clay. It was to such sugar boxes that the captain was referring when he noted the carrying capacity of various vessels. The *Abbot Lord* was loaded with both kinds of sugar, although traditionally Havana was the noted clayed sugar port and Matanzas the muscovado.[7] Six days after his first letter, Blaisdell wrote to inform Daniel Lord of the change in his plans.

I wrote you a few days since informing you of my arrival here &c and my intentions of going to New Orleans but the same day I got accounts from N. Orleans of the 8th Inst. wich showed a decline of freights there and an arival of a Bark at Havana from Apalach[icola] in Balest and Other things combined to change my mind, and I have taken a freight to load at this Port a full cargo of Sugars in H.h.ds & Boxes for Cowes & a market @£2.17.6- Per ton with 5% Primage with the customary additions & Differences if Ordered to any Other Ports then between London and Hamburg, but I think it Probable I shall go to London direct. I may have ben to hasty possably in Excepting this freight, but time will show. the Abbot Lord is rather to large for this market and might lay here a long time with Out gitting an Offer unless there was a scarcity of vessels wich was the case when I ingaged, but this morning we have got a fresh suply three large vessels of 3000 Boxes all came in togeather and should there be as meny more come in tomorrow morning I doubt if I should be able to chose to so good advantage monday as I did saturday. they wanted me to limit the Bark to 3000 boxes wich I would not for she will probably carry something considerable Rising of that number. Messrs. Sanchez & Co Charters me

I wrote you in my last that the salt would probably pay a little something but I am afraid it Will not—the quantity is to large for this market and to have to ship it to Havana the freight and Other Expenses attending it would be as much as it is worth, we shall know tomorrow the result and I will let you know. I got a letter from Mr Tyng yesterday and One from J.C. Burnham & Co. in answer to my said they had nothing to Offer me at Preasant. the last ingagement at Havana Mr Tyng wrote me was a bark for Leghorn @£3.0 and the last ingagement here was a bark of 2200 Boxes for Triest

My Expenses here will be high having provitions to buy at a high rate and the Tonage duty under the new act is about a quarter more than formally but I will git along as cheap as I possably Can Your kind letter of the lst Inst. has Jest come to hand, and I am glad my calling here met your vewes rest asured that it shall be my cheaf study to promote your Intrest or the Intrest of the Owners of the Bark Abbot Lord If I Err in jugement you must Excuse me.[8]

Despite bleak market prospects the captain did manage to dispose of the salt, which was measured in fanegas, a Spanish measure (abbreviated in his letters as fan.) equal to slightly more than a bushel and a half.[9] Overall he appears to have been satisfied with the business he had conducted in Matanzas. He had secured his freight before the number of vessels in port had increased, causing rates to fall, and the proceeds realized from the sale of the salt were a pleasant surprise. On the negative side, however, were certain necessary expenses that caused him real concern, as he noted in a letter on 25 April.

> I wrote you dated the 18th Inst. informing you of my having taken a freight of suger in H.hds & Boxes @£2.17.6 per ton for Cowes & a market. since wich I have sold the salt and landed it, the fine @ $3.75 per Fan.- of 200 lbs. spanish wieght, and the course at $2.25 per fan. the duty is $1.87 1/2 cts. per Fan.—after paying all the Expenses the net proceeds Will probably be about $1000. so I shall not loose any thing On it. the fine salt pays well, but the course is nearly a total loss after paying all the Charges, I shall commence loading day after tomorrow, and am in hopes to be away by the 10th or 15th of may,—I have ben under the necessity of colking the Bark Out side from the Copper up the seams being Very Open and at a high rate, I have got to discharge part of the Crew here and ship Others. but I shall probably be able to git them as low as the Others but it will make my Expenses high here I have also got to buy all my provitions here for the passage Out but you may rest asured that I shall be as Economcale as possable— both Matanzas, and Havana is now full of vessels, and poring in dayly. So I think I should not done any better by holding On any longer, a ship of the size of the Abbot Lord cleared today for New Orleans it is verry dull here at preasant. there is no demand for vessels now Only of the smaller Capasity.—I shall keep you advised of my proceedings Everry Oppertunity. . . .
>   P.S. the Swiss boy sails tomorrow for Gibralter.[10]

The *Abbot Lord* was fully loaded and ready to sail shortly before the captain's predicted date in the middle of May. As was not unusual when trading in Cuba, Captain Blaisdell did not make enough from the sale of the bark's salt to meet all his expenses and so was forced to take an advance at a high rate of interest on the freight to Europe. This shortfall, and the need to caulk the bark, lent a tentative tone to his report to Daniel Lord on 9 May.

> I take this Oppertunity to inform you that I am now loaded and ready for sea. shall be dispached On the 12th the next day after the steam packet leaves Havana, I have about 600 payable tons in @£2.17.6 per ton - my freight and primage will be about £1800 - on wich I have to draw about $2200 @ 11 1/2 % prem. Wich amount I have to Insure in London—
>   I have not yet got my a/c, cannot until day after tomorrow, but as there is a vessel sails today for Baltimore I write you on account of the Insurance if you wish to git any on the freight, I have not yet got the returns of the salt but there will probably be a balance in my favor of about $1000 after paying all Expences On it. wich will be a little above the Invoice cost, my Expences here is high On account of having to pay Off my crew and Shipping another and having all my provitions to buy at a high price. but I hope my a/c will be satisfactory when you see them.

my colkers Bill is $300- and Seamens wages and advance is Over $700- Tonage duty about $800- So you can see where the most of it is gone, if I can git my accounts in in time to make Out my a/c I will Send you a coppy—the Bark is verry deep drawing 18 ft. aft & 17 forward. She leaks some yet notwithstanding She has ben fathfuly Colked. the man has lost fifty dollers by the Job. I dont know but you will blame me for Colking her at such an Expence, but had I not done so, I think I should have had to unloaded again for the seams was verry Open and I found some verry bad places under the counter had to put in some graving pices—

freights now is low about £2.10 per ton. there has ben a great number of arrivals within these last 3 days some is about to leave for New Orleans—I have discharged Goodridge and given him an Order On Perkins & Moody for the balance of his wages—[11]

Although the captain's tone was apologetic, the work done to the *Abbot Lord*'s hull was obviously needed, and later events would show that, if anything, greater overhaul and expense could have been justified. Soon after leaving Matanzas it was evident that the bark was in trouble, but the captain held to his course, perhaps under the mental admonition that "the safest rule is for the master to remember, that his duty is to prosecute the voyage, and that he must act in good faith for the accomplishment of this object."[12]

A week after clearing Cuba, however, matters took a turn for the worse and the applicable admonition became that he should "exert himself to save and preserve all the lives and property entrusted to his care."[13]

Portland June 2nd 1846

Daniel W. Lord Esqre
Dear Sir,

it is with regret that I inform you of my having to put in here leaky. I left Matanzas On the 12th of May Soon after I got Out She commenced leaking badly so that we had to keep One pump going all the time When it was rough, but I kept On my voyage in hopes that the leak would not Increase, but On the 19th I took a gale of wind from the Northward With a heavy Sea When the leak increased to such a degree that we could scarcely keep her free and I beleave had the gale continued She would have gone down. I Expect the water got to the sugar for she has got two or three streaks list, On the 21st the Crew all came aft and requested Me to put in to port as they did not feel safe to continue the voyage. I Expostilated with them but to no purpose. So I had to comply and made the best of my way for this Port it being about as near as any Other and I presume the best for all concerned Where I arrived today—in smooth Water she does not leak much, but as soon as it becomes rough she commences leaking and the rougher it is the more she leaks, Where the leak is I am not able to say, but I am induced to think it is in her bottom that she strains and Opens her seams. I had her uppers thoroughly Colked in Matanzas from her Copper up to the plank Shere and the Spanyards has the reputation of being the best Colkers in the wourld at any rate it cost anough, she was very Open and we found some bad places under the counter—I have written Capt. Patterson thinking possably you mite be Out of Town and consequently not git this. I have noted a protest and taken Everry nessacry precaution and await your arrival Or Orders.

P.s. I lost One man On the Passage and have got another sick on board / I have ben off here in the fog nearly a week with the Wind to the Eastward.[14]

Under such adverse conditions Portland was an ideal haven for the *Abbot Lord*. As Maine's largest city and port, the facilities for the repair of the bark would be readily available. Its close proximity to Kennebunkport and Boston meant that Captain Blaisdell could have the benefit of the owners' input on exactly what measures should be taken to insure that their vessel was seaworthy. Costs for repairs would probably be a bit less expensive than in Boston as well.

Upon his arrival, as he stated in his letter, the captain noted a protest. Made to protect a vessel's master and owners from liability and to insure their standing in case of a settlement for damages, a protest was a sworn written declaration giving the circumstances under which some injury occurred to a ship or its cargo. It was recommended that masters file a protest in every instance of an accident that was to the disadvantage of anyone interested in the voyage. The protest had to be made in the first port the vessel arrived at following the accident. Within twenty-four hours after his arrival the master had to appear before a notary public or the collector of the district and with some members of the crew swear that the losses sustained were for the safety of the ship and goods and for the preservation of the lives of those on board.[15]

After handling the details of the protest, Captain Blaisdell left Portland for home to better consult the owners. Arriving in Kennebunk he found only Robert Towne in residence. After a brief meeting the captain headed back to Portland, while Towne forwarded Captain Blaisdell's letter to principal owner Daniel Lord with an update of his own.

My Clark will hand you a letter from Capt Blaisdell that was brought to my house this morning at 7 o Clock. also one for Capt Patterson I immediately carried Capt. P letter to his house & found that he started for Saco early this morning with his family. Capt. Blaisdell took a horse & chaise last eveg. He has been over here & I told him he had better call & see Capt Patterson at Saco also Mr. Thornton. Capt Blaisdells letter to you will probably explain every thing in relation to his putting in to portland. He started for P. about 9 oClock & I told him he might expect you there this eveg or at fartherest by tomorrow noon. Capt Patterson may go into Portland with Capt Blaisdell but will not probably make any arrangements for discharging & survey &c until you get there Capt Blaisdell says it will not be necessary for him to enter for 48 hours after he arrvd.[16]

For the next two months the *Abbot Lord* remained in Portland, being repaired and overhauled. The job of overseeing the work on the bark fell to Captain Acter P. Patterson, and during the ensuing weeks he faithfully kept Daniel Lord informed of the progress. The initial task was to unload the bark, and in the first week two small vessels ferried boxes and hogsheads of sugar from the *Abbot Lord* to shore. As the bark was emptied, Captain Blaisdell's fear of water damage to the cargo was confirmed. Captain Patterson noted: "The cargo comes out of the lower hole in better order than from between decks the tier of Boxes along the wings in the lower hole are some stained The ground tier appears to me to be dunaged very high and I am of the opinion that these will not be much damage[d] from water There is now laid on one side between decks 25 Hds and 80 Boxes partially damaged."

By 11 June the bark was sufficiently unloaded to allow her to be towed to Union Wharf, where the remainder of the sugar was taken off and put into storage.[17] Once the unloading had been completed, actual repair work could begin. A month after the bark's hold had been emptied Captain Patterson reported: "we are going on rather slowly with the repairs the weather is so excessive hot that the men keep braking off some owen to sickness and others will not work. we shall make out about 115 or 120 days Labour this week The clamps & Beams are all in (seven new beams) and about all hanging knees on labauord side and most of deck knees (we shall have forty six new deck knees) The lower hole on stabaourd side will require about twenty five the counter will be shut in by to night."[18]

In addition to these structural repairs, the *Abbot Lord*'s bottom was recoppered and her hull was salted.[19] Salting was a method of wood preservation akin to pickling. Salt was packed on salt stops between the frames from the waterline up, producing a brine that inhibited the development of rot in the frames.

By early August the overhaul of the bark was nearing completion, and she was issued her certificate of seaworthiness. Portland businessman Thomas Jones reported to Daniel Lord that he had "just left Capt Patterson at the Bark. He says that he feels quite relieved that he is ready to launch and seems pleased that matters are going on with pretty good dispatch."[20] Finally, on 12 August, at one in the afternoon, the *Abbot Lord* was launched into Portland Harbor. The reloading of the undamaged sugar began almost immediately. On 17 August Captain Patterson issued his final report.

The "Abbot Lord" is hauled off into the stream this evening and we now have the Brigs Clio & Henery Leeds to discharge I hope will not take more than three days. The Carpenters cleared out last week and Caulkers to day. we have the painters at work they will probably finish tomorrow The Barque leaks about five hundred strokes [of the pumps] in twenty four hours. I returned to the Revere Copper Co 45 Sheets 24 oz copper and 1 Sheet Stem plate and sold the Shokings with the old Bolts at 17 c per lb 233 lbs copper 26 lbs old nails & Spikes. I should like to know if there is a 2d mate and what number of men are coming from Kennebunk The Shipping Master here says that he can ship a crew at an hours notice by paying $16- pr month he is at present only offering $15 for the A.L. but I expect he will have to pay $16. If we can get the bills all in and papers in order she may go to sea

next Saturday Capt Blaisdell came down to day. I should be pleased to see you
here as soon as you can make it convenient.[21]

Captain Blaisdell's arrival to take up his command of the *Abbot Lord* may not
have been totally voluntary. Shortly after his arrival in Portland the captain
had become involved with a new vessel being constructed for William Lord.
Lord and his Boston agent, George Callender, had decided jointly to build a
bark in Kennebunk. The bark was nearing completion and Lord invited
Captain Blaisdell to buy an interest in her and to go as her master. By now the
command of the *Abbot Lord* had lost whatever luster it may have had, and the
captain gladly accepted Lord's offer. The arrangements seemed finalized in
June when George Callender wrote, "I was very glad to hear Capt. Blaisdell
had agreed to take a part of the Bark & to go in her—If I can hear of any good
business for her I will let you know."[22]

But only two weeks later a change of plans had occurred. Evidently the
owners of the *Abbot Lord* would not allow the captain to leave the bark and
insisted that he finish the voyage. Callender wrote, "I am sorry to hear Capt.
Blaisdell cannot go in the Bark—I hope he will buy 1/4 or 1/3 of her at all
events—I have no doubt Capt. Joshua Perkins will do very well."[23] In the end
Captain Blaisdell purchased a 1/8 share in the bark.

The new bark was named *Francis Watts* in honor of William Lord's brother-
in-law and insurer. One can only speculate on Captain Blaisdell's opinion of
the choice, considering the dealings he had had with Mr. Watts in the *Swiss
Boy* affair. Constructed in the Landing yard of Robert Smith, Jr., under master
carpenter Isaac Hall, the 256-ton *Francis Watts*'s hull cost $6,700, or about
$26.00 per ton.[24]

In mid-July the captain traveled to Boston and with George Callender
purchased material for the *Francis Watts* that could not be supplied in Kennebunk. On his return the vessel was launched and given into the care of Jesse
Towne, a man who was well versed in the hazards of the narrow Kennebunk
and who generally piloted the craft launched at the Landing downstream to
the wider basin near the river's mouth. Towne was reportedly an excitable man
who would dance upon the deck of the newly launched craft shouting directions, encouragement, and admonitions to the men maneuvering her from
the river's banks, "Pull on the starboard side, boys, or copper-bottomed ship
will go to the bottom! Pull hard, boys, pull all together! There she goes right
into the bank, into the mud, can't get her off, have to wait 'til next tide.
Heave ho!—see if you can't start her again! Splendid ship, boys, all gone to
destruction, so much money lost."[25] It took four tides and nineteen men to
transport the *Francis Watts*. For getting the bark from the yard to the docks
Jesse Towne was paid $47.60, $8.00 of which was his; the remainder was
divided among the men depending upon how many tides they had worked.[26]

Once at dockside in the Port the bark's masts were stepped, and she was
rigged by Thomas Maling.[27] On 12 August 1846 she was officially registered.

Her capacity was listed as 255.38 tons, her master was Captain Joshua Perkins, and her principal owner was William Lord.[28] With a load of lumber she set sail for Havana, in spite of it being the height of the Caribbean hurricane season.

Not long after the *Francis Watts* had sailed from Kennebunk, the *Abbot Lord* cleared Portland. On 22 August she was piloted out of the harbor, and "with a pretty good breeze from about southwest" she resumed her interrupted passage to Cowes on the Isle of Wight.[29]

Waiting at Cowes the captain found a packet of papers from Daniel Lord, who counseled him:

> you will receive herewith all the accounts and vouchers relative to the Expenses on the Cargo of your vessel, and the sale of the damaged part of her cargo at Portland together with an adjustment of the average . . . should you go to the Continent it is probable that the principles of Law and usage prevailing there will accord so nearly with those adopted by the Broker here, that no revisions will be asked—but should your Cargo be landed in England it is probable that exceptions may be taken to the allowance of Wages and Provisions, and you will be obliged to submit to the local Laws.

In all, a total of 119 hogsheads and 101 boxes of sugar had been so damaged that they were not worth shipping to Europe.[30] They had been sold in Portland. Under maritime law, any loss sustained by the consignees of the damaged sugar, along with certain expenses incurred while the bark was in Portland, were to be shared by all parties directly interested in the voyage.

From Cowes the *Abbot Lord* carried the sugar to London. As Daniel Lord had warned, the English authorities objected to the figures worked up in Boston. However, the difference was evidently minor, as Captain Blaisdell remained unperturbed.

While in London, the captain took the opportunity to write to William Lord in Kennebunk with news of the *Swiss Boy* and questions concerning the *Francis Watts*. His expressions of gratitude at the letter's end undoubtedly referred to Lord's bringing him into the *Francis Watts* project, and probably also alluded to his inclusion in the venture of a new ship Lord planned to build the following year.

London Octr 12th 1846

> I called on messrs. Baring Brothers on the 8th Inst. to inquire about the Swiss Boy they informed me that Capt. Perkins had remited £800- and that there was a letter in the Office for him that they Expected that he was bound for London but they did not know, I have not seen him reported as sailed from Triest yet, nether have I had any accounts of the New Bark or from Havana, since the 8th of aug—it apears that freights was good at that date, and I hope that she found some good good imployment,—I am up for New Orleans shall probably sail in about a week I shall not make much freight—several ships has ben chartered to go to Bremen and take passengers to New Orleans @ ten dollars per head, but it is gitting rather late in the season to go there Especialy for so small amount. Capt. Willson

in the Marcia Cleaves is here I beleave has got to copper his ship. I beleave he has not desided what to do yet—My [general] average business is not settled yet, they will Not settle by the statement made in Boston, but I think I shall have no difucilty or detention on that account.—I think freights will be good this fall in the States. there must be a great quantity of corn and flour shipped this year, flour and corn has risen at a tramendious rate, it is now 40 shillings per Bble and dayly rising they want to charter some ships here to go for corn I beleve ten shillings per quarter has ben given and now dear Sir I feel it my duty to Express my gratitude to you for the Interest that you have Ever taken in my welfare and now Especialy the last time that I was at home, and I trust I shall Ever prove my self worthy of your confidence at any rate I shall Ever my best indevor to do so. and I feel verry greatful to you for your kindness to me

Wishing you and all yours health
hapaness and prosperity. . .[31]

Any anxiety felt about the *Swiss Boy* was soon put to rest as she was reported as sailing from Bordeaux to New Orleans soon after, but the *Francis Watts* was another matter. Even as Captain Blaisdell wrote she was experiencing the full fury of the sea.

Captain Perkins had arrived in Havana to find a very dull market. He finally succeeded in selling his lumber, and took on sugar, coffee, and tobacco bound for New York. He described the events that followed his departure from Cuba in a letter sent to Kennebunk.

> I sailed from Havana on the 9th and on the 11th I encountered a hurricane which has wrecked me. Both fore & main mast are gone to the deck, jib boom, head sails & knees & the topsails. After I lost the masts I drifted in on the coast of Florida, came to anchor and parted the larboard chain. Let go the other which held her, this being the 13th at 5 o'clock in the morning. At 10 a boat with four men came from Key West and I made an agreement to take me to Key West for 500 dols. We got jury mast & yesterday arrived at this place in a dreadful state. Everything that was afloat was in some (way) or other wrecked. I have heard of something like 5 sail which has been wrecked at sea or on shore.
>
> I was knocked down in the Lee & had my arm dislocated and it has been so for 4 days. Last evening I had two doctors and five men to set it. I can assure you that I have had a hard time. . . .[32]

But Captain Blaisdell would not learn of this disaster for several months. Despite the deprecating remarks he had written from London, November found Blaisdell and the *Abbot Lord* in port at Bremen. Apparently passengers at ten dollars a head was the best business to be had.

Bremen Nov. 3d—1846

> I take this Oppertunity to inform you that I am Now ready for sea with my full compliment of Passangers Onboard bound for New Orleans. shall sail to morrow wind and Weather permiting. I have 175 passangers Onboard at $10.00—$1750. I have sent a Bill to Baring Brothers for £300. I have had to git a spanker here wich costs about $80 Bremen dollers. advanced seamen $140- Provitions and

William Lord's 468-ton ship *Hartley*,
built by Jacob Perkins in 1845. Oil
painting by Frederic Roux, Havre, 1848.
(Courtesy Brick Store Museum)

Crude wooden pens were constructed to
house passengers in the 'tween decks of
ships chartered in the emigrant trade.
Illustrated London News, 10 May 1851.

stores is about—90- Board Bills $64-. Cordage @ $25. making in all about 400 Bremen dollers. Or $320- the commutation And hospital money will be paid here wich I shall take with me to pay at New Orleans, I thought it nessacery to buy more Provitions then I should have done had I not taken passangers but I have bought nothing more then what was realy nessacery the Old spanker was verry bad and not fit for a winter passage, I notice by the latest accounts from the states That Freights was advancing. and I think the prospect looks faverable for good freights this year, and I hope I shall Be there in time to imbrace the highest rates—[33]

The *Abbot Lord*'s passengers were but a handful of the thousands of Europeans who quit their homelands, victims of the social upheaval that resulted from the Industrial Revolution and burgeoning populations in agrarian areas. Beginning in the decade of the 1830s, and showing marked increase during the 1840s, emigration rose steadily. Compounding Europe's problems, in 1845 a blight destroyed the potato crop all across the northern tier of the continent. In the following year Germany suffered again as adverse weather conditions caused the potato and grain harvests to fail once more. Successive crop failures during the next several years worsened the plight of the people and gave added impetus to the emigrant trade. Eighteen forty-six saw the number of Germans emigrating to the United States rise to 93,000, and in 1847 the total peaked at over 100,000 for the first time.[34]

By late December of 1846, the 175 souls transported by the *Abbot Lord* had reached New Orleans, and many undoubtedly made their way up the Mississippi to join compatriots in establishing farms in the growing Midwest. Finding business to be fair, Captain Blaisdell wasted little time in securing a return freight for the bark. The makeup of his cargo reflected the demands of grain-hungry Europe. During 1846 and 1847 countries such as Germany, which usually exported grain, were forced to import large quantities. Blaisdell reported to Daniel Lord on 29 December:

I wrote you two days since informing you of my arrival at this Port &c sence wich I have taken a Freight for Liverpool That is I have ingaged 3000 Bbls of Flour @ 6-shillings per Bbl, and 3000 Bushels of corn @ 1s-6d- per Bushel Wich is about as much Heavy Freight as I can take to pass the [Mississippi] Bar with safety, I have not ingaged any Cotton as yet I think it Probable that I could ingage the cotton now @ 5/8. but I am in hopes to be able to git more, I dont know but you Will think I have ben too hasty. but I thought it Better to secure part of my freight at a fair rate then to run any risk, I have got as high rates as has Ben given yet, I consider it nearly Or quite Equel to 3/4—but that I must leave to your better Judgement to decide, at any rate I have done what I thought for the best, I shall probably git my cargo Out this week, and commence loading, you will Observe that Exchange on England is verry low about 4% I dont know what way you wish me to draw to pay my disbursements here—

Mr. Nason [the mate] is sick with I supose the small Pox, and I am afraid that I shall have trouble it is imposable to keep it a secret. I have got clear of my passengers. . . .[35]

An outbreak of infectious disease among the crew or passengers of a vessel meant a quarantine. Any invalids would be removed to a hospital, while the vessel and those remaining on board her were segregated from the general activity of the port to prevent an epidemic. A fixed fee known as hospital money was routinely paid for each passenger a vessel carried, and standard monthly deductions were taken from seamen's wages to pay for the care of the sick and disabled and to build marine hospitals. However, should a seaman become ill in the course of a voyage the expense of his treatment fell to the ship.[36]

The delay and expense entailed in a quarantine were the troubles Captain Blaisdell feared, but there was some consolation in the fact that the passengers had been discharged. Keeping them on board and feeding them for the duration would have been an added strain.

The *Francis Watts* further complicated Blaisdell's life. William Lord wrote to him relating the wreck of the *Francis Watts*, and, after further correspondence and negotiations, the owners decided to sell her at the first opportunity.

At Key West the bark was refitted and then continued on to New York. On arrival at New York she was taken over by William Lord's brother Tobias. In February of 1847 she was sold to the packet firm of Woodhull, Minturn, & Wendell of New York City for $14,000.[37]

January of 1847 had passed, and the better part of February, before all matters were squared away and the *Abbot Lord* could sail. Blaisdell sent a final accounting to Daniel Lord on 22 February.

I am at length loaded and Ready for sea shall sail to night if I can git My crew Onboard. wich of late ships have had great Dificulty in doing. you may think that I had Ort to have ben away before. but realy I have used my utmost Exertions to git filled up and to git Off. but I could not do it with Out taking low rates. I have at length succeded in gitting the highest rates as they advanced, I wrote you that I had ingaged at 7/8d—but there was Only 593 Bales and then I wanted about 120 bales more to fill up and I found great dificulty to git that small lot, after I had given away the consignment, wich detained me nearly a week but I have at last succeded, and @ 1d- for the balance My freight and primage will amount to about two thousand six hundred pounds as near as I can calculate, the last 120 bales I have not yet got the weight so I have averaged it with the Other lot, I am drawing 17 ft. Wich is full deep anough to cross the bar, you will learn better by the price currant Respecting freights then I can tell you I sent you One yesterday, I think there is a good chance for freight to advance but too late for me to profet by it now, but it is the General Opinion that freights will keep up here all through the summer and I hope to git back in time to imbrace them, and make up my loss for this time a report has Jest came up that 20 ships is in the river and 11 in the offing,—

I will send you annaxed account of disbursements as near as I can git at it. some of the bills I have not got in yet and therefore have to Guess at them you will percive the $240. was paid for Hospital money On the passengers wich makes

it run up higher. but I am frightened to find my disbursements so high & still I
have gone to no unnesacery Expence and ben as prudent as I possably could—
I have Jest got my accounts in and my freight & Primage amounts to £2559.5.0—
By Freight from London as per freight

		List £112.9.11 @$4.80		$ 539.98
"	"	Less charges, Commissions,		
		discharging collecting &c	33.93	
"	"	Advertising Recieps—		
		Books &c	5.00	
"	"	Entering at the custom house	17.35	56.28
				$483.70

By—cash brought from Bremen as
per a/c £45.0-0 sold @ $4.85 .... 218.25
By my draft On the freight £599.16.8
@ 4 3/4% Premium 2792.54

	$3494.49
Balance—	33.76
	$3538.25

Charges
To Paid		seamens wages inward cooking &c	440.00	
"	"	Advanced wages Outwards about	220.00	
"	"	Mairs fees On the Passengers	27.87	
"	"	Hospital money On the passengers ...	220.50	
"	"	Compress Bills	415.00	
"	"	Stevedore Bill discharging &		
		loading	497.00	
"	"	Towage Bills up & down the river	445.00	
"	"	Pilotage in & out	106.75	
"	"	Levey fees	100.00	
"	"	Harbour master & Port wardens fees .	18.10	
"	"	Stores Groceries ship chandlery		
		&c about	350.00	
"	"	Bakers Bill	48.00	
"	"	Repairing Camboos, tinware &c	19.00	
"	"	Butchers Bill marketing &c	25.00	
"	"	Bending sails & laibour	10.00	
"	"	Brokers Commissions On the Freight .	566.63	
"	"	Negotiating On $2792 @ 1 1/4% ...	34.90	
			$3538.25[38]	

The amounts of his disbursements in New Orleans would continue to be an
endless source of amazement for Captain Blaisdell throughout his years of
command. While comfortable in the knowledge that he had obtained the
highest rates then available, the shadow cast on his efforts by the still higher
rates rumored for the future caused him to downplay his success and justify his
actions. Notwithstanding his protests, at nearly $12,500 the freight was a

respectable one, especially when compared with others taken during his career.

After her arrival in Liverpool the captain chartered the *Abbot Lord* to carry freight and passengers to Boston. The potato blight that had spread across northern Europe in 1845 had struck especially hard in Ireland, causing widespread hunger and deprivation. With each succeeding year the number of people trying to reach America increased. Many of these emigrants crossed the Irish Sea to Liverpool, which soon became a major embarkation point for them. Several charter companies there offered to transport them across the Atlantic. Of the four million people who emigrated to the United States between 1840 and 1860, the Irish and the Germans accounted for far the largest share.[39] United States laws set down the regulations governing the transport of emigrants to her shores. The codes attempted to stem gross overcrowding and its accompanying disease and suffering. One such act was passed by Congress in February 1847. Far from home in Liverpool, Captain Blaisdell and other masters taking passengers bound for the States were keenly interested in the bill and its ramifications. Blaisdell explained their position on the law in a letter to Daniel Lord on 23 April.

I wrote you by the last steamer to Boston dated the 15 informing you of my arival, and having chartered the Abbot Lord for Boston for a lump sum of £800. to take freight and passangers, & load to 15 ft. to give the charters 15 days after the ship got a Loading berth, since wich I have delivered the cargo in good Order and ben On a loading berth 8 days, I shall probably be away from here about the 10th of may, there is a great Excitement here relative to the New Act respecting passangers there is various opinions wether it is 14 ft. clear of the berths Or 14 ft. inclusive. but as Our consuls here has not had any Orderes from Our Government transmited to them, they dont consider the law takes affect until the 31st of may here so the most of the ships are taking there full compliments by the Old law, or alowing Each passanger 14 ft. wich amounts to about the same—

I wrote you in my last that I should take the freight money With me, about £2000. but as my weight falls short of the Invoice nearly £100 I shall not probably have above £1900 to take with me. I dont know but I have done rong in Not shipping it by the steamer agreable to your Instructions but I thought when you wrote me you had no Idear of my coming to the North. Otherwais you would have prefered shipping it by the Abbot Lord. If I have Erred it was for want of due reflection. my Intentions was good I thought it would be to your Intrest to ship it in your Own ship as it saved the freight and could be Insured here as low by the Abbot Lord as by the steamer. however I have reflected On it since I wrote you last and dont know but I have done rong, but my motives was pure.—

the Inspecters passed the Bark with Out any hesatation and prononsed her better then meny new ships. we have accounts from the states up to the 5th of April it seams that flour & Corn freights was good at that time. and I hope I shall be in time for you to Obtain a good freight for the Bark. I should like to spend the summer at home if it is no Inconveniance to you to git an Other master. but at the same time I will not put you to any inconveniance. for I feel my self under an

Obligation to you for your kindness in giving me the ship When I was Out of imploy.[40]

When fully enacted, the 1847 law called for the number of passengers a vessel could carry to be determined by a ratio of one person for every fourteen feet of clear deck space. The amount of deck space required increased slightly if the clearance between decks dropped below six feet. Should the orlop deck be called into service, thirty feet of clear deck space was mandated. Such a precaution could do little to mitigate the unsavory accommodations afforded by the lowest deck in a ship, a place usually reserved for coils of cable and other stores.

Previous and subsequent bills set forth specifications to cover most aspects of the travelers' physical environment, including such things as the dimensions of berths, proper ventilation, cooking facilities, and adequate provisions.[41] Despite such official minimum standards, the overall accommodations could only have been cramped and uncomfortable. The willingness of these people to undergo the hardships of an ocean crossing reflected the hopelessness they were leaving behind and their dreams of opportunity in America.

The 173 passengers on board the *Abbot Lord* began their Atlantic crossing on 12 May. The letter Captain Blaisdell wrote from Liverpool the day before detailed his last minute financial arrangements, and included news of Daniel Lord's ship *Excelsior* and William Lord's bark *Diantha*.

I am now ready for sea and shall sail tomorrow morning wind and weather permiting for Boston, I wrote you that I had Chartered for a lump sum of £800— but the charters after gitting the ship down to the draft stipulaited had some freight left Out. and I agreed to take it On half the freight or divide it with them wich makes it amount to about £850. £481 freight to be collected at Boston as per bills of Lading. the balance they have paid me in cash here. I have about £1,800 in soveriegns Wich I take with me, I wrote you that I should probably have £2,000. but they got more freight then they Expected consiquently did not have so much to pay me here. my freight from New Orleans fell short about £90. as I did not git settled and git my bills in until late, I have not time to make out an a/c to send you but hope all will be satisfactory at my return to Boston, the Excelcior arrived here On the 8 Inst. the Diantha has got a freight for Havana makes £400, wich I think is verry good for that port, I notice by the last a/c from New york that freights was down. but dont doubt but there will be a reaction and hope the Abbot Lord will be On the spot in good time I have Onboard 173 passengers. wich gives 14 ft. to Each including the berths. wich is the Way it is Generaly understud here—
the ship is drawing 15 1/2 ft.[42]

There were countless matters and details that required Captain Blaisdell's careful consideration before he sailed. His attention to the number of passengers is understandable in light of the law's penalties for overcrowding. A culpable master was subject to a fifty-dollar fine for every passenger carried above the vessel's legal capacity, and he would also run the risk of serving a

one-year prison sentence.[43]   The nuances of the financial agreement made in
the charter party demanded special scrutiny.   Although unknown to him at
the time, the terms of the charter party negotiated in Liverpool, and the fact
that the balance of his freight was to be paid in Boston, would provide
difficulties for Captain Blaisdell at the end of his passage.

A little over five weeks after clearing Liverpool, the *Abbot Lord* lay in
quarantine off Deer Island in Boston Harbor, where a temporary quarantine
station had been established because many shiploads of arriving Irish were
ravaged by a virulent fever.   Uncertain how long he would be detained, the
captain dispatched a quick report to Daniel Lord on 20 June.

> I arrived here On the Evening of the 19- 38 days from Liverpool with passengers
> and acording to the new regulation am put in quarentine for how long will
> depend upon circumstances. the passengers are prety healthy. I lost two On the
> Passage One adult with Consumption and One Infant With a coald. but the
> health Officer has put me Down for 20 days, if this finds you in Boston I Supose
> you will write me by the health vissit to morrow. I have about £18.00 Onboard
> Wich I supose you can take Out providing I am not cleared. . . .
>
> P S Messrs. Harndon & Co is the Passengers agent.[44]

By the following day, after checking with another master whose vessel was also
in quarantine, the captain had a much better idea of his situation.
Though, due to misinformation, Captain Blaisdell did not have the facts
strictly correct, the news was not good.

When entering an American port, a vessel carrying immigrants expected to
pay a tax.   Collected by the individual states, and known colloquially as head
money, the tax was levied on passengers arriving in the United States for the
first time.   Massachusetts collected the tax until 1872, when the state legisla-
ture abolished it in an effort to make Boston more attractive than New York as
a port of entry for steamship lines.   In 1876 the United States Supreme Court
struck down the nationwide practice as unconstitutional.[45]   Captain Blaisdell's
initial impression that new regulations had superseded the payment of head
money was some twenty-five years premature.

It was the bonding of passengers that apparently took him by surprise.
Passenger bonding laws differed from state to state.   In Massachusetts the
master of any vessel carrying passengers was required to report their names and
port of embarkation to the municipal authorities.   The city officials could then
demand that the master post a bond of $1,000 for any individual with no
apparent means of support, in order to prevent their falling to the public
charge.   The bond could be reduced to the nominal amount of two dollars, or
even waived, at the discretion of the proper officials.[46]   The dilemma was, who
would post the bond?   Until that question was resolved the captain, the bark,
and the passengers would all remain in official limbo.   Such a situation would
in turn breed new concerns for the continued health of the passengers, on

Boston July 2° 1847

Mr. Lord.
Dear Sir.

We have not commenced Discharging yet. I was at the Customhouse this morning to see if I could git a general permit to commence Saturday morning but the Collecter told me I could not have it before monday and as there is but free permits out. and as monday is a holy day we cannot commence til Tuesday. I got a letter from Mr. Nason to day saing he should be here Tuesday. and then if you have no objection I should like to go home. — I forgot to name to you When you was here about the Windless bring broken if you will authorise me I will set a carpenter about Repairing it, I dont know that the ship needs any other repairs at present.

I remain your Obedient Servant
Jotham Blaisdell

which the length of the quarantine depended, and the added expense to the bark of keeping them on board. None of these problems escaped the captain's notice as he wrote to Daniel Lord on 21 June.

Sir I wrote you a few lines yesterday By the health Visit to inform you of my arrival &c as the health Officer stoped but a few minuets onboard I could learn but little from him respecting the new regulation of passengers. I have since seen Capt Knox [Knapp] of the ship John Courrier who informed me that the Citty authorities required bonds for all the Passengers instead of the head money Or Commutation as formaly and that the agent refused to give bonds Consequently his Owners was Obliged to give bonds. this is bad business had I have known this at Liverpool I should not have taken this charter. I wrote you that Harndon & Co was the Passengers agents. I hope this Will find you in Boston so that you can attend to it the commissioners will probably be Onboard to morrow the Passengers are all in such good health I am in hopes that they will let me Out of quarantine soon but should they persist in keeping them Onboard any length of time they will be sure to git sick this hot Wether. besides they have nothing Onboard to Eat but Bread and but very few any money to buy with. I Wrote you that I had about 1,800 soveriegns Onboard I think it will be well to git them Out.

They have jest ben Onboard and counted and Examined the passengers and they made such a good appearance that I think there will be but few if any that will require bonding. and if they do not git sick before we are cleared from quarentine I am in hopes there will be but little Or no Expence On them. but this whet weather is rather unfavorable for them by keeping them confined below—

if ther is any letters for me I will thank you to send them Off by the docter. my letters Generaly comes to the care of Mr. Callender.[47]

The anticipated letters undoubtedly brought news from home, updates of events in Kennebunk that had caused the captain in April to ask to leave the *Abbot Lord* at the end of the voyage. Surely there would be a letter relating the progress made on William Lord's new ship, a vessel Captain Blaisdell held an interest in and would command. Most certainly another letter announced that in May, while the captain was at sea, his wife had given birth to a son. The contents of his letters, pleasurable as they were, could only have increased his impatience to conclude his business and return to Maine.

On shore, Daniel Lord and his legal and financial representatives, N. & C.B. Dana, were working to get the bark out of quarantine. Since the English charterers, Pilkington and Wilson, had given Captain Blaisdell no funds to defray the expenses of head money and bonding, Lord applied to the passengers' Boston agents, Harndon & Company. Negotiations between the two parties were not resolved quickly. Initially, Harndon & Company were reluctant to cover the costs as they feared they might not recover their outlay from Pilkington and Wilson. They wanted a bond from Lord to hold as surety they would suffer no loss.[48] As the days passed with expenses and the risk to the passengers' health both increasing, Lord acted and gave his own bond to the city authorities. Shortly after doing so he was able to come to terms with Harndon & Company. They agreed to pay the head money and post the bond with the city. Lord for his part pledged to refund their costs if it should prove that the vessel, rather than the charterer, was liable for the expenses. Harndon & Company's bond was substituted for Lord's, and Monday, 28 June, found the *Abbot Lord* alongside Battery Wharf in Boston at last, where her cargo of iron, steel, and other merchandise would be discharged.[49]   A week later Captain Blaisdell made a final report to Daniel Lord.

> We have not Commenced Discharging yet. I was at the Customhouse this morning to see if I Could git a General permit to commence saturday morning but the Colecter told me I could not have it before monday next and as there is but few permits Out, and as monday is a holy day we cannot Commence til Tues.d. I got a letter from Mr. Nason to day saying he should be here Tues.d. and then if you have no Objections I should like to go home.—I forgot to name to you When you was here about the Windless being broken if you will autherise me I will set a carpenter about Repairing it. I dont know that the ship neads any Other repairs at presant.[50]

Having survived his bout with small pox, Mr. Nason had been named to succeed Captain Blaisdell, who was only too happy to turn the bark over to his command. Finishing up his business in Boston, the captain returned to Kennebunk to rejoin his family and renew his association with William Lord.

SIX

The Ship *Mount Washington*
1847-1848

THE FATES appeared to smile on Captain Blaisdell and his endeavors as he arrived home that July, but any satisfaction he may have felt as events unfolded was undoubtedly tempered by the all too familiar knowledge that they were fickle and could quickly frown. Crossing the threshold of his home, he found his family waiting with its newest addition. On 16 May Elizabeth Blaisdell had delivered her sixth child, a boy. The natural joy of the proud parents was amplified by the fact that, at last, fifteen years after the death of young Jotham, they again had a son. The child was christened William Jotham in honor of his father and William Lord.

The happiness occasioned by the little boy's birth was soon overshadowed by the fact that the health of both mother and son was far from good. As the summer progressed and their conditions did not improve, a decision was reached, and arrangements were made for Elizabeth to accompany her husband on his upcoming voyage in the hope that the change of atmosphere and sea air would prove beneficial.

The new ship Captain Blaisdell would command was already under construction when he returned to Kennebunk. The keel of a vessel was generally laid in the spring, and she would be ready for sea by late fall. William Lord had initiated plans for her construction and had decided on a full-rigged ship. He brought three other men into the venture, but remained the principal owner, holding a 3/8 share. The other owners were Robert Smith, Jr., in whose yard she would be built, with a 1/4 interest, Captain Charles Barry also with 1/4, and Captain Blaisdell with 1/8.[1] When the ship was registered, Lord did Captain Blaisdell the honor of allowing him to appear as the principal owner of record.

The name chosen for the new ship, *Mount Washington*, was probably suggested by Captain Barry or his wife Sarah, who was William Lord's daughter. The couple, married in June 1845, had spent their honeymoon in the White Mountains and were very impressed with what they had seen there.

The *Mount Washington* was built at the Landing yard of part-owner Robert Smith, Jr., under master carpenter Asa Durell, with Captain Blaisdell supervising. While Smith was a part-owner and was held in high regard, it is

57

evident that Blaisdell's role was to look out for the owners' interests. As Captain Barry noted to his father-in-law Lord: "I have no doubt Mr. Smith will build a good ship, but he is such a good-natured, easy soul, that I think you will require to look after his workmen a little to see they do not share in poor pieces & sap. I hope he will have a good foreman as it makes considerable difference if he has good taste in turning off the ship because with good taste he can do a great deal to the well appearance of the ship without adding to the cost."[2]

In light of Captain Barry's concern, it is interesting to note the reaction of one of his Boston acquaintances after seeing the *Mount Washington*, "She is a good, wholesome-looking ship but can't say much as to her Beauty; and her finish would not suit a Man of your taste to go in—'tis my opinion."[3]

Work continued on the *Mount Washington* all through the summer and fall. Captain Blaisdell kept William Lord advised of progress and periodically sent him updated lists of needed articles. Shipbuilding and its allied trades were the life's blood of the local economy. Apart from the carpenters and laborers who worked on the *Mount Washington* in Smith's yard, many local artisans and merchants contributed to her construction. Palmer Walker made cushions for the cabin; Joseph Sargeant did her gilt work; Thomas Maling prepared her rigging. Jesse Towne and a crew of local men took her down the river where her rudder was mounted, her masts were stepped, and she was rigged out. When ballast was needed it was supplied by Asa English, Samuel Boothby, Joseph Gooch, and others.[4]

When at last the *Mount Washington* was completed her total cost amounted to $31,128.52, and for his 1/8 share Captain Blaisdell paid $3,891.06, a considerable investment for him.[5] But it was with a feeling of accomplishment that he could look upon the new ship as she rocked on the gentle swells of the lower river. She was a symbol, something real to show for the years of hard work and sacrifice. He still had his share in the *Swiss Boy*, the investment in the *Francis Watts* had been recouped at her sale, and now there was the *Mount Washington*. If all went well he could increase his holdings in the future.

The *Mount Washington* was a two-decked vessel 143 feet 3 inches between perpendiculars, 28 feet 8 inches in beam, and had a depth of 14 feet 4 inches.[6] Work continued on her all through the summer and into the fall. Nearly square at bow and stern, the *Mount Washington* was built to carry cotton. Maine shipyards were especially noted for the construction of cotton ships. The vessels' bottoms were made broad and flat to facilitate crossing the shallow water of the Mississippi bar. They stowed well and carried 2,000 pounds of cotton for each registered ton. Traditionally, they had the reputation for being good sailors when before the wind.

The 1840s and 1850s were boom years for Southern cotton. From the days of its beginnings, the trade had evolved into what became known as the "cotton triangle." Vessels registered in New England and Northern ports would sail down the Atlantic coast to the commercial centers of the South—Savannah, Mobile, and especially New Orleans—deliver Northern goods and then load cotton. The cotton was purchased from the plantations by American merchants who then sold it to European (or New England) spinners through the agency of brokers in the major ports who received a commission for their services. Due to commercial ties and the restriction of foreign vessels from the coastwise trade, American vessels had an advantage in transporting cotton to its European destinations. From Europe the vessels returned to the ports of the Northeast, carrying manufactured goods, coal, or raw materials, thus completing the third leg of their voyage and the last side of the imaginary triangle.

The importance and growth of the trade cannot be overestimated. Volume increased by a factor of four from 732,218 bales shipped in 1830 to more than 3,000,000 in 1859. In 1852, 800,000 tons of American shipping and 40,000 men were employed in the foreign cotton trade. Those figures represent 47 percent of the registered fleet at that time.[7]

When she was registered on 20 December 1847 the 547-ton *Mount Washington* embarked on her career as a trader. A trading vessel carried a cargo belonging to her owner, and for her first cargo William Lord had purchased a load of hay for her to take to New Orleans. Such trading voyages had characterized the American merchant marine in the first part of the century, when vessels were small, but by the *Mount Washington*'s time they were relatively rare. After her initial passage, the *Mount Washington* joined the bulk of American vessels as a general cargo carrier, transporting the goods of others in consideration of freights.[8]

While the ship's hold was being filled, the Blaisdell family made its preparations ashore. Captain and Mrs. Blaisdell entrusted their younger daughters to the care of their aunt and uncle, Leonard and Sarah Webber. The eldest, sixteen-year-old Elizabeth, would sail as companion and nurse to her mother.

Once aboard the ship, Captain Blaisdell remained on deck as the pilot guided her down the river. Elizabeth and the children soon retired to the warmth of the cabin. Though not large, the cabin had been made as comfortable as possible. It was carpeted, and the furnishings included a desk, two upholstered chairs with ottomans, a mahogany table, a mirror, and even a spitoon.[9] To these Elizabeth may have added personal belongings to give a more home-like appearance, but most moveable or breakable objects were stowed away during a voyage and only displayed when in port.

Leaving Kennebunk in the last week of December, the *Mount Washington* arrived at New Orleans on 22 January. Already in port were the Kennebunk ships *Lucy* and *Howard*, as well as the *Henry Ware*, which belonged to William Lord's brother George. Captain Blaisdell wrote to William Lord giving him the particulars of the voyage and his opinion of the new ship.

this is to inform you of my arrival at leangth at the city this morning I arrived at the Bar On the 12th and sailed up the River with in 9 miles of the turn where I have ben Ever since in hopes to be able to sail all the way Up, but the wind continued dead ahead and I got tired awaiting any longer so I took steam the rest of the way wich cost me $140-

I have had rather bad luck with my crew two of them was taken sick the 2d day out with the Small Pox & One died the 12th day the Other has ben sick all the Voyage—respecting business here I have not yet had an Oppertunity of Informing my self, but I beleave prety dull I find plenty of Ships amongst the rest is the Henary Whare, Lucy & Howard. I hapened to drop into the same Pier with the H. Whare and found her a loading for Liverpool @1/2[cent per pound]. Wich he tells me is the highest noch of rates and scarce at that. I fear the hay has come to a Poor market.—Respecting the Qualities of the Mt. Washington so far as I have ben able to Juge She is a good comfortable ship a verry good Working ship & a good sea boat steers verry Well and sails as well as could be Expected She is not fast but midling. I have not had a good Chance to try her. She leaked some more the latter part of the passage but it has stoped since I have ben in the river, I had One heavy wind and a bad sea in the Gulf but not a drop of salt water has come Over the rail during the passage.—I supose your vewes respecting freights remains the same as when I left, that is not to take the presant Rates that is 1/2. I hope you will keep me advised as Often as convenient, I will write you again as soon as I have time to look round a little and see what the prospect is,—I think that my wifes health has improved since she Left home thanks to your Generosity in permiting me to take her.[10]

Business continued to be poor in New Orleans. Captain Blaisdell waited, a victim of the law of supply and demand; as the number of ships in port increased in relation to the amount of cotton to be carried, the freighting rates fell. There was an additional complication in that the demand for Southern cotton in Britain was also down. While waiting for a change in rates the Captain had other business to attend to. He bought and shipped a personal order of goods for William Lord, and sold the cargo of hay he had brought from Kennebunk.

The hay was carefully separated into six different categories, which sold at varying rates. There were the gradations of coarse hay: good, stained, and crossed (mixed), as well as good fine, stained fine, and crossed fine.[11] The captain sold it all, except three of four bales that were rotten, for $875.42.

Three weeks later business had still not improved, and the captain informed William Lord of the situation on 12 February.

I have Omited writing you from day to day in hopes to have something more favorable to communicate. but I have waited in vain, the prospect looks rather worse then better, since I wrote you last British Ships come poring in by the score—there is no change in the rates of freights 1/2 a 1 ct. but few engagements made for the last three days, the decline of cotton in England has brought business to a stand for the present.—I have sold the hay and delivered it and got paid for the most of it, I will send you the a/c as soon as I git the weigers a/c.—it will average about $15 per ton in all there is about 54 tons in all there was a large proportion stained and damaged. I have Executed your Order viz—2 Bbls. molasses, 2- of Flour l of Sugar, 2 1/2 Bbls Mess Beef, & 2 Kegs of Lard and shipped it in the Bark Attica, Capt. McLullan for Boston. Consigned to George Callander Esqr and send him a Bill of Lading, the following is the Prices I paid

```
2 Bbls flour of the best quality @ $5.75  . . . . . . . . . . . . . . . . . . . . . . . .   11.50
2- do Molasses—82 Gall. @19 cts  . . . . . . . . . . . . . . . . . . . . . . . . . .   15.58
1- do sugar, 242 lbs. @ 5 3/4 cts  . . . . . . . . . . . . . . . . . . . . . . . . . .   14.17
2 Kegs Lard 85 lbs. @ 7 1/4  "  . . . . . . . . . . . . . . . . . . . . . . . . . . . .    6.16
2 1/2 Bbls famaly mess Beef @ $5.50 . . . . . . . . . . . . . . . . . . . . . . . .   11.00
                                                                            $58.41
```

the freight is $4.30 wich is to be paid On delivery I think you will find them Good articles and they will Be stowed nearly on top of the cargo—

I hope to git a letter from you soon and git your Opinion respecting the prospects of Freights here,—My idear is not verry high at presant,—

the Henry Ware is loaded and will probably go down to night, She has 2044 bales of Cotton and 400 sacks of Corn wich I think is verry good carrying,—hoping soon to have something more favorable.[12]

Before he could receive an answer from Lord the captain acted. Seeing no signs of improvement in the near future, he decided to take the best offer he could find and hoped to make up any loss once across the Atlantic.

New Orleans Feb,y 24—1848

I wrote you a few days since giving you my vewes of things here respecting the Prospects of freights. Since that things has Grown Worse instead of better as you will see by the Price Currant there has ben two Or three ships taken up for Havre at 15/16 of a cent, and some for Liverpool @ 15/32—and british ships cant git Even that. ships are increasing and the General Opinion is that there will be no improvement this year Or at least for a long time to come I have ben in treaty for a freight of cotton for Cronstadt for some days, there is Only three cargos goes there per year, two has already gone, and this is the last, and I have taken it at the Low rate of 15/32 of a cent that is shaving pretty snug when we have to cut a cent up into 32 parts, but such is the case I was in hopes to have got 1 1/4 c. but this is all I could squeese Out of them, I think that any chance for freight back will be better then Eather Liverpool Or Havre, as I have a rainge of all the Baltic & North sea ports before me I am in hopes that I shall find something at Cronstadt as I shall be Early or amongst the first ships, Ether to the States Or som bye Port last year there was a large quantity of Grane shiped from Rusia to the north sea and some good freights given, I shall write from Elsanore to different places On my way up so that I can git an answer at Cronstadt and see Where I can do best, perhaps you may be able to make a charter in Boston for the ship, this is a Verry poor business but I have done what I thought was best, the prospect looks so bad I was afraid to hold On any longer for fear it Would git worse instead of better the difference wich I git is rather more than they make in sugar frieghts between the

North Sea and the Baltic, I think if you was here to see how things is that you would not advise me to lay any longer but make the best of it and be Off, the most of the ships that are Loading here now are hung up cant git Cotton to fill up at the rate they began at,—I have not yet colected all my pay for the hay the whole amount is $820- and I have got $700-, there is a little difference in the weight but I think I shall git it I will then send you the a/c that you can Settle with Peas,—I have nothing more of importance to communicate. I shall write you again how I progress in Loading &c—[13]

Lord informed the other owners of the captain's course of action. They felt that in the given conditions what had been done was the best they could hope for, but with Lord they agreed that not much could be done in the way of a charter. Captain Barry expressed their view when he wrote:

I was glad to hear that the Mt. Washington had got as good freight as she has although rather low figures—but I think it is a great deal better than to any of the other ports as his ship will be early there & likely to get a much better return freight than from either L'pool or Havre.
My own impression is that Capt. B- would be quite as likely to do full as well there as we can here—as he is well acquainted there (New Orleans) & most charter parties are of a speculative character.[14]

A charter party was the written contract between a vessel's master or owners and those who wished to hire her for the transport of their goods. Depending upon the circumstances, a vessel could be taken by the month, the voyage, or the ton. The rate of payment agreed to by the contracting parties was her freight. Generally the terms called for the master to have his vessel in good general order and adequately manned and stocked to perform the voyage. Above all else, he undertook to deliver the cargo at the designated port in good condition. The shipper could be obligated to load or unload the cargo within a specified time and was expected to pay the freight upon the arrival of his goods at their destination. If a vessel was hired under a single contract by a merchant or group of merchants she was known as a chartered ship. However, if she carried the goods of several independent shippers she was correctly termed a general ship.[15] Captain Blaisdell hoped a charter made in Boston by Lord or his agent would guarantee a return cargo for the ship from Russia. While subsequently offered one himself in New Orleans, however, he turned it down.

Once the arrangements on the Cronstadt cargo had been finalized the captain began having the cotton loaded. In all, the *Mount Washington* took on 2,250 bales of cotton, weighing 983,105 pounds or 441.5 tons. Her resulting freight and primage came to $11,938.50. Against her freight were charged her disbursements or expenses while in port. Two of the largest expenses were preparation and loading of the cotton. Before they could be put into the ship's hold the bales of cotton had to be compressed, to take up as little room as possible in the hold. Captain Blaisdell paid a press on Canal

Street the rate of fifty cents per bale for a total cost of $1,125.00. After the bales were compressed, stevedores were hired to manhandle and wedge the 400-pound bales into the hold. The stevedore's bill for stowing the *Mount Washington*'s cotton came to $792.30. In addition to these two major items were the expenses incidental to any voyage, such as pilot fees, port charges, seamen's wages, and provisions. In the end the disbursements for the *Mount Washington* while in New Orleans totaled $3,446.25.[16] As the sale of the hay had only brought about $800.00 to offset the expenses, Captain Blaisdell found it necessary to borrow against the freight to pay them.

Nearly a month after having accepted the cargo, Captain Blaisdell was ready to sail. Overall, he considered that he had made the best of a bad situation.

New Orleans March 27th 1848
I am at leangth loaded and ready for sea shall go down to night if I can git my crew Onboard. you will no doubt think I have ben a long time aloading and so I have but I have tried my best to git dispach the cotton pressed so drove that we cannot git cotton. I have had to wait ten days for a lot of 50 bales wich was in One of the presses—

I have got in 2250 bales of Cotton 983105 lbs wich I think is prety good carrying considering the poor lot of cotton that have in the Bales runs very large and light no doubt with a fair run of Cotton she would carry 100000 lbs, and of small Tenesee cotton 2400 bales My Freight amounts to $11367.15 & Freight & primage to $568.35 Total $11935- My Expences is higher then I expected but I have got along as cheap as posable I have had to lay in a larger stock of provisions for this Voyage then I should have done for Liverpool or Havre and laying here so long it increased the Expenses. I have had to draw on the freight for £740.- on Baring Brothers @7 1/2 percent if I am fortunate anough to git a good freight home I shall make a saving go of it yet, I dont know but I may consider my self fortunate after all in Excepting this freight as bad as it is,—the newes from Europe has had a bad Efect here has put Every thing to a stand. and will probably remain so til the next steamer arives, it is the Opinion of some here that Freights in american ships will improve On the strength of the Revolution in france, there is no change as yet, I saw your Son to day he is quite well and harty

I have 17 Bales on deck wich you can insure Or not as you please. the ship draws 14 1/2 feet On an Even keel. I was offered a charter to day from St. Petersburg by the way of Rio & to New Orleans of about $9000, but I prefered taking my chance, if I am detained at the Bar I will write you again and give you a coppy of my disbursements, they brought me in for my second Wharfage.[17]

In New Orleans at the same time as Captain Blaisdell was William Lord's son Hartley. A captain himself, he would go on to take over the handling of his father's interests and become a successful businessman. He and Captain Blaisdell were well acquainted and he naturally took an interest in the captain and the new ship. On 23 March he observed to his father: "The Mt. Washington most loaded. Capt. B- has some trouble getting his cargo—like all others as all vessels have been detained in the same way. His family are pretty well, I am much pleased with the ship—model, etc. only think her a little too sharp forward."[18] Later, when the ship sailed on 28 March, he noted:

> The Mt. Washington went down river this evening and I have a letter for you from Capt. B- which I shall mail with this one tomorrow—His family were all pretty well—The child looks sick and was rather slim in health as well as body—I should think as it is very small indeed—But I hope it will take a start at sea and grow stronger.—The ship had in a good cargo and will carry well I should think—Capt. B- has of course told you the particulars—but I should think it not an average of N. O. cotton and with a fair lot would carry much more the bales being larger and spongy—all that I saw—and I hear there is a great difference in this lot and the H. Ware's cargo bales being larger & lighter in the Mt. W—The ship looks as well as any of the cotton ships here—and appeared stiff & is I think in many respects better than the Hartley—a better looking ship—as large a carrier and will be stiff I think—but I don't believe she is so strong or well built as the H—but good enough for the times and trade.[19]

When ready for sea, Blaisdell engaged a steamer to tow the *Mount Washington* down the Mississippi. Just before sailing he wrote a quick note to William Lord.

> S. W. Pass march 29—1848
> This is to inform you that I am now over the Bar and to sea—I send this up by the steamer—I think that the ship will be midling stif
>   I wrote you yeaterday giving you the amount of my freight & I have nothing now of any moment to write. I trust to Git a letter from you at Elsinor Or Cronstadt and that you have ben able to Effect a good Charter for the ship home if not I hope I shall be able to git something that will be profitable Ether to the states Or some Out port,—if Mr. Elwell Or Leonard Webber should want a little Money to buy the children some clothes during my Absents—will you have the kindness to let them have it and Charge it to me I thought I should have had a chance before I got Out to take Out an a/c of my Expences here but we made no stop inside of the Bar, my Expences was much higher then I Expected I had to pay sea and Levee dues for One thing and laid in a large stock of Provisions for a long voyage for I may have to to to some Out ports wich will prolong the Voyage, but I hope that my a/c will be satisfactory to you.[20]

At the outset of the voyage it had been the opinion of both Blaisdell and Hartley Lord that the *Mount Washington* would be stiff. A stiff vessel had good initial stability, being able to carry sail in strong winds without heeling dangerously or capsizing. However, the *Mount Washington*'s passage across the Atlantic proved to be a frustrating one. April passed and much of May before the ship made an unscheduled stop at the Isle of Wight off the southern coast of England in a crank condition. The opposite of stiff, crank implied that she was topheavy and awkward to handle, perhaps because she carried too little ballast.[21] Blaisdell described the situation to William Lord.

Hartley Lord (1825–1912), the shipmaster son of William Lord, frequently corresponded with Blaisdell. Oil painting, artist unknown. *(Courtesy Brick Store Museum)*

Cronstadt, the port of entry for St. Petersburg, Russia. *Gleason's Pictorial*, 8 July 1854.

Mother Bank May 20—1848
I put in here yesterday in a Gale of wind from the South. I was off the Isle of Wight near in when it came On to blow heavy dead On shore so that I could not clear land on Eather tack the ship being verry Crank so I deamed it the most prudent to make a harbour. I start again this morning with the wind from the westward I was 50 days from the Bar to the Isle of White I have had a great deal of head winds and calms On the pasage. the ship is rather dull in light winds But she works verry well and appears to be verry strong You have undoubtedly heard of the war between Denmark & Germany all the German ports is Blockaded and it is Only a few days that the Blockade has ben taken off the Baltic it is thought that the dificulty will be settled soon, I fear that my long passage will be against me On account of gitting a return freight but I have got along as fast as posable.—22

The war that closed the Baltic had been brought on when Denmark tried to annex the duchies of Schleswig and Holstein. Although they nominally belonged to the Danish king, their populations were largely German, and Prussia objected to the Danish action with force of arms. The outcome of the 1848 war was indecisive, and it was refought a few years later, resulting in a German victory.23

With the blockade lifted, the *Mount Washington* continued on her way. In the view of the ship's owners the anticipated advantages of an early arrival had been the one positive aspect of the passage to Russia, but with each passing day of her long crossing the captain saw their hopes evaporate before his eyes. It was not until 14 June, nearly 2 1/2 months after leaving New Orleans, that the ship arrived at Cronstadt.

Before entering Cronstadt, the *Mount Washington* came to anchor near the guard-ship stationed outside the harbor. Captain Blaisdell submitted the ship's papers, including her bill of health and cargo manifests, to the boarding officers for inspection. The papers were then sealed and returned to him, and an official entry was made for the ship giving her name, master, nationality, and cargo. The customs officials then set about sealing all the hatches, making careful note of their number and location as they did so. When their preliminary duties were completed they returned to the guard-ship, leaving behind a pilot who took the *Mount Washington* into the harbor.

After reaching his assigned anchorage, the captain had twenty-four hours to deliver the sealed ship's papers to the customhouse. He was also expected to present a full and detailed report on his vessel. Her port of origin and length of passage had to be given. A list having the names and nationalities of all persons onboard—captin, crew, and any passengers—had to be drawn up. He also had to submit a complete accounting of every article the ship carried, from the cargo to the personal effects of the crew. Along with his declaration he had to hand over any letters then in his possession.

Excepting the captain's trip to the customhouse, no person was allowed to board or leave the *Mount Washington* until she had been officially inspected.

The superintendent of vessels and his deputy would arrive bearing the manifest submitted by Captain Blaisdell. After being inspected for tampering, the seals would be broken and the contents of the hold checked against the manifest. When all was found to be in order, inspectors were assigned to oversee the unloading of the cotton. The crew was then free to go ashore after being searched for contraband.[24]

The impatience Captain Blaisdell felt because of his lengthy passage and the further delay caused by the formalities of the ship's entry into port turned into frustration when he discovered business in Cronstadt was as poor as that which he had left in New Orleans. It was a far from rosy picture that he painted for William Lord.

Cronstadt June 21st 1848

I arrived here On the 14 Inst 78 days from New Orleans, the most teagous passage that I have Ever had but the most of ships have had verry long passages this year, two Brigs arrived today 82 days from Havana the ships Botton got verry foul the latter part of my passage wich made her verry dull with light winds, you may rest assured that I got her along as fast as I could, I have received four letters from you, two at Elsinore and two here I have commenced discharging and have got Out about 800 Bales, shall probably finish in about five days if the weather is good, I have jest returned from St Petersburg, I have seen all the Brokers & shipers I fear the prospect for a return freight is small in fact at preasant there is nothing for the states, the ship Bangor nearly the same sise of the mt. Washington Chartered for New York for $1500- wich is small business, the Broker thinks he will be able to git a load of deals for some port of france or spain at a low rate and there is another has a load of Bones for England wich he thinks he can git twenty shillings per ton it is a dirty stinking Cargo but still it is the best thing I can hear of, but I hope something better may Offer by the time my cargo is Out, if I can git a freight of Deals to Cadis and there take salt to some port in the states perhaps would do as well as anything, however I will try and make the best of it. this is unfortunate as it is likely to turn Out I could not have chused a worse port, but it is impossable to fore see Events, I thought when I ingaged this freight I was taking the best step to secure a return freight I will write you again as soon as I decide What to do or where to go, the Cotton comes Out in good Order so far, the decks leeks a little mostly about the houses, but she is verry tight in her bottom she is a good strong ship but not verry swift.—You write that you have sent Capt. Perkins out to settle the Swiss boy affair, I realy hope he will succead to your sattisfaction, I think as you observed they are all a lot of swindlers I wonder how Capt. Perkins lawyer undertook the suit without the hundred pounds, if we got a verdic in Our favor it was jest as well as though Capt. Perkins and the mate had been there—I forgot to mention in my last letter the diffucilty I have had with the compasses, there is some attraction wich makes the larboard binicle quite useless it being 5 points Out of the way the starboard One varies some times is nearly two points Out of the way and some times correct acording to the direction of the ships head I dont know what to lay it to Eather the stearing apperatus Or the tin On the bread lockers, wich is cloast by the binicles I shall take the tin off and deter-mane—it is verry dangerous I hope to be able to give you some more favorable account in my next.[25]

The *Swiss Boy* affair alluded to had begun the previous year. Captain Perkins had delivered a cargo to Belfast, Ireland. The consignee of the goods withheld £1,300 of the freight money on the grounds that they were damaged through the fault of the master and the brig.[26] Because of distance and other difficulties, litigation would drag on for quite some time.

While the cotton was being unloaded Captain Blaisdell continued to search for a cargo for the ship. He and his family made six trips from Cronstadt to St. Petersburg. For such trips a special pass was required in security conscious Russia. The Blaisdells took lodgings in the capital, where they could sleep and take their meals, and where Elizabeth and the children could wait while Jotham visited the brokers and shippers.[27] Although business consumed a great deal of time, an opportunity must have been found for the obligatory sightseeing.

Sometimes called the Venice of the North, St. Petersburg covered nineteen islands at the mouth of the Neva River. Along the canals were the opulent palaces of the nobility, and everywhere the golden domes and crosses of magnificent churches. On the northern shore of the Neva stood the great fortress of Saints Peter and Paul. What could have been farther from the small village they called home? Even the days were foreign to Elizabeth. In the summer St. Petersburg receives twenty-two hours of daylight. By eleven in the evening the sun had set; yet by midnight signs of approaching dawn were evident.

Lurking amid the seeming magic of this city of endless days with its palaces of yellow, blue, and white was the sinister reality of stalking death. Cholera had broken out in the capital and during the Blaisdells' stay reached epidemic proportions. Asiatic cholera is highly contagious, and the physical danger was very apparent to the captain and his wife. Captain Blaisdell was also aware that he stood the risk of a long quarantine, which would mean further delay and difficulties. At last he secured a cargo of deals (boards of fir or pine) destined for Bordeaux, France. He wrote to Kennebunk informing Lord of the arrangements.

> Cronstadt July 5th, 1848
> I wrote you by the last steamer advising you of my arrival the prospects of business &c since wich I have delivered the cargo in good Order and have Chartered the ship for Bourdous to load Deals at Whyburg about 50 miles from this @ 70 franks & 15% primage wich is verry low I am aware but this is the Only thing I could git and I thought it better then leaving in Balest, at Bourdoux I may git a small freight to New Orleans, I think I shall make Out nearly $4000, on the deals I have to give them 35 runing days for loading and discharging—150 franks dimurage I shall probably be 10 or 12 days loading—I have sent Bills to Baring Brothers for [£]2058-17-10 reserving money anough to pay my Portcharges at

Whyburg, I have bought Canvas enough to make a top sail & top Galt. Sail as it came some cheaper here then Elsewhere, I have also bought some Cordage and paid the Crew about $300—
   the Cholory is araging here verry bad   at St Petersburg there has ben 800 to 1000 Cases per day & from 400 to 500 deaths—wich is verry alarming, my wife is verry much alarmed.   I fear that I shall be subject to a quarantine in France but I hope not long—I will write you again before I leave Whyburg. I leave for there to day.[28]

The mention of demurrage and running days referred to the terms of the charter party drawn up for transporting the cargo.   In order to close the deal Captain Blaisdell had to give the charterers a total of thirty-five days for the loading of the deals in Vybourg and unloading them in Bordeaux.   If they exceeded the time allowed they agreed to pay 150 francs in demurrage or compensation for the delay.[29]

   After calling at the port of Vybourg to load the deals, the *Mount Washington* made the required stop at Elsinore during the first week of August. Soon she was on her way to France.   Although Captain Blaisdell was far from satisfied with the business he had concluded in Russia, there were no serious complaints from home.   George Callender wrote, "I think the Mt. Washington may do pretty well with the freights to Bordeaux & what she may get there."[30]   And part-owner Captain Barry, who was on a voyage to India, while not ecstatic, was satisfied with the captain's proceedings, as he informed his father-in-law Lord.   "Sarah writes me the Mt. Washington left Cronstadt for Bordeaux & New Orleans—I have tried to see some account of her in the papers but did not succeed.—I feared she would not be able to leave Cronstadt before all business was knocked in the head by the Cholera & thought she would be hardly able to do anything for home or anywhere else. I think she did quite as well as could be expected from N. Orleans and if she manages to pay her way this year will be all that can be expected."[31]

   In mid-September the *Mount Washington* arrived at Bordeaux, sixty miles up the Garonne River from the Bay of Biscay.   There had been sickness on board the ship again, perhaps cholera, but the exact nature of the illness and the fate of the sick man are not known.   At Bordeaux, a doctor visited the vessel sixteen times to treat a sailor and perform two bleedings, all at the expense of the vessel.   The doctor also returned on one occasion to vaccinate the Blaisdells' son William.[32]   The anxious parents were taking every precaution, having inadvertently exposed him to both small pox and cholera during a voyage that had been intended for his health.

   Despite any sickness, business went on.   The deals were unloaded and the captain made arrangements to carry wine to New Orleans.   While waiting for the casks of wine to be assembled and loaded he and his family had some time to relax.   He commissioned marine artist Richard Faxon to paint a picture of the new ship, and with his wife saw the city and did some shopping.   Both he and Elizabeth were susceptible to French fashion, having clothes made there and buying quantities of material to take back to Maine. In early November all was in order and the *Mount Washington* set sail for America almost one year after leaving Kennebunk.

The ship made much better time on her return passage, and by mid-December she was waiting to be towed up the Mississippi to New Orleans. Constantly shifting sand bars formed at the mouths of the Mississippi delta passes, so it was impossible to give masters accurate sailing directions for entering the river. For safety's sake they were advised to drop anchor and wait for a towboat when they reached a depth of ten fathoms as they approached the delta bars. Anchored inside the bars, the steam towboats ventured forth during daylight hours, cruising out ten to fifteen miles in fair weather. Stiff competition meant a sharp watch was kept, and vessels were seldom delayed for want of a towboat and river pilot. Before proceeding up river under tow, or under sail if the wind allowed, masters often stopped to report their arrival and pick up the latest market information at the telegraph station at the delta settlement called The Balize.[33]

The prospects that awaited the *Mount Washington* in New Orleans were no better than those she had found the previous February and March. In fact, the whole voyage had been marked by disappointment and ill-fortune. The annoying mishap during the tow upriver, which the captain recorded almost as a matter of course in the letter announcing his arrival, seemed almost to be a fitting end to a frustrating year.

> New Orleans Dec. 27—1848
> I take this Oppertunity to inform you of my arrival. I was 38 days to the S W pass, have ben nearly a week gitting up the river, the steam boats in gitting me over the bar broke all my horsers in three Or four peces, So as to compleatly spoil them & ran me On shore coming up the river Stearn first and has Injured the rudder & the stearing apperatus, so that I fear that I shall have to unhang the rudder—I fear I shall have to wait some time for a berth to discharge in, the Ship Radius has ben in twelve days from Bordeaux and has got no berth yet, respecting the freighting business here the prospect at preasant looks bad—I wrote you from Bordeaux previous to my sailing, stating that I should take the balance of my freight money here I shall have about $4000, please to write me what part of it I shall Remit to you, and if you would prefer my taking a Coastwise freight providing I can git a good or deacent One the Cholery has subsided a little the last two days, in hast
>
> I remain your Obedient Servant
> Jotham Blaisdell[34]

Steam towboats were essential for the passage of
sailing ships through the Mississippi delta. Here
off the Balize, the *Panther* tows the ships *Shirley*
and *Julius* up the Mississippi. Oil painting by
James Guy Evans and Edward Arnold, 1850.
(Courtesy Peabody Museum, Salem, Massachusetts)

Liverpool, on England's west coast, became that
nation's principal port of entry for cotton and
port of departure for emigrants. Painted by
George Chambers, engraved by James Carter,
published by Thomas Hague, 1841.
(Courtesy Mariners' Museum, Newport News, Virginia)

SEVEN

Home the Hard Way
1847–1848

THE CAPTAIN'S initial pessimism moderated somewhat after his arrival. He found freighting rates not as low as he had expected and rather on the increase. Unable to conduct any negotiations for a new freight until his cargo of wine should be unloaded, he attended to the damage suffered by the *Mount Washington* as she had been towed up the Mississippi. After viewing the damage himself, and consulting with a carpenter, he decided against replacing the rudder or steering mechanism. At the time it probably seemed a wise decision, not only materially, as the rudder could apparently be soundly repaired, but also economically. Before the year was out, however, he would have cause to regret his careful husbandry.

Once the *Mount Washington* was in port, Captain Blaisdell notified the cargo's consignee of her arrival, and after making a report to the health officer he went on to the customhouse. Because the ship was laden with wine the captain had forty-eight hours to file a special written report with the revenue inspector. The revenue inspector or the port surveyor would then inspect the cargo, carefully noting the contents and proof of each cask in the hold. After a permit to discharge had been issued, one of these officers or their deputy would oversee the unloading. For most cargoes the duty payment had to be made in cash before a permit would be given. A consignee of wines had the option of either paying the duty owed at once or of removing them to a public warehouse where he had a year to draw on his supply, paying the duty as he did so.[1]

Still awaiting the permit needed to discharge his cargo, Blaisdell closely followed the day to day fluctuation of rates. Both coastwise and European freights seemed on the rise, but, as he wrote to William Lord on 3 January, his preference seemed to be for a coastwise charter.

> I wrote you a few days since informing you of my arrival, and yesterday I recd your letters of the 14th & 22d—of Dec—the first to the care of J P Whitney I did not think to call there as you had never sent any to his care before consequently I did not git it until yester,d. I have not commenced discharging yit, I cannot git a General permit til tomorrow and then I Expect it will take me at least ten days to discharge Coastwise freights have improved of late and I beleave that $1- per bbl

for Pork has ben paid for New York for small lots, but it is useless for me to ingage
a freight with this cargo in—Eurapean freights is with Out change viz 15/32 in
am. ships if there is not too many ships comes in and the weather continues good
for business I think that there will be 1/2 given by the time I am unloaded and
then as you recomend I think I shall not lay long with Out ingaging Something, if
coastwise freight keeps up I shall give it the preferance—

   Mr. Jenkins is about to draw on Mr. George Lord of Boston for disbursements of
the ship Holy Oak for $1500- $1600- to day Or to morrow and I shall buy the Bill
for you.[2]

His predeliction for a freight to New York or Boston is understandable.
Having been absent from Kennebunk for more than a year, both he and his
wife must have had a strong desire to stop at home. Despite the helpful
presence of her daughter, Elizabeth did not attempt the journey north on her
own; although when sailing on the *Swiss Boy* ten years earlier she had changed
vessels at sea in order to return to Kennebunk. In consolation, there was an
opportunity to receive firsthand news from home. In January a bark arrived in
New Orleans from Kennebunk. On board was Eben Mitchell, a near neighbor
of the Blaisdells. His social calls would have given much pleasure to the
captain and his family.

   After one such visit Mitchell wrote to his parents: "New Orleans is very
sickly with the colerry consiquently shell bee home by the middle of march if I
live Last Sunday I was on board of Capt Blaisdell's ship and spent the fore
noon & diner with them they are all well & look fine Elizabeth is as large as
her Mother & will [be] the Bell of Kennebunk if she lives to get home I had a
vary agreeable visit."[3]

   As agreeable as such occasions were for them all, Captain Blaisdell could
afford them little time. He took the freight money he had on hand from the
Mount Washington's passage to Europe and bought bills of exchange drawn
on George Lord of Boston. The bills were due for payment seventy days from
their date of issue, and accrued interest during that time. The captain sent
them on to William Lord in Kennebunk, along with a letter that again
sounded him out on the idea of a coastwise freight.

New Orleans Jan,y 5, 1849
I wrote you On the 3d Inst. acknolaging the receipt of your favors of the 14th &
22d ult—I have Just commenced discharging & I fear I shall have a long Job of it
for a Bordeaux Cargo is the verry worst of Cargoes for dispatch, but I shall do my
utmost to make dispatch—coastwais freights at the preasant is fair, say
5/9 ct. for cotton for Boston & 85- to 90- cts for Pork, and if I was ready to receive
Cargo now I think I should take a freight for Boston Or New york, but before I git
ready there may be a change however it is the General Opinion that freights will
advance rather then decline & I think I had better wait the result, then to Except a
freight now with a full cargo in to discharge & posably it may take me three weeks
to git clear of it. I here send you inclosed a Bill of Exchange drawn by T. C.

Jenkins On Messrs. George C. Lord & Co. of Boston, for $1687.83—at 70 days from date, this the first, the Secand I Shall send tomorrow.[4]

The cargo of Bordeaux wine came out slowly, and as the hold was carefully emptied it was discovered that some of the casks had been split or broken, causing the loss of their contents. The master and owners of a vessel were liable for all damage caused during either the loading or unloading of a cargo or resulting from improper stowage. Casks of wine were expected to be well bedded in dunnage and stored uniformly on their sides with the bung up. Wooden wedges were used to keep them from rolling about in the hold, and to prevent breakage due to pressure a prudent master did not stow them in tiers of more than four casks high.[5] Upon the discovery of the damage in the *Mount Washington*'s hold, the port warden was called in. Following an inspection, he ruled that the wine had been properly stowed and transported and found no fault on the part of the captain.

As soon as the ship's hold was emptied Captain Blaisdell began to seek a new cargo for her. Weighing all the prospects and offers, he decided that a European freight had the greater advantage for the ship, despite his preference for a coastwise passage, so he accepted a cargo for Liverpool of cotton and oil cake. Oil cake—cotton seed from which the oil had been pressed—was used as a cattle feed and fertilizer.

January had passed and February was nearly done before the ship was ready for sea. Once on his way the Captain hastily wrote to William Lord on 24 February.

> New Orleans Febry 24—1849
> I write this On the river going down you will no doubt think it is high time that I was going down, but I have done my best to git dispatch. the whole amount of my freight & Primage is £2480.11.3 wich is fully as much as I thought I should make when I began the Oil Cake proved to be better freight then I Expected I have got in nearly 400 tons of Cakes & 1613 bales of Cotton weighing 722206 lbs I got 1/2 [cent] for 900 bales & 9/16 [cent] for the rest I think that my freight is Equal or better then 9/16 for all Cotton I regretted after I took this freight that I had not waited a few days longer and taken a Coastwais freight, but this may turn Out as well in the End, I hope I Shall be able to git a good return freight to help Out the voyage a little—my Expences has ben tramendious high here and I was astonashed when I came to Settle up to find I had to draw [£]699-8.4 On my freight, but I hope that my a/c will Explain it to your Satisfaction I will send on ahed a scetch of My Expenses I owed a large sum for wages On my arrival & haveing to pay /75 Compress bill for the most of the Cotton full towage in & Out &c the draft will be insured in England.[6]

Although fairly satisfied with the freight he had secured and the prospects awaiting him in England, the captain was very concerned with the amount of his disbursements while in New Orleans. The tally sheet he sent to William Lord provided a detailed list of expenses, which totaled nearly $6,000. His alarm is evident in a postscript on the sheet in which he wrote, "When I came to figure up I was frightened & Could hardly beleave it til I went Over & Over it again, I am completly disgusted with New Orleans and all there is in it, I shall be afraid to see the Owners after they see this and yet I have gone to no unnessacery Expence that I know Of what alarms me is that my disbursements is so much higher then Ever before."[7]

At the mouth of the Mississippi the captain concluded his letter: "I have nothing more to say of importance you are in posession no doubt of all the news here there was not One kennebunk vessel in port when I left, freights rather On the decline hoping soon to be able to give you some favorable account from Liverpool."[8] With that he was on his way.

Before he left though, his wife had put together a package containing presents purchased for her daughters in Europe, and this, along with the painting of the ship done at Bordeaux, was sent by sea to Boston. The packages' arrival a month later was noted by Hartley Lord when he wrote to his father that "on Saturday [arrived] a box containing a picture of the Mt. Washington from Capt. B- via "Howard" also a box for Capt. B's daughters. I opened the box and took out a package marked for me—which you will please mention to them."[9]

At about the same time that the forwarded parcels were reaching Kennebunk the *Mount Washington* was nearing the southern coast of Ireland. It had taken her thirty days to cross the Atlantic from New Orleans to Cape Clear. Off the Cape she ran into rough weather and took shelter in the harbor of Cork, where she lay at anchor for three days. With the return of fair skies and favorable winds she was on her way again and arrived at Liverpool on 14 April 1849.[10]

Located three miles upstream on the Mersey River, Liverpool was the major port of entry for the cotton that fed the textile mills of Lancashire. The harbor, a scene of unending activity, was filled with the clamor of men who labored in and about vessels in various stages of arrival and departure. The docks along the waterfront could accommodate 300,000 tons of shipping, with each individual wharf being given over the the handling of a specific product or trade. At the time of her unloading the *Mount Washington* would have been warped into the King's Dock, where cotton ships discharged.[11]

Following regulations, which in most respects mirrored those of the other ports he knew, the captain filed the necessary documents within the twenty-four hour deadline of his arrival. As was universally required, he gave a full accounting of his cargo. He reported the *Mount Washington*'s tonnage and her places of construction and registration. A roll detailing the names and nationalities of the crew rounded out the major portion of the mandatory paperwork. No goods could be either landed or shipped except under the surveillance of a port officer. At least one was stationed on board the ship during her entire time in port, and Captain Blaisdell was expected to provide them with sleeping quarters below decks.[12]

The *Mount Washington*'s passage to England had been uneventful except for the foul weather off the Irish coast and the earlier loss of a head sail. However, the ship was leaking some more, which made the captain decide to have some caulking done. Once the ship was docked, little time was lost in getting her unloaded. There was some water damage to the cargo, but the captain wrote that he did not anticipate any problems on that account.[13]

Three days after the arrival of the *Mount Washington*, the *Swiss Boy* appeared at Liverpool under the command of Captain Moses Maling. She had had a rough passage out, and Captain Maling was relieved to finally reach his destination. He sought out Captain Blaisdell soon after his arrival, as William Lord had instructed him to consult with the captain about business for the brig. The original intent had been to find a cargo for Havana, but nothing worthwhile was available. The two men then looked into the carrying of emigrants to the States, but because of her age the *Swiss Boy* was deemed unsafe to carry passengers. They settled at last on carrying railroad iron to Boston. Throughout the early nineteenth century, America was a major importer of iron and steel products, and Britain was the primary source of such manufactured items. With the advent of the railroads, English rails were in great demand.

The *Mount Washington* was also advertised for Boston, and she too took on a quantity of iron, but the greater part of her space was set aside for passengers. Despite the difficulties he had encountered while carrying emigrants in the *Abbot Lord*, Blaisdell was determined to go to Boston, and passengers offered the best opportunity. In all, the *Mount Washington* took on 236 men, women, and children.[14] The passengers would not board until the ship was ready to sail, and as the departure date neared Captain Blaisdell penned a quick note to William Lord on 5 May 1849.

> Liverpool May 5—1849
>
> I wrote you by the two last steamers advising you of my proceedings Since wich I have colected my freight and paid Over to the Barings £1.400—I have got in nearly all my heavy freight Shall probably sail On the 10th Inst—freights have declined Since I chartered the ship so I could not have struck in a better time. Capt williams sailed last Sunday, and the wind has ben to the Eastward Ever Since so he must have made a good run, there has no Other k.k. [Kennebunk] ships arrived yet.[15]

The discomfort of close quarters was not the only hardship the passengers had to contend with, as the crossing proved to be a long and often rough one. Arriving at Boston on 2 July, Captain Blaisdell lost no time in informing William Lord.

> I take this Opperunity to inform you of my safe arrival after a long teagous passage of 45 days from Liverpool, the ship is at quarentine yet. but I Expect to git clear to day and git to the Citty. I shall have to give bonds for some 20 passengers but I do not think that any of them is destitute I have got Mr Callender to sign

the bonds, I have a verry good set of passengers. the docter said he never saw a cleaner & more healthy set in the Port and gave me my clearance before he left the ship,—the ship has leaked some on this passage, I had heavy weather On the first of the passage & she laibored verry heavy in consequnce of having such a weight in the bottom of the ship—I hope soon to hear from you in the meantime I shall go On discharging my wife is quite unwell is not able to set up.[16]

In the end, twenty-seven of the *Mount Washington*'s passengers had to be bonded.[17] Captain Blaisdell, as well as George Callender and Hartley Lord, began to seek out work for the bonded emigrants so as to be relieved of their financial responsibility as quickly as possible.

On Independence Day 1849 Hartley Lord wrote a most interesting letter to his father in Kennebunk. He began by seeking places for two of the *Mount Washington*'s passengers, but went on to give a glimpse of the opinion that both he and his father held concerning the abilities of Captain Blaisdell when compared with another local master.

I was down on board the Mt. Washington this morning and Capt. Blaisdell asked me if I thought you would like a girl—inst.—as he said there was one or two aboard the ship he thought would make good girls that wanted places. I thought I would drop you a line to see—I think Mrs. Hilton would like her—and if you think it would be worth while I will have her sent down—please send an answer in the morning as they will probably be off tomorrow—of course Capt. B- cannot tell how they will do but he thinks from what he has seen of them on board they will make good girls—all is if you think someone will take her or if there should be chances for two I will have them sent down & pay their passage—Sarah thinks her mother will take one if you do not. There is nothing new here—The painters are at work on the Ocean Star and we cannot very well do anything until after the paint gets dry. But really, I do not see any need of cleaning the ship's bottom when it is apparently clean as nearly as clean as when she was new as far as we can see it is not foul at all—but Capt. W- wants it done—whether or no—I hope you will not say anything about it to them but between you and me I do not think Claudius is fit to take charge of such a ship—he is negligent and careless—and goes smash through everything—haphazard—trusting to luck and thinking as a matter of course all will be right. I am glad we are not any more interested and have wished a good many times since she has been in we did not have anything to do with her. I like to see things attended to and not neglected but Claudius never seems to know about anything of course—as he never does and makes the best of everything, but it pains me to see everything left at loose ends—call a man smart because he carries away masts and makes good passages I think the business part is of as much importance—It is one thing to be smart and another to exercise good judgement and good management. But I do not think Claudius has any system or particular management about him. You can judge something perhaps by what you have seen. The ship looks well but she might have looked better—Claudius perhaps suits many of his friends—and I have no right to say anything but I have only said to you what I think about him and it will go no further—I know we shall not find it so aboard the Mt. Washington and things will be taken care of and in their places. We have been obliged to make allowances on cargo damaged etc. which I do not believe we shall have to in the Mt. W- and which was entirely through neglect and carelessness on the part of mates & captain. I want you to know just how it is but not to think any less of Claudius for what I have written. I suppose Capt. Charles would want to put another brother in Master if his funds would stand it—but I hope there are some who will object to it. I don't doubt he thinks Albert would make a good master. It is rather a noisy day here today and we shall be glad when it is over. Hope to see you up before the Mt. Washington goes.—Please burn this letter—[18]

The weather proved to be very hot, which slowed down the work of unloading the *Mount Washington*. As the iron the ship carried came out, it was found to be very rusty, despite Hartley Lord's comments in his letter of the fourth. His reaction was "the iron seems to be considerably rusty and damaged but I hope we shall get through with it without making much allowance as it is all apparently well stowed and every proper care taken of it while on board the ship—but there always are some things which are obliged to be allowed as they cannot be avoided."[19] One man found his iron so rusted that he refused to pay the freighting charge. The reaction of Captain Blaisdell and fellow-owner Captain Charles Barry, then in Boston, was to take the man to court. George Callender explained the situation to William Lord in a letter written on 21 July.

There is one consignee of Hoop Iron who says his iron is damaged $300- or $400- & although the port warden certified it was well stowed he refuses to pay the freight $98.00. He says it must have been injured by water spilt by passengers or by soda ash & shows some white spots on it which he calls soda. But there were only 9 casks of soda on board & that was stowed clear forward & out of reach of the Iron. We suppose from his talk he might settle by our giving up the freight but if we contest it he would try to make a claim of $400-. The iron is no doubt badly damaged but it don't appear to be from any fault of the ship & there seems no reason in giving him up the freight. We wish to know whether we shall sue him if he won't pay. Capt. Barry and Capt. Blaisdell appear to be in favor of doing so & we should like to hear from you before commencing a suit—We think it would be better to sue him than give it up, though it would cost about all of it if you get your case & might cost a good deal more if you lose it.[20]

The outcome of the dispute in Boston is unknown, but William Lord did decide that the *Mount Washington*'s continued leaking was a problem and ordered the ship coppered while in port.[21]

After seeing that the *Mount Washington* was coppered, Captin Blaisdell took the train to Kennebunk, where he would remain until the ship was loaded and ready to sail. He may have returned earlier with his wife, although she too may have remained in Boston through July, recovering her health, which was so poor on her arrival. While at home the captain attended to business. Plans were completed to offer the *Swiss Boy* for sale, and the captain settled his accounts with William Lord. As master he was paid a monthly salary of about $20.00, in addition to which he received his primage, a percentage of the freights the ship earned. For the time he had spent on board the *Mount Washington* his primage came to $1,177.70, from which he had to subtract $200.00 as the passage fee for his wife and children.[22] Beyond his primage and his salary as the ship's master, as a part owner he received his share of the ship's profits.

As August drew to a close, George Callender wrote that the *Mount Washington* was just about ready for sea and that the captain should plan to return to Boston soon.[23] When Captain Blaisdell arrived in Boston he found two matters that required his attention before he could sail. One was the possible sale of the *Swiss Boy*. In the event that he was at sea when the sale was made, he gave his power of attorney to William Lord and left it with George Callender.[24] In the other matter, some of the emigrants brought over in July still had not found employment. He met with Callender and Lord's son Hartley; the latter reported to his father that, "we have talked with Capt. Blaisdell about the passengers here from the Mt. Washington and he leaves it for you to settle and shall be governed accordingly when you write—but I should think the best course would be to take them down to Kennebunk and get places for them there—They ought to be able to earn their livings I should think—If could find anyone willing to take them."[25]

On 31 August the *Mount Washington* sailed. George Callender was among those who saw her off, and he wrote to Lord, "the Mount Washington sailed this morning with a good S.W wind, makes about $2,500 freight & $95 passenger money which is quite as well as we expected for some time past." The ship's destination was New Orleans.[26]

By mid-September news was reaching Kennebunk from New Orleans that Captain Blaisdell had taken on a cargo of cotton bound for Havre, France, at the rate of one cent per pound.[27] When he was ready to sail the captain informed William Lord on 26 October 1849:

I wrote you yesterday that I was loaded I thought then that I should git ready to go down that night but I got disapointed, consequently I shall not leave til to morrow Evening my freight and primage amounts to $9070- passager money $500- I have 29 bales On deck wich I have not insured wich I advised you of in my last letter. about 13,000 lbs cost about 10 cts per lb—I have drawn against the freight for $1,800 wich will be insured in france.—

I have settled with Mr. Pearson but in consequence of 4 Boxes and 3 bales being missing as I wrote you before and give you the marks, I had to settle subject to any claim that may be made for the missing goods if they are not found, but I hope that they will be found, there was some Other draw back for short measurement and damage to the amount of $44- and after taking Out the above & Commisions, and passage money and some freight paid at Boston left a balance of $2287.28

I hope to git some return freight and passangers to make up or help out this low freight—at any rate I shall try hard for it.—and I hope by the time I git back

freights will be better for it is bad anough at preasant please to write me to Havre
and tel me in what way to mak remitance I beleave the Exchange between france
& England is against us—When you write will you please to call at my house and
tell my wife if it is not to much trouble that she may know what time to write
me—there is quite a fleet of Kennebunk here now, as you see New Orleans papers
and have Newes from here by lightening spead, it is unnessasry for me to say any
thing on the subject, hoping to give you favorable account from Havre—[28]

It was wise for a master to supervise carefully the loading of his vessel, as he was
accountable for all the cargo put aboard her. With each delivery of goods a
signature of receipt was made on the bill of lading. When the cargo was off-
loaded at the ship's destination the contents of her hold were naturally expected to conform to the bills of lading item for item.[29] The fact that Captain
Blaisdell had been in Kennebunk during the time the *Mount Washington* was
being loaded did nothing to exempt him of responsibility. The missing goods
that he noted as giving him so much trouble were located several months later.
In Boston they had been put aboard the wrong vessel and shipped to Texas.
Upon their discovery they were forwarded to New Orleans.[30]

It was not until 30 October that the *Mount Washington* did get to sea. In
addition to the cargo of cotton, she carried some tallow and lard. The first
week and a half was uneventful, and the ship sailed her course for France, but
the eleventh of November brought change. The day dawned with fair
weather, and the ship was off the eastern coast of Florida, making her way
under all possible sail. Some difficulty was noted with the steering, and upon
inspection it was found that the rudder, which had been repaired in January,
was in very poor condition, the wood being "split and splintered." The captain ordered repairs made, and it was wedged and caulked and made as sound
as possible.

The *Mount Washington* continued on her way until the fourteenth, when
she encountered moderate gales and squally weather. The crew began to
shorten sail and prepared to weather the storm. During the next four days the
ship struggled against a high sea and continual heavy gales. At the approach
of the storm the crew had sent down the mizzen topgallant yard and mast;
then they double reefed all the topsails and took in the outer jib. Still the ship
labored heavily. By Friday the sixteenth the ship lay to under her main
spanker, and later that same day the men took down the fore topgallant yard
and mast and unbent the flying jib. Saturday, the seventeenth, the gale
continued unabated. Under the wrenching stress of the heavy seas, the rudder
head, already weakened, finally gave way. While the crew labored to rig a jury
rudder, Blaisdell decided to make for the nearest port, which he reckoned to
be Charleston, South Carolina. He ordered the foresail and main topsail set
and with the jury rudder headed for Charleston, which they reached on 21
November.[31]

The battle with the elements had severely taxed the endurance of captain,
crew, and ship. In addition to experiencing both mental and physical fatigue,

the captain was very ill when the ship made port. Upon reaching shore he telegraphed George Callender, informing him of the ship's condition and requesting that a new master be sent out to replace him as his health would not permit him to continue the voyage. While he waited for an answer, other problems demanded his attention: a new rudder had to be made and hung; his first mate, badly injured during the storm, had to be hospitalized; he had to file a protest with the French consul to protect the ship and her owners against any charges of negligence that might be filed by consignees due damage or delay of the goods shipped, and to protect their standing in case of a settlement of averages.

William Lord agreed to send a new master and chose Captain Willliam P. Stone to assume command of the *Mount Washington*. When Captain Stone arrived at the end of November, it was a thankful Captain Blaisdell who wrote to Lord on 29 November.

> Capt. Stone arrived here yesterday morning and handed me a letter from you, I was glad to see him I think you have made a good choice. I feel bad to be Obliged to leave the ship but realy I dont feel able to perform the voyage, I wrote you a few days ago stating that we had at last got the Rudder unhung with Out discharging the Cargo wich I was verry glad of, we are gitting along pretty well with the Rudder I am in hopes if we have no difficilty in hanging it to git away Satterday. but they work verry slow, I shall stop here til the ship is ready to start, I dont know what the Expence will be here yet, it cost me $60- to tow in, and if we have to tow Out will be probably 50- more—Pilotage in and Out will be about $70- the Rudder and all the fixing Will be at least $150- shall have part if not all of the Crew to ship as half of them has ran already and I Expect the rest of them will to before she gits away—the Cargo should pay a large proportion of it as it is Worth probably nearly or quite $150,000-
>
> Capt. Stone thinks to take Adam McCulloch for his mate, and I think he will do verry well he is young yet but he has done verry well since the mate hurt him self, my Old mate got verry badly hurt like to lost his leg is going to the hospital.[32]

The Adam McCulloch mentioned as becoming first mate was the son of Captain Blaisdell's old friend and benefactor Adam McCulloch, Sr. It is unclear how long he had been serving previously under Captain Blaisdell, but he would continue as the *Mount Washington*'s first mate until 1851, when his departure would compound an already trying situation for the captain.

After repairs at Charleston totaling $713.00, the *Mount Washington* was fit for sea by the first of December.[33] On the eve of his departure Captain Stone communicated with William Lord on 2 December.

> I have neglected writing you untill now as Capt. B tolde me he had writen you all concerning the Ship. I am in hopes the Carpenters will get through time Enough to go to Sea tomorrow Capt B will stop & settel the bills & if tis A good chance to go to sea I shall have to go withouth them—you will pleas forward them to Havre if I leave them behinde, we cant tell how much the bill will be but I think from 700 to $800 I had to Ship part of A crew & Second officer I have taken Mr

McCaullock as chief Officer as Capt B Discharged his mate he had with him. I have made an agreement with Capt Blaisdell for $15 per month & half the primage for the present voyage Capt B is quite out of health but may get better after he gets home, his complaint appears to be on the liver, you will pleas write me my Enstructions to Havre Concerning business for the Ship, hoping I may have a good & prosprous voayge.[34]

On the morning of 4 December Captain Blaisdell watched the *Mount Washington* sail for Havre. He reported to Lord that day:

I take this Oppertunity to inform you that the Ship went to Sea this morning. we had to take a boat Out as the wind was light. but there is now a good breeze from SW and I hope she will have a good chance, I have drawn On Messrs Callander & Co for Seven hundred & thirteen dollers. @ 30 days sight I could not git the average papers ready to give Capt. Stone so I will take them With me and send them from New York or Boston She has now got a verry good rudder they made a verry good Job of it, but rather an Expensive one I have got duplicate Bills of Every thing—
I think I shall start for New York to morrow Hoping soon to have the pleasure of Seeing you.[35]

On the fifth Captain Blaisdell boarded a steamer for New York and from there made his way home to Kennebunk.

Le Havre, at the mouth of the river Seine,
was a frequent port of call for American
ships. Stone jetties led into the outer
"basin de la barre" with its commercial quays.
Engraving by Martens and Calow, ca. 1840.
(Courtesy Mariners' Museum, Newport News, Virginia)

The bustling port of New Orleans, looking
upriver from the Lower Cotton Press, 1852.
During the height of the cotton season a wall
of river steamers and ocean sailing freighters
lined the city's levee. Lithograph, drawn
by J.W. Hill & Smith, printed by Sarony &
Major, published by Smith Brothers, New York.
(Courtesy Mariners' Museum, Newport News, Virginia)

EIGHT

A Duty to Take Charge
1849-1851

CHRISTMAS OF 1849 was a holiday of note, one that found the entire Blaisdell family gathered safely under one roof. Such gatherings had occurred infrequently during the years of the Blaisdells' marriage, and with the continued passage of time their finite nature would have become apparent. In 1850 Jotham became fifty-seven years old and Elizabeth was forty-one. At seventeen and fifteen their older daughters, Elizabeth and Sarah, were entering young womanhood, and the younger children, Maria eleven, Eunice seven, and William already three, were maturing rapidly. Because of the long intervals between his stays at home, the captain perceived as more dramatic the natural changes that occurred gradually to his family. As he observed his wife and children move around him in the course of their daily activities, he would have realized that many of the moments that he had experienced as husband and father so seldom and cherished so deeply were numbered and therefore all the more precious. But as important a role as the captain's family played in his life, it alone could not suffice.

With returning health Captain Blaisdell's thoughts once more turned to shipping. Unlike most of the vessels in which William Lord held a controlling interest, the *Mount Washington* was managed mainly from Kennebunk rather than through George Callender's office in Boston. While Captain Blaisdell was in Kennebunk, Lord kept him advised of the ship's proceedings and forwarded Captain Stone's letters to him. The *Mount Washington* had completed her passage to Havre and returned to New Orleans in the spring of 1850, where Captain Stone took on a cargo bound for Europe. The missing cargo from the fall of 1849 had still not been located, and when returning some of Captain Stone's letters to William Lord on 28 June 1850, Captain Blaisdell included a few remarks of his own.

I send you here inclosed Capt. Stones letters togeather with Mr. Pearsons a/c, it seams that Capt. Stone has had to pay another claim on the cargo from Boston When I settled with Mr Pearson the freight was not all colected and I could not obtain a Settlement without the clause spaisfied in the a/c for reclamation for gods short, damaged or over measured, I had no other remedy but to submit to the clause or detain the ship and go to law with the parties to bring them to a

Settlement, it seams that Mr Pearsons opinion is that the two cases of boots was never put onboard of the ship, and providing they were onboard they were lost through the neglect of Pearsons Levy clark consequently we had no right to pay for them, I feel verry unpleasant about it althougt I dont know that I could have avoaded it or acted any differant under the circumstances that I was placed, I trust that the two cases of boots may be found, I think the ship got in a verry good cargo that is she carries well and made as much as could have ben Expected at the costs I hope please God she may git a good freight back. . . .[1]

The *Mount Washington* was not the only business matter to require Captain Blaisdell's attention during his stay at home. Soon after his arrival back in Kennebunk the old and faithful *Swiss Boy* had been sold. Her owners, McCulloch, Lord, and Blaisdell, had wanted to sell her for some time, but though there were several inquiries throughout 1849, a deal was not closed until June of 1850.[2]

After her sale, the *Swiss Boy* left Boston and made her way around Cape Horn to the West Coast, where she eventually became employed in the lumber trade. In 1857 she was sighted by one of her former officers, probably Captain Moses Maling, who was then in the Pacific. He described her as "looking so old and queer, with her great head, short, deep model, channels a foot or more wide, and stern cabin windows." She was by then twenty years old and quite rotted, and though her pumps were in constant use she listed notice-ably.[3] Her end came two years later, on the west coast of Vancouver Island.[4]

Captain Blaisdell certainly did not concern himself with the subsequent career or ultimate fate of the *Swiss Boy*. His immediate concern following her sale was how to reinvest his share of the proceeds. It may have been at this time that he purchased a share of the ship *Ocean Star*. The 714-ton *Ocean Star* had been built by Clement Littlefield at Kennebunk in 1848. She hailed from Boston rather than Kennebunk, though she was owned by local men.[5] Both William Lord and George Callender owned shares in the ship at the time of her launching, and Captain Blaisdell, while not an original owner, at some point acquired a share for himself.

The details of the sale of the *Swiss Boy* were soon taken care of and the captain's responsibilities concerning the management of the *Mount Washing-ton* and perhaps the *Ocean Star* were far from demanding, as William Lord handled most of the details. Such inactivity did not agree with the captain, and by the fall of 1850 he had become quite restless. He informed William Lord of his desire to rejoin the *Mount Washington*. Lord was happy to put the ship back into his charge and late in November sent a dispatch to Captain Stone in New Orleans advising him of the impending change.

Capt. Blaisdell sails from this port in a few days in a new brig built this season by the Wards (viz. passenger) he has got tired of staying at home and goes out to take the ship. We would not have you think that we are in any way dissatisfied with your proceedings, but as Capt. Blaisdell has recovered his health and being an owner in the ship he thinks it his duty to take charge of the ship again. Should you receive this letter before Capt. Blaisdell arrives you will go on in discharging the ship and have her ready for business and if Capt. Blaisdell should not arrive there by the time you are discharged if business will justify then your engaging a freight for the ship you are to do so and go on the same as if you were going on the ship.[6]

On 29 November Captain Blaisdell sailed down the Kennebunk River as a passenger on the new brig *Tehuantepec*. Her principal owner was Eliphalet Perkins of Kennebunkport, and on her maiden voyage to New Orleans her master was Captain Sylvester Brown.[7] The brig made a good passage to New Orleans, and Captain Blaisdell was soon in command of the *Mount Washington* again.

He lost little time in securing a cargo for the ship. His surviving dispatches to William Lord make clear the difficulties a shipmaster faced when seeking profitable employment for his vessel. Clearly evident is the element of calculated risk that accompanied each of his decisions. Was the deal struck at the most opportune time: were the present rates going to rise or fall after he chartered? Did he choose the right commodity to carry or was another going to offer a better return tomorrow? Would a profitable return freight be waiting at the vessel's destination: would a cargo to Liverpool offer greater advantage than one to Havre? And after all the thoughtful consideration and careful weighing of the transitory evidence available to him, would his actions meet with the approval of Lord and the other owners? His tone throughout bordered on being apologetic. He was aware that to a large extent each choice was a gamble, and his analogy between the business he had concluded and die being cast was very apt indeed. On the last day of 1850 he notified Lord:

> I wrote you yesterday giving all the newes that I could think of of Interest, and intimating that I had some Idear of closing for Havre, which since I have done. given away the consignment for 1400 bales of cotton at 7/8 ct. for Havre, since which we have got 300-bales more making about 1700 bales ingaged. and I am in hopes I shall git good dispatch, I dont know that my proceedings will meet your views or not but I dont see much prospect for improvements verry soon and if we calculate to make two voyages to Europe this year it is time that we was about it, and I thought I mite be in Havre about the time the passengers began to come in and think my chances for a return freight will be as good as at Liverpool as there is so many ships up for that port—I have ingaged my balest at $1.25 per ton put On board, shall want about 150 tons—There was 5000 bales of Cotton sold today. one am [American] ship has been taken for Havre at 7/8 ct and a british ship for Liverpool at 3/8. no other change has transpired since yesterday.[8]

Meanwhile, in Boston Hartley Lord studied the business reports from New Orleans and reached the same conclusions as had Captain Blaisdell, writing that, "Should think Capt. Blaisdell had rather take 7/8 [cent] to Havre than lay—as there is no prospect of an immediate improvement."[9]   His father, however, had other views, at least initially, as Blaisdell acknowledged on 2 January 1851.

> your favor of the 24—ult—has jest come to hand. am sorry that I did not git it sooner or on my arrival, I Should have then ben guided by your advice. but the die is cast now and cant be recalled. I wrote you a few days since advising you of my having taken a freight for Havre @ 7/8 c for cotton. since that there has ben no improvements in freights here as yet but I cant help thinking that there will be before long now, but at the time that I ingaged the prospect did not look so good, as you see accounts from here almost dayly it is useless for me to make any statement of the rates of freights, for the last ten or fifteen days or since I have been here, Ships have ben taking the going rates as fast as they could git them that is 7/8 ct for Havre, and 13/16 for Liverpool, I could not have made an ingagement here to go to mobile at 1 c for Havre or any quarter. if I had went it would have ben on my own risk and I did not like to take the risk,—since I wrote you I have bought my balest and got the most of it in at $1.25 per ton and got in about 100 bales of cotton and 1900 bales Ingaged and a prospect of good dispatch,—Capt. Stone has not settled his freight Inward yet, it is his Intention to do so before he leaves and settle the bills Inwards,—I suppose you have given him direction What to do with the balance as you have not mentioned it to me. I dont know but you will think me to hasty in taking freight for the ship. but you see what the prospect was at that time. I mite have held on here a month longer with out gitting any higher rates, or then have to take the same, if I calculate to make two freights this season I have no time to spare. It is true that one good freight is better than two bad ones but I had no garantee for that one good one, one thing I am sure of I have got one poor one and now my only hope is to git the good one next time. We have teligraphick dispatches from the North that there has been some dreadful heavy gales there. I Expect it will be a hard winter as the fall was so mild, it has ben verry cold here and a great deal of rain of late,—I shall keep you advised of my proceedings. . . .
> P.S. you wrote me to send you ten bbls molasses at 23½ cts per Gall. I shall comply with your request if I can buy it at that price but at preasant a good article is a little above that mark. I bought one bbl for my self to send home and had to pay 26 cts but to take it from the Levy it may come something less—tomorrow I will look around and see what I can git it for—[10]

Captain Blaisdell awaited with some trepidation the arrival of the letter that would contain William Lord's reaction to his proceedings in New Orleans. The details of preparing the ship for sea consumed most of his waking hours in the interval.

Of special concern was the matter of the *Mount Washington*'s ballast. Without enough ballast to provide sufficient counterweight in her bottom the ship would be restricted as to the amount of sail she could carry and could be in danger of capsizing. Stone, metal, and sand were usually available to ships as ballast in most ports, with sand being the ballast of last resort. Sand could become lodged in a vessel's pumps, blocking them and causing water damage to the cargo. If a cargo was damaged due to a master taking on sand ballast when stone or metal had been available he was liable for that damage.[11] The captain also concluded the financial aspects of the voyage, and his freight and primage seem to have met his expectations. He included a report on the new ship *Osborne*, registered at Kennebunk in December and expected in New Orleans, and an update on the progress of the ship *Ophelia* belonging to William Lord, Jr.[12]

yours of the 22—Inst. has jest come to hand. I wrote you a few days since in answer to yours of [?] since that I have made rather slow progress in Loading on account of the presses being so much drove that they could not press it. but I am a going on now prety well have got about 1400 bales in and on the Levee and about anough Ingaged to fill up the ship—I bought 130 tons of balest at 1.25 per ton. with 50 tons which was in the ship before makes 180 tons and I have got 1200 Hydes wich will be Equal to 40 tons more. so I am in hopes that the ship will be stiff anough.—The ship Try. Mountain of Boston One of the three deck ships after being loaded has had to discharge and take in more balest. She would not stand up with out tackles to the next ship. I dont have a verry good opinion of the three deck ships,—since I wrote you last there has ben no Improvements in European freights, there was a little improvement for heavy freight for Boston but there was so many ships laid on for that port I doubt if they dont go down again L.H. Gale has got ships anough on to carry 30000 bbls of Pork. and I dont beleave that he has got 2000 to put in to them the preasnt rates for Boston is /70 cts for pork and 1/2 ct for cotton at that rate this ship would not make over $5000-

Cotton is light this year and I fear I shall not carry as much as the first voyage. but I hope to come up to $9000 freight & primage

Capt. Stone has settled the bills inwards and left a balance with me of $1555- which I supose you wish for me to retain to go towards dfraying the ships Expences as you did not write for me to remit it. I gave an Order on you in favor of Adam McCulloch for $100- and an Other in favor of Capt Stone for $238.39 for his half of the primage agreable to your Instructions.—It seems that you are having a hard winter of it I got off in good time to clear it but I supose I shall have to take some of it yet. It seams that they are making preparations to build more large ships this year. wich I dont see much incouragement for so far—I dont know but you will blame me for being hasty in ingaging so low a freight but you see that there is no improvement yet, in fact ships are taking the same rate that was given when I ingaged as fast as offered and in some instances less.

I thought some ten days ago that freights would improve as the number of ships had got reduced so much and the stock of cotton had increased. but I do not now think as favorable of an improvement as I did ten days since, ships drop in about a fast as they are wanted and so many laid on for different Ports with but a small part of their Cargoes ingaged with bad accounts from Europe, Everry thing seems to combine to keep freights from improving The Osborne has not arrived yet out 26 days. I beleave that the Ocean Star goes down tonight, the Ophelia is loading for Boston I beleave has all her cargo ingaged @ 70 cts per bbl for Pork & 1/2 ct for cotton,

> We only get mail once in four days here now I supose in consequence of bad
> roads, thinking of nothing more of Interest—[13]

When the letter from Kennebunk arrived the captain was relieved to learn that
Lord approved of his actions. The pleasure he may have taken in this turn of
events, however, was somewhat subdued by the high disbursements incurred
by the ship while in port, as he reported to Lord on 24 January.

> your kind favor of the 14th Inst. has Jest come to hand. I am glad that you
> approve of my proceedings in taking a freight for Havre. but I am hardly satisfied
> with my self for since I wrote you last freights have improved. When I wrote you
> last in answer to your last letter, it was very slack in freights and Every One was
> taking what was Offering but within a few days freights have improved on 1/16 of
> a ct. & 1/32nd I am loaded and go down to night if I can git my crew on board I
> have 2163 bales of cotton Onboard. thirty Eight of wich is on deck at the risk of
> the ship wich you of course will act as you please as to the Insurance, and 1200
> salted hydes @ 20 cts a pice, the whole amount of Freight and Primage is $9055-
> wich comes to about what I wrote you I thought it would, cotton in general runs
> light this year my cotton is verry large and light, for the sise, but is a fair average
> for this year, I git no passengers this time to help me Out.—and I Expect my
> disbursements will astonish you. but I am only responsable for the Outward
> disbursements. I shall only share half the blame I hope, but I hope there will be
> none attached to Eather of us.—Capt Stone settled the Inward disbursements
> which he will account to you for.—I have drawn On the freight for $2,150 @ 30
> days sight at 5.27%—I have not spent one cent more then was realy necessary, I
> had to pay Extry advance for men In consequence of there being scarce. but there
> wages per month dont Exceed $15- per month.—Capt. Stone bought a New
> Combunse or Cooking stove, which was neaded in consiquence of the Old One
> being burnt Out, and I had to git a little cordage and a full suply of provitions for
> the voyage which makes my bills tilt up. besides having to buy balest and paying
> higher rates for Stowage in consequence of high wages which all combines to swell
> up Expences for your sattisfaction I will give you a scetch of my disbursements on
> the next page It seems to be poor discouragements when it takes all of one freight
> and a good part of an Other to pay the Expence on One low freight.—By all
> apearances I think that the ship will be pretty stiff notwithstanding the deck load
> and a smaller quantity of balest than she has Ever had before. . . .

Transporting Ship	10.00
Levee dues for 2d m.ty	45.00
Compress bill for 2163 bales of cotton @/50	1081.00
Stevedores bill for 2150 bales of cotton@/35	757.00
130 tons of balest @ $1.25	162.00
1200 Hydes @ 3 cts per bundle	36.00
Black Smith bill	11.50
Bidwell Grocery bill Including bakers bill	469.19
Shipping master	321.19
Rating chronometor & almanack	3.25
Towage down & to Sea	155.00

T.C. Jenkins Commission 431.00
top Sail yard 18.00
Clearance bill of health 12.45
Advertising &c 5.00
T.C. Jenkins commission on Exchange 26.90
Sundry Expences probably 30.00
Recvd my self the balance or short 168.46
                                                         $3805.00

By cash recvd from Capt Stone as per a/c
                                1555.00
of Adam McCulloch draft on you 100.00
Draft on Havre .... 2150.00   .... $3805.00

The above is merely to let you know what has become of so much money. I
thought it might be some satisfaction to you—Capt. Stone will render you his
a/c of Inward Expences &c—[14]

In March the news of the *Mount Washington*'s arrival at her destination was
heralded by Hartley Lord with the observation that, "I see the Mt. Washington arrived out in fair passage I should not think the prospect very good for
return freight but don't know how it will be when he is ready."[15]

Le Havre, situated on the right bank of the Seine, handled the lion's share
of France's American trade. Her harbor became dry at low tide, though the
force of the river's current across its mouth delayed the fall of the water for
three hours after high tide. To accommodate shipping, three basins had been
built. The outer one, known as the "basin de la barre" was reserved for
commercial activity. Vessels could remain at anchor there unless red flags
appeared on the bridges in warning that the basins were to be drained for
cleaning.[16]

Once ashore at Havre, Captain Blaisdell found a letter from William Lord
waiting for him. In it Lord stated his own preferences on business and offered
what guidance he could respecting the course of action the captain should
follow in taking a return freight.

I think you had better go back to New Orleans provided you can get enough to
make it an object. However rather than go back in ballast, if you are sure of
making some five thousand dollars $5000- and upwards to New York or some
Northern port, I mean from Havre (it might do)—I should not think it would be
an object to go after rail road iron to come north even if you could charter for
thirty shillings per ton or not less than this rate—I should prefer going south with
a small freight or in ballast to either—if you should go south in ballast I think it
would be well to touch at Mobile if you can do so without too much inconvenience. Its next to impossible to make any calculations about freights but I cannot
but think there will be an improvement this season but it may not last long. Any
remittance you have to make you can deposit in the hands of Green, Paris
provided you are satisfied the house is in good standing—I believe Mr. Green is

dead—but I suppose the house or firm still exists in business—sometimes we sell
the exchange here (I mean in Boston) to be paid in Havre or on account to some
firm in Boston, should I do that I will let you know in time.[17]

By the end of March Captain Blaisdell had concluded his business in Havre.
One of the final transactions he had to undertake before his departure was the
handling of the proceeds from the freight to France. It was his usual practice
when in Europe to remit any funds to the banking firm of Baring Brothers in
London. Whether through habit or caution, he chose to have no dealings
with the House of Green in Paris, but went through the customary channels.
On 27 March 1851 he sent to London a collection of bills of exchange and
Bank of England port bills totaling £892, or about $4,280. The firm at his
request forwarded a receipt to his next port of call and sent a letter of notifica-
tion to Lord in Kennebunk.[18]

With the last details taken care of in France, the *Mount Washington* cleared
Havre for Cardiff, Wales. Earlier in March Captain Blaisdell had succeeded in
chartering the ship to carry railroad iron. Having been unable to locate any
significant cargo in Havre, he had written to different brokers in search of
business. Through the agency of Charles Gumm, a London broker, a charter
party was negotiated with the shippers, Palmer, McKellop, Dent & Company.[19] The cargo of iron was consigned to New Orleans, which complied
nicely with William Lord's stated preferences. Lord had objected to the ship
carrying iron only if it meant calling at a northern port, as that would put the
ship out of the way of the cotton markets at a time when freights might be
expected to rise. A line from a letter written by George Callender to William
Lord concerning the insurance on the *Mount Washington*'s freight gives an
indication of the reaction at home to the turn of events: "We think Capt.
Blaisdell was fortunate in getting this freight."[20]

He was not as fortunate in getting the rate of thirty shillings per ton
specified by Lord, but that had been a condition for coming north. Under the
terms of the agreement the ship was to carry the iron at twenty-five shillings
per ton, using the long or metric ton measure of 2,240 pounds. In qualifying
the payment of the freight, the monetary exchange rate was fixed at $4.80 per
pound sterling, and the captain was given 5 percent primage. The iron was to
be loaded in Cardiff and then unloaded in New Orleans at the shippers' risk
and expense. In the contract they were given thirty running days for the
loading, which would cost them £8 per day in demurrage if exceeded.[21]

A week after leaving Havre the *Mount Washington* entered at Cardiff.
The Kennebunk ship *Nathaniel Thompson* had been in port there during
January and February. The *Nathaniel Thompson* had been launched a few
weeks after the *Mount Washington* and was of almost identical tonnage.[22]
She had also carried iron to New Orleans, and Captain Blaisdell used her as a
gauge for his own vessel's cargo capacity, when he wrote to Lord on 10 April
1851.

I take this Oppertunity to inform you of my safe arrival at this Port On the 8th 7 days from Havre. I had to beet down the british chaniel against a Westerly Wind, and after I got to the lands End the wind set in from N E and I had to beet up the Bristal chaniel against a strong N E Wind, I Shall git my balest Out tomorrow and be ready to take in Iron the next day after tomorrow if I can git it, I am in hopes to be dispatched by the 25 inst.—I noticed the Nath,l Thompson took 848 tons of Iron, and I suppose I shall take about the same quantity, I received a letter from Barring Brothers yesterday acknowleging the receipt of the [£]892.3- which I remited from Havre, Iron freights remains about the same—I notice by the last accounts from New Orleans freights was good and I hope they may continue so til I git there. but I fear not. I shall make all possible dispatch and advise you of my departure. . . .[23]

It was not until the end of June that the *Mount Washington* crossed the bar at the mouth of the Mississippi ready to make the hundred-mile journey up the river to New Orleans. Once the ship was at her berth alongside the levee, Captain Blaisdell wrote to William Lord on 30 June, advising him of the ship's arrival and the current prospect for business.

I take this Opertunity to inform you of my arrival after a teagous passage of 58 days to the Bar. and 61 to the Citty. I have had a great deal of Calm weather. I arrived yesterday—and Telegraphed yesterday—I rec,d your letter of the 25 ult. and the 7 Inst. I find freights Exceedingly low and dull, but rather on the improvement, One ship was taken last week for Liverpool @ 3/8 & 40. has ben paid for staves for Bordeaux. I cant think that freight will be any lower, so I shall wait til I git my Iron Out, unless there is some improvement before it is the General Opinion that there will be an improvement. but it is hard telling ships keeps dropping and taking what ever is Offered so long as that is the case there will be no improvement at preasant I think the stave freights is rather the best, Espeacialy for ships that has no balest, balest is three dollars per ton, and scarce at that,—I got Over the Bar with One Boat but took the ground several times. I mite have taken 50 or 100 tons more if I had have known the water was so good.—I shall commence discharging tomorrow and I supose it will take two days to discharge and by that time I hope to hear from you again, I realy hope that I shall git a deacent freight. I have ben so unlucky here to fore.—the Ocean Star & Orlando is loading staves for Bordeaux.—it is verry warm here but healthy, . . .[24]

There seemed to be no silver lining in the dark cloud that shadowed the *Mount Washington*'s prospect. The cotton rates then being offered were roughly half of those given six months earlier when the ship had last been in port. In Cardiff, Captain Blaisdell had disposed of a large portion of his ballast, giving the space over to iron, which provided the needed weight at a better return. In New Orleans he was faced with replacing that ballast, for which he had paid $1.25 per ton, with ballast priced at $3.00 per ton. He did manage to diminish the expense somewhat by purchasing fifty tons of ballast at $1.75 per ton from his fellow townsman Captain John Gould, master of the *Orlando*.[25] The ship remained in port throughout July and into the first week of August. It proved to be a very discouraging time for the captain, and in each letter that he 'wrote back to Kennebunk he detailed the poor business, hot weather, and recurring ill health that plagued him. On 9 July he complained to Lord:

> your letter of the 28 ult. was duly received— Since I wrote you last there has ben no change in freight for the better. if any thing rather duller and I dont see any chance for improvement this year I am still disingaged. have got Out nearly half of the Iron the weather is so hot that it is difficult to git men to work—you will notice by the list that the number of ships in port keeps good whilst the stock of cotton is reducing fast there is some little cotton shipping for Liverpool @ 5/8 and Tobacco at 35 shillings Staves for Bordeaux @ $40- per—Tobacco for the meditrainian @ $8 per H.h.d. nothing shipping for Havre, Coastwise freights dull, too many ships loading, I expect I shall have to take a stave freight if I git anything the prospect looks gloomy,—I shall look for a letter from you to morrow in answer to my dispatch, of the 29 ult—
> the weather is verry hot here and the musketoes verry numerous I am now all alone it is so hot I can keep no one Onboard Mr. McCulloch wanted to go home. He found a good chance and I let him go. Since that the S.d mate has left.—I wish I had something good to communicate, but I have not. so I will close.[26]

There continued to be a paucity of good news to communicate. As he had expected, Blaisdell's search for a cargo concluded with his chartering the ship to carry staves to the wine port of Bordeaux. All in the same predicament, the other Kennebunk ships then in port were in various stages of loading staves, though one, the *James Titcomb* under Captain John Hill, was taking on cotton.

Alone on the *Mount Washington*, Captain Blaisdell chafed under the stagnant weather and frustrating business conditions. He directed his ire at the shipping brokers and in particular at one Levi H. Gale. Brokers acted as middlemen between merchants with goods in need of transport and masters with vessels in need of cargo. Some brokers were retained by European or Northern businesses for whom they purchased and shipped produce and commodities. Others were independent brokers. All received as payment a commission based on the value of the transactions they facilitated.[27] Captain Blaisdell was of the opinion that the brokers were conspiring with the shippers to keep freighting rates low and receiving financial kickbacks for their efforts. His recounting of the plight of broker T.C. Jenkins, with whom he had done business in the past, hinted at feelings of retributive justice, but he was especially goaded when Gale thwarted his attempt to bypass the brokers and their commissions.

Tired of dealing with a situation in which he felt powerless to effect anything positive, and worn down by the heat and a rather nonspecific ailment that centered on his liver, the captain lost heart. Young McCulloch had unexpectedly returned, and on 21 July Blaisdell sounded Lord out on the idea of turning the ship over to him.

I wrote you a few days since informing you of my having chartered the ship Out to Bordeaux to load with staves for the sum of $7,200- I have commenced loading have got in about 20,000 it is verry slow work and the weather is so hot it is dificult to git men to work. I shall not probably be loaded before the 5th or 10th of augt I think I shall git a few passengers probably from three to four hundred dollers, to help me out a little,—I have settled the freight Inwards the Iron came Out in Exelant order it over run several bars and I git paid freight for One ton Over delivered 859.5 freight and primage amounting to $5,413.44 my draft at Cardiff including Intrest & Insurance—$787.76— leaving—$4625.76, of which I think I shall remit $2000. or 2500 and if I should run short I can draw On the freight at par or perhaps something less my Expences loading with staves will be much less then any other cargo Espeacialy cotton. something like $1,800 less—there is no change in freight since I wrote last, but there has ben no arrivals of late for several days the ships have got thined off and there is but a few disengaged ships, but as the stock of cotton has got reduced down to 47,423 bales which will not be much more then anough to fill up the ships now loading. there is nothing now but Tobacco & staves to go On, and I doubt if there is much if any improvement this season. there is a number of ships due here but it has ben calm in the Gulf for several days so that they cant git along—Capt. Gould sailed day before yesterday, Capt. Lord in the Ocean Star is about 2/3 loaded he gits a verry good lot of staves and should think will carry considerable over two hundred thousand, Capt Hill the James Titcomb is loading cotton for Liverpool, 3/8—four or five ships has ben taken for Liverpool within two or three days. I should not be surprised that they will git on so many ships that they will reduce the rates to 5/ 16- again that apears to be the game that the shippers & Brokers are playing and have ben all season, they have got so many on for Boston that they have cut freights down to nothing, and some of them are taking out what they had in and shipping it by Other ships it apears to me that freights will never be any better here as long as there is so many Brokers and they working for the shipers and against the ships. I was in treaty for this freight that I have got with the shipper, I asked him $8000. and have no doubt should got it but Gale came in and Offered the ship Granada which is forty or fifty tons larger for $7,200. and cut me Out, he was watching me when I went in to the shipper and sticked right in, consiquently I had to go to Gale at last, the shipper gives my ship the prefferance as he had loaded her before and knows what she would carry, Jenkins has discarded his old pardner Berdendorff that cheated him out of about $20,000 and has taken another pardner in which is a Dutchman also, and I should not wonder but he will play the same Game with him,—the weather is verry warm here, but not much sickness, my health is not verry Good. I have the bilious complaint which I am so subject to in warm climates but I hope when I git to sea I shall git better of it I will mearly surgest to you that providing my health should be such as not to be able to go to sea if you are willing to trust the ship with Mr. McCulloch the mate, to take charge. for my Own part I have confidence in him so far as I am interested Or I would not surgest it. I know he is young but yet I would reccomend him before I would some Older, now sir, if you disapprove of it Or wether you aprove of it please to answer by Telegraph and I shall git it in time. If you disapprove it would be as well to say nothing about it, at the same time if I find my self able to go the voyage when the ship is loaded I shall go, at preasant I am not able to stop at home nor go to sea, should you approve of Mr. McCullochs taking charge Of the ship—I trust in your goodness in using your influence in putting me into some other ship when my health will permit me to go to sea again, that is if I have given you sattesfaction, I know I have ben unlucky of late but not through any misconduck thank God, this is an unusial long letter and I fear a tiresome One to you, but I hope that you will Excuse my persumption as my pretention to letter writing has always ben small, or to any thing Els, I would not give you any unnessacery trouble if I could avoid it, nor will I now, if you disaprove of what I have surgested you nead not give your self any trouble about it and I will to the voyage sick or well as it may be, . . .[28]

Two days later the captain transferred the net proceeds of the iron freight to Lord in Kennebunk. With each bill of exchange he included a brief report on the dismal market conditions as well as on his progress loading. He found some small consolation in the fact the the relatively small number of staves the *Mount Washington* was apparently going to carry would result in a fairly low stevedores' bill. As the amount of the freight remained the same regardless of how many staves were loaded, it was to the owners' advantage.

I send you here enclosed a Bill on [Magoun & Son] of Boston at 60 days for [$1780.]
I shall probably send you from five hundred to a thousand more in a few days.—
I wrote you two since giving the state of things here, since that there is no change Expect the Ships here got thined of and there is but two Or three disengaged ships in port, but still there is no improvements in freights, there has ben no arrivals for several days. there is a number of ships due here, but it has ben calm in the gulf so that they cant git along,—I make rather slow work of loading. I dont think that I shall be loaded til the last of next week. I have no news of Intrest to communicate.[29]

Two days later, on 25 July, he reported:

I wrote you on the 23d Inclosing you a Bill of Exchange of Messre. Magoun & son Boston for seventeen hundred & eighty dollers which I hope you received, and I here Inclose the 2d of the same.—Since I wrote you last there is no change in freights Everry ship in port is taken up and no improvement Even the last ship that was taken Only got 3/8. there has ben no arivals here for several days it being calm but the Wind is now strong from the Eastward and several ships is tele-graphed at the Bar, it is singular after the ships got thined of and Only two disengaged ships in the port that freights did not advance but, the unfavorable accounts from Liverpool had a bad affect, besides the stock of Cotton is too small. I am about half loaded, but it is verry slow work loading staves, the staves that I am taking is verry large and the most that we can git in in a day is ten thousand, I dont think that I shall carry over 140,000 but it will be all the better as I shall not have so much to pay the stevedors.—[30]

As the end of July approached the loading of the *Mount Washington*'s hold neared completion. The captain, still in low spirits, had received no reply from Lord concerning the possibility of Adam McCulloch taking charge of the ship. With the time of departure nearing, Blaisdell again broached the subject on 29 July. Though he craved a respite from the cares of command he was well aware that his financial standing in the world would not permit him to remain permanently ashore.

your letter of the 18th came to hand to day. it seems that you had not then heard of my Ingagement, I wrote you a few days since inclosing the second bill of Exchange On [Magoun & Son] Boston for $1785.- I git On slowly loading, it is slow work loading staves, we have had considerable rain of late which has put me back some. I am in hopes to be nearly loaded this week, since I wrote you last there has ben but little or no change in freights. I beleave that one small ship got 7/16 for a small lot of cotton for Liverpool, but there has ben several new arrivals and I dout if that rate is sustained. One of the Brokers I understand reported 25 ships due yesterday I expect it was Gale, one ship that was loading for Boston had a small part of her cargo in after waiting fifteen days, took it out again and took a cargo of Tobacco for Rotterdam @ forty shillings per H.h.d.—the Ocean Star is about loaded & will go down tomorrow, she takes a verry good cargo, Capt Lord told me he should have in about 200,000 staves, and 100 H.h.d. of Tobacco. he must have had a small lot of staves. my staves Runs verry large, and I dont think that I shall carry much over 160,000, but it will be all the better for me as the stevedores Bill will be less. I wrote you dated the 21st Inst. as my health was poor if you had any abjection to Mr. McCullochs taking the ship provided I did not feel my self able to go and if you had not to answer by Telegraphick dispatch at the receipt of my letter, I have not named it to him nor shall not if you Object, I wrote you soon after my arrival that he had left me it was mutual, his folks wanted him to come home, and he got a mates berth in a ship bound for Boston, but as I could not git any mate at that time and finding that I was alone he came back again with his own free will, I did not ask him to come back I thought as his parents was desirous for him to come home, that I would not persuade him to stop. but as he was so considerate as to sacrifice the pleasure of seeing his friends for my sake and the Owners I feel some gratitude for him. and he is a steady young man and some Experience too considering the time that he has ben to sea, I have considerable confidence in him, but at the same time if you have not, and wish for me to remain by the ship I shall of course do so. I have not hinted this to no one but yourself and if you disaprove of it perhaps it would be as well to say nothing about it unless I have presumed to much already, but as I abserved in my letter of the 21st that I am not able to stop at home nor at preasant go to sea, unless my health improve—but should you approve of Mr. McCullochs taking the ship, and I find my self able to go to sea again as I said before, I trust in your goodness in your using your Influence in placing me in another ship if I have given sattesfaction, for I have no other friend that I know of to lean on. Mr. Jenkins to day made me a bet of a hat, that freights would be 3/4 during the next season, and I hope that he will win, more Espeasialy if the mount Washington is here to improve it, but I hope that they will not be so short lived as they wher this

year, the Cotton bids fair to be great this year so far, but I think that the crop of
ships bids fair to be full as great, as the cotton, . . .[31]

Evidently the captain's suggestion that McCulloch take command of the
Mount Washington did not meet with Lord's approval, for when the ship
sailed Captain Blaisdell was still her master and McCulloch still first mate.
McCulloch, only twenty-one in 1851, was the son of Adam McCulloch, Sr.,
and the captain may have been overly eager to repay the family for his own
promotion so many years before. Indeed, within the next three months events
would transpire that transformed the captain's feelings of gratitude toward
young McCulloch to those of disappointment and disgust.

By the end of the first week of August all was ready aboard the *Mount
Washington*. Before heading down the river Captain Blaisdell wrote on 6
August to apprise William Lord of the final outcome of the ship's affairs in
New Orleans.

> I take this Oppertunity to inform you that I am now loaded & ready for sea I shall
> go down to night if I can git a boat. I have drawn On the freight for $700.- you
> will Please to insure my Primage if you Insure the freight the ship draws 17 feet,
> which is a light draft for staves, I Expect that she will be rather tender, as I have
> only about 45 tons of Balest, there has ben no change in freights since my last,
> little or nothing offering at preasant,—I have not received any dispatch from you,
> my health is not verry good but I hope it will improve after I git to sea, I have not
> time to send you my account from here but I hope Everry thing will be sattesfac-
> tory I have got disapointed in my passangers, it being late in the season they are
> afraid of the Hurycanes,—I hope I shall be more fortunate in a return freight then
> I am in this,—if my wife should be in want of any money will you please to let her
> have it.[32]

Hindsight gives the line "it being late in the season they are afraid of the
Hurycanes" a premonitory ring. Two weeks out of New Orleans the *Mount
Washington* was caught in the grips of a hurricane that nearly destroyed her,
and the ensuing course of events nearly destroyed Captain Blaisdell as well.

NINE

An Unfortunate Business for All Concerned 1851

Key West .. Augt 27, 1851

William Lord Esqre
Dr Sir,
I am under the disagreable necesity of informing you of my arrival at this place
with loss of fore mast fore topmast fore and main top Gall. masts Gib boom with
all the rigging & sails attached and leeking badly. I left the S.W. Pass On the 7
Inst. had light winds from the Eastward and calms til the 20th of Augt when it
commenced blowing from the Eastward being then in Lat. 23.42 N. & Longitude
82.40 W. at noon.—at 8 P.M. being then under cloast reeft fore and main top
sails Juging my self well Over On the Cuba shore I wore ship to the N.N.E. the
Gale increasing and a tramendious heavy sea runing Commenced leeking badly.
took in fore and main top sail and lay too under bare poles. the ship laying Over
Verry much, all hands at the pumps working both pumps.—
    at midnight Gale increasing sounded the weather pump found two & half feet
of water. Ship laying with the lee rail under
    at 6 A.M. gale still increasing shiped a sea that broke the main rail and lifted it
of the stantions stove in the bulwark and hove the ship nearly on her beam Ends.
found something must be done Speadly to save the ship to keep her afloat. after
a consultation of the Officers, we deamed it Our Only resort was to cut away the
masts. after the fore mast was gone the ship wrighted some. the main top Galt
masts and gib boom went with the fore mast. all hands was kept to the pumps
and both pumps was kept to work til Friday morning with Out sucking. Friday
augt 22d at day light found we was in White water. sounded and found ten
fathams of water.
    the ship was unmanagable, would not whare nor stay. consequently we got the
anchors off the bow & found we had shoaled the water to 7 fathems it was still
blowing strong dead on to the reef, and a heavy sea running, thick rainy weather.
preasantly Saw breakers to leeward not above a half mile dist. let go both anchors
and brought her up in five fathems of water, nothing in sight but Breakers and a
Bark that had drifted in On to the reef. got an Observation and found we was in a
verry dangerous place not twice the length of the ship from a shoal of quick sand
with not above ten feet of water On it. and with poor holding ground. the wind
had moderated but continued to blow toward the shoal got up a Jury fore mast

and got some head sails rigged in case the wind should change to try and git out of our dangerous situation. nothing came in sight til Sunday morning when two wreckers came along side. I tryed to make arrangements with them to give me a pilot to take me out of this and up to Key West but could make no arrangements with them. the only thing they would do was to keep their Schooners by me til they got me in to Key West and then leave it to arbtration Or the decision of the court which I was under the necessity of complying with, knowing if it should come on to blow I must unavoidably go On to the Shoal. Monday we got under way and got two schooners ahead with the help of what sail we could set On the ship we got her into safer anchorage betwixt the reef and the Marquis Keys. and to day we arrived at Key West, where I noted a protest and called a survey. I find that there is no spar here fit for a mast nor no cordage large anough for shrouding &c on the top mast Stays & back stays, consiquently I have decided to leave the ship in charge of the mate and to take passage in the steamer tomorrow morning for New York. to consult you what is best to be done, I send this by Brig - which sails for New York in the morning in case of any acsident to the steamer, hoping to see you in five days from this,

I remain sir your Obedient Servant
Jotham Blaisdell

P.S. augt 29 the steamer did not pass near anough to key west for me to git onboard, consiquently, I have decided to take passage in the Bark Em[ily Miner] for New York and I leave this to be put Onboard of the first steamer that passes for New York. if you should git this before my arrival you can git the mast & spars, rigging & sails, in progress. Everry thing was lost that was attached to the fore mast, fore top mast, fore & main top Gallant masts & Gib booms & martingale spars, Rigging &c, I should think it would be best to git the draft of the ship from Mr. Maling and Everry thing can be fitted by that I think it would be best to have Everry thing fited at Boston or New York. Or where Ever you send them from so as to be all ready to go On as soon as it arrives Out here.[1]

The protest had been filed, and in anticipation of a claim for salvage a survey had been called to appraise the value of ship and cargo. With the posting of the letter informing Lord and the other owners of the *Mount Washington*'s plight Captain Blaisdell fulfilled the last of the most pressing responsibilities that had faced him upon his arrival in Key West. However, this granted no respite for he was still confronted with a bewildering array of details and problems that required his attention.

Following the preliminaries in Key West, his main priority was to confer with William Lord. Taking passage aboard the bark *Emily Miner*, bound to New York from Mobile, he arrived in New York two weeks later on 12 September. He lingered only long enough to leave a letter for Lord's brother Tobias, dealing with the possibility of securing in the city the materials needed for the refitting of the ship.

The next day he was in Boston. He called on George Callender and the two of them presented the claim to the insurers, who, without delay, granted permission for the purchase of the necessary masts, spars, and rigging.

Before he took the train to Kennebunk, he also saw Hartley Lord. Hartley immediately wrote to his father, "You will have seen Capt. Blaisdell before this is received and get all the particulars about the Mt. Washington—It is a bad job and I was sorry to hear of it—but there is no help for these things—I have been expecting to hear the same of the Ocean Star & J. Titcomb but Capt. Blaisdell thinks they were ahead of it."[2] The *James Titcomb* did not totally escape the storm, but her only reported damage was the loss of three casks of water.[3] Echoing Hartley Lord's rather fatalistic tone, George Callender noted, "This is an unfortunate business for all concerned but it can't be helped."[4] Captain Blaisdell's opinion on the matter, shaped by his experiences as the episode ground on, was that his own misfortune grew in direct proportion to the amount of his concern and involvement.

The captain did not remain long in Kennebunk. He and William Lord decided that the needed materials for the ship could be procured in New York with the greatest dispatch and least cost. He stopped at home long enough to gather up his family, and then they all set out by train for New York City. Once in New York, the captain settled his family into a hotel and went to see Tobias Lord. Tobias's business sense and connections in the city would be invaluable. Throughout the proceedings, Captain Blaisdell kept William Lord fully posted. On 17 September he reported:

> I arrived here on Tuesday morning and called on Tobias Lord Esqre went together ameaditly and Saw the sparmakers and bought the spars, viz. fore mast, topmast, two top Galt masts, Gib boom fore yard, fore top Galt yards and martingale all compleat for $359 which I think is less than we could have bought them at Boston the fore mast was $110- the cordage we paid 9 cts per lb for american hemp menella 13 1/4 per lb the Riggers bill for fitting $100- we have also bought the canvas at reasonable prices, all @ 6 months the sail maker makes the sails @ $4.50 per bolt & find all they have ingaged to have done in a week the Black Smith asks 12 cts per lb for the iron work—there is a vessel advertised for Key West so I am in hopes we Shall make good dispatch.—I suppose that your Brother will write you by the Same mail I supose Mr. Calender has advised you of the arangements in Boston with the underwriters, the Agent is a going out to Key West, there will be no [steamer] coming over to Key West til the 1st of Oct consequently I can git no letter forwarded nor git On myself before that, I shall keep you advised of our proceedings. . . .[5]

Obvious from the outset, but becoming more evident daily, was the magnitude of both time and aggravation that the settling of the *Mount Washington*'s affairs would entail. That prospect, coupled with his indifferent health, caused the captain to waiver in his commitment to the command which he had been so eager to take up nine months before. On 19 September he wrote to Lord. Once again, but in slightly more pressing tones, he requested to be relieved from the *Mount Washington* and the overwhelming complexities of her situation.

I wrote you a few days Since informing you how we was gitting along &c Since Which we have bargined with a Black Smith @ 10 cts per lb for Iron work and all the blocks compleat for $85. we have not got a vessel yet to take them Out but think we Shall have no difficulty in gitting One as there is Several up for differant ports in Florida—

the first conveyance to Key West that I can hear of is a steamer leaves Charleston on the 1st of Oct for that port and there is a steamer leaves here for Charleston tomorrow but as I should have to wait some time in charleston for the Key West boat, I think I shall stop here til the 24 or 25 and go On by land. by that time we shall have Everry thing Compleated and I hope On the way for Key West, and after we git the materials Out there I think She can be dispatched in fifteen days. Capt. Tobias is a first rate man to Cheapen the mechanicks I think that he has got things as low as they Possably could be got,—I have had no chance of answering the letter from Key West as there has ben no conveyance but presume they will not do anything more then to calk & repair the upper works till I git there, and as it is the wish of all concerned not to strip the bottom there providing she can be made safe to perform the passage to Bordeaux where it can be done with better dispatch and much less expense, I shall indeavor to do so if possable—as my health is bad I fear I shall not be able to perform the voyage to Bordeaux. if it is agreable to all concerned I wish you to send On another master. as Capt. Maling is at home and you have no Objections to him, I have no doubt he would be glad to take the ship. I feel greaved to leave the ship but my health at preasant will not admit. if you approve of Capt. Maling Or any One that you may Select I think had better go On by the first Conveyance as there is but One in fifteen days, I shall Start by land about the 25 or 26 Inst. and Capt. Maling or whom Ever goes could take passage in the vessel that takes Out the spars &c—the Rigger has commenced fitting the Rigging, and it is Exelant Rigging upon the Whole I think we have got Everry thing reasonable and probably Cheaper then at Boston or Kennebunk Espeacialy the mast.[6]

By the following day a vessel to transport the materials had been secured, and the captain's own travel plans had been altered.

I wrote you yesterday informing you of Our proceadings &c Since that we have got a vessel the Bark Lluallyn to take Out the spars, Rigging & sails & Blocks &c for which we pay him $356 and if he is detained after the 24 Inst On Our account we have got to pay him thirty dollers per day damages but I am in hopes we Shall not have to pay any damages as I hope Everry thing will be ready by that time. this is the first vessel to go and I think it is an object to Secure her as we mite have to wait some time for another vessel. I wrote you in my letter yesterday that I thought I should not be able to go the Voyage on account of my health which is poor & mentioned Capt. Maling, but if he dont meet your aproval, whom Ever you may send, if he can git ready had better come On ameadently so as to take passage in the Bark which takes Out the spars &c. she will sail probably next thursday the 24th Inst—I think that I shall go Out by the same vessel as the Steamer from Charleston for Key West will not leave til the 1st of Oct. and probably the Bark will git there as soon as the Steamer as she is a fast sailer.[7]

Upon receiving the captain's request to leave the ship William Lord consulted George Callender who answered, "We hope Capt. Blaisdell will conclude to go in the ship as we think it very important the same master should go in her to Bordeaux to settle up the loss and as you say another reason will be having to copper her there but the most important is to explain & settle all that grows out of the putting into Key West. If his health will in any way permit & we should think it would—we trust he will go in her from Key West."8

William Lord soon wrote to Captain Blaisdell that he thought it best if the captain remained by the ship as he understood and could handle the problems concerning her better than another master would. That Lord was unsure of the captain's reaction is evident by the fact that he wrote to his brother Tobias asking how the captain took the news. Tobias answered that, "Capt. B- did not say much on account of your not being willing for him to leave. He knows best his feelings but to appearances he is not dangerously sick—in fact I did not know he had wrote you for a discharge 'til he got your answer, then he spoke of it."9 In Captain Blaisdell's written reply to William Lord his regret at Lord's decision was clear, although Lord had attempted to sweeten the bitter pill of staying with the ship by offering to allow Elizabeth Blaisdell to join her husband on his voyage. The captain responded to Lord's letter in a melancholy vein.

Your letters of the 21- & 23d has ben received the Bark Lluallyn sails to day with all the Outfit for the mt. Washington and I leave on Saturday for key west in the Steamer Florida by the way of Savanah we have got in about all the Bills In. the whole amount will be about $2,500- or $2,600 including Stores for the Ship which is about $95- Capt Hoyt the Agent goes Out with me. I should have gone out in the Bark that takes the rigging Out but I thought it was important that I should git Out there as Soon as posible. I am much disapointed in your not being able to ingage Capt. Maling or some other master to take charge of the Ship as my health is so bad but I hope it may improve but wether it does Or not if I am alive I will stop by the Ship and do the best that I can as I Observed before I am not able to Stop at home nor go to Sea I am about worn Out in the Sea Servais and before Or without making a fortune that is a Secret that I have yet to learn. but it is hard to learn Old dogs new tricks and I heartly thank you for your kind Offer in allowing me to take my wife to Sea with me but having a large family to look after and many of them young it would be dificult for her to leave home. it is verry important that she should remain with the children and as much as I value her company I must deny my self of that pleasure for the Childrens sake.

As the underwriters agent is a going Out to key west I hope that all will be settled to the sattisfaction of all Concearned, I hope that you will write me as Often as Convenient and give me all the counsel that you can advise Mr. Callender sugested taking the specie to pay the salvage On the staves, France is a ticklish place to settle adjustments and there is more law there then Justice. the average will have to be made up in france as they willl not settle by an adjustment made up in the States. . . .10

Somewhat resigned to what lay ahead of him, the captain concluded his business in New York. He sent his family back to Kennebunk and saw the bark that carried the *Mount Washington*'s rigging off to Key West. On 27 September, after ten days in the city, he departed New York, accompanied by Captain John Hoyt of Boston who went out to protect the interests of the insurers. Before Captain Blaisdell left he notified both Lord in Kennebunk and George Callender in Boston.

New York Sept. 26, 1851

Messrs Geo. Callender & Co
Gentlemen
    Undoubtedly Mr. T Lord has kept you advised of the proceedings here, so I can give you nothing new, but as we have now got every thing dispatched I thought I would drop you a few lines   We shipped every thing on board the barque Llewellyn for Key West On the 24th so there was no detention to the vessel, but as the wind has been ahead she has not yet sailed but will sail the first chance of wind. I leave tomorrow in company with Capt. Hoyt in the steamer Florida for Savannah from whence we take the Isabel for Key West I did think of going out in the barque, but I thought finally—as it is so important that I should be there as soon as possible—that this will be the quickest way to get there. We have got the bills all in and I take the duplicates out with me The whole amt. is something over $2500. Every thing is fitted ready to go right ahead as soon as it arrives there I fear that the making of the rudder out there will be the longest job, as we cannot load till the rudder is hung. I shall endeavor to make all possible dispatch, and settle every thing to the satisfaction of all concerned. I am glad that Capt. Hoyt is going out with me as he is well acquainted with the place, and better able to detect any imposition. . . .
    P.S. Please write me to Key West and any information you can give me will be very acceptable Respecting the adjustments of the Genl Avge will it be necessary to have it made up here or at Bordeaux—Please to advise me. I believe they will not settle by adjustments made up in the U.S.[11]

New York Septr 27 - 1851

Wm Lord Esqre
Dr Sir,
    I wrote you day before yesterday, but as I leave to day I will send you a few lines. I leave to day in the steamer Florida for Savannah and frome thence in the Isabella to key west, the Bark that takes Out the spars &c sailed yesterday, but she has had a dull chance, as the wind has ben to the S.E. I stated in my last that the bills here would be about $2,500 but they Excead that, some considerable
    I will Send you the amount & following—

Rigging Bill—$1251.03—Duck do $497.74	1748.77
Black Smith $248.02—sail maker $183.05	431.08
Riggers bill $104.75 Chains—$52.64	157.39
Block maker $85.00—Sheaving spars $30.58	115.58
Advertising	1.00
Spars &c	366.19

```
Rudder Stock  ..........................................    26.35
Commissions on $2846-96—@ 5/c  ..........................   142.34
                                                          $2988.70
Cash taken my Self  .....................................   110.00
                                                          $3098.70
```

I remain Sir verry respectfuly your Obedient Servnt.

Jotham Blaisdell[12]

It was October before Captain Blaisdell returned to Key West. Two months had already slipped by since the *Mount Washington*'s departure from New Orleans in early August. Upon his arrival from New York the captain found that Adam McCulloch had put the time to good use by attending to many of the ship's needs. He was well satisfied with the nature of the repairs and their workmanship. However, as he inspected the completed work and contemplated what still needed to be done, his apprehension concerning costs grew. Key West was notoriously expensive. Indeed, the maritime authorities of the day cautioned masters to have only the most vital and pressing repairs made there and strongly recommended that anything that could possibly be put off until the vessel reached a larger and more economical port should wait.[13]

Until the early 1800s Key West had been a haven for pirates. These first denizens were eventually eradicated, and in 1822 the island passed from Spanish to American ownership. The area known as the Florida reef, in which Key West lies, was considered to be the most dangerous stretch of coastline in the United States. Its impact on shipping was magnified by the large number of vessels that crossed it on their ways to and from New Orleans and the Gulf ports. During the 1840s and '50s it was estimated that an average of fifty vessels came to grief in these waters each year. Because of its location, Key West became a major ship salvaging center, and a court of admiralty was established there in 1828.

As there were no other ports of entry on the reef, Key West enjoyed a monopoly on the salvage business. The livelihoods of virtually all her citizens depended to some degree on wrecks and wreckers. Like enterprising people everywhere, they naturally became adept at promoting their own interests. Not surprisingly, their interests and the interests of a crippled vessel's owners and insurers did not always coincide, and there were frequent charges of conflict of interest and corruption. Certainly the conditions, especially in the earlier years, seemed to invite abuse.

Generally, from twenty to thirty vessels were employed as wreckers and could be found cruising the waters of the reef. Usually small craft, either sloops or schooners, they were in many instances owned either in whole or in part by merchants in Key West. These wreckers were in the habit of anchoring inside the reef, well out of the sight of any passing commercial traffic. Each day at dawn they would comb the reef in search of vessels that might have grounded during the night. When a merchant ship in distress was sighted, the wrecker immediately made for her. It was financially more advantageous to the wrecker, and his owners and backers, if the injured vessel was beyond help. He would then set about salvaging the cargo and ferry it to Key West. In situations where the grounded vessel might possibly be towed off the reef and saved, some unscrupulous wreckers were not above attempting to buy her master's acquiescence in the staging of her destruction. Using the argument that to take her into Key West would incur great expense, one third of which her owners must bear, while the insurers alone would pay if she were a total loss, and armed with a substantial bribe, they often found their mark. When they had, the ship was lightened by removing some of the cargo, ostensibly to aid in getting her off but in reality allowing her to drift farther in onto the reef. Then boats would be used to try and drag her over the reef bow first to open water. Ultimately she became hopelessly stuck, and there she bilged.

The prime concern in either case was to gain control of the cargo. If it became a little wet or water stained in the transfer so much the better. For some convoluted reason a higher rate of salvage was at one time paid on damaged goods than on dry. Once in Key West, the goods were consigned to a merchant; not improbably the merchant who owned the wrecker. With the ship a total loss the cargo must be disposed of, and the port marshall would set the date for an auction. Because of distances and poor communication, the bidders at the auction were often just the merchants of the island. Loath to inflict financial hardship on each other by actively bidding, they would amicably divide the cargo among themselves at a fraction of its value.

Often acting as agent in the matter for the absent insurers was one of the Key West merchants, who at best would have had divided loyalties. The judicial system itself was not above suspicion, as the judge of the court of admiralty could be chosen from among the lawyers of the island, who had of course in their time represented wreckers and received large fees in return. And should the case go to arbitration, there was no guarantee that the persons chosen were not secret owners in the wrecker or financially interested in her in some other way.[14]

By the time the *Mount Washington* was at Key West, many of the problems had been redressed. An observer in 1848 had noted that there were twenty-four Key West wrecking vessels, "all having licenses from the Judge of the Admiralty Court. These are not obtained with very great facility; an eye is had to the character of the man who commands the vessel, and, whenever any dishonesty is detected, he is deprived of his license. . . . The aim of the Judge seems to be to make it profitable for these crafts to assist in saving vessels—not in 'wrecking' them. . . ."[15] The judge of the admiralty court was William Marvin, who had literally written the book on wrecking and salvage procedures.

Wreckers at work in the Florida Keys.
Harper's New Monthly Magazine, April 1859.

Key West was a small but thriving port in the 1850s.
Local wreckers kept the docks filled with derelict
vessels and the court filled with salvage cases.
Lithograph, drawn by J.C. Clapp, printed by
Chandlor & Company, Boston, ca. 1855.
(Courtesy Mariners' Museum, Newport News, Virginia)

Nevertheless, the insurers were unwilling to rely upon a long-distance agent, and sent Captain Hoyt to look out for their interests. It was under the apprehension of the traditions and reputation of the place that Captain Blaisdell labored as well, and his constant vigilance against being "imposed upon" is evident in the letters he wrote to Lord during his time on Key West.

Key West Octr 8th 1851

I take this Oppertunity of writing you by the Steamer Isabel which leaves here this Evening Or Early in the morning for Charleston,—and the same Steamer will leave Charleston again for this Port On the 22d Inst. if you wish to write by her. I arrived Out here on the Evening of the 3d inst. and found the Ship nearly ready to commence loading, they have calked her from the Copper up—in side & Out found her verry Open took nearly 1000 lb of Oakum, the main rails was broken on both sides and three of the Chanels the Chacks On both sides forward was also gone the monkey rails & boards nearly all gone and a good deal of the main bulwarks gone, which have all Ben repaired, the fore & main topmasts was both found to be badly sprung & have ben condemned and replaced, the work is all well done the quarter pieces & Curtain rail has ben taken Off and calked under them and put On again, the head rail and knees was mostly washed away and have ben repaired, some of the hanging knees are sprung & broken and no doubt in the late gale, the Copper looks to be badly strained and renched up, and some of it stove off by the spars. the survay recomends it taken off in the first convenient Port, and calked & recoppered, but are of the Opinion that it will be safe to procead on the voyage, for the passage,—I can form no Idear yet as to the Expences, but I fear it will be heavy, but there has nothing ben done but was realy nessacery, and had she ben in any Other place then this, and under your Own superintendance I think that you would have had Still more done then has ben done here but as I consider the Ship safe to go On the preasant voyage I do not wish to incur any further Expence here, which is all ready heavy, but I think that it will be nessacery to have some thing done to the hanging knees betwisct decks in the first convenient port Where it can be done,—as the winter season is aproaching and I have got to go On a winter passage I thought it nessacery to have more balest in the Ship, consiquently I have ben Ever Since I have ben here scraping up all that I can find, which is verry scarce finely I have made Out to git about 40 tons, including about 5 tons of pig Iron Or kentleage which I have bought @ $15- per ton, which no doubt will at any time bring more then I paid for it, but I should not have bought it if I could have got stone balest. but there was no more to be had. I paid $2 pr ton for what I have got delivered alongside I have commenced loading to day I Stow with my own Crew, and have to hire men to put them on board, I think I shall git them about all in again, I have lost four of my crew, some ran away, some was sick and I discharged them, and one poisined him self by drinking two Ounces of Laudinum, the Others work well and behave well, the Bark has not yet arrived with the spars rigging, sails &c but I look for her now dayly, the Carpenter sais he can make the Rudder & hang it in a week after he gits the stock, we find the old one badly broken and nearly twisted off, the ship is quite tight now and I am in hopes that she will proove so, I saw Mr. Carson the shipper of the staves in New York, he told me that he had jest rec,d letters from bordeaux and that freights were Extreamly dull then, but said I should now be there in good time for a good freight as I should find no vessels there on my arrival I hope that it may turn Out so, and that all may prove for the best I hope that you will write me by the return of the boat, and give me all the instruction that you can. I shall write you Everry Oppertunity and that is not verry often, for the boat stops 8 days in charleston this trip, consequently will not be Out here again til the 25 Inst—my health has not much improoved, and I fear it never will,—Capt. Hoyt the underwriters agent is here, and I find him a verry agreable man and am verry glad he is here,—as I have to stow the staves with my Own crew, I have ben trying to git the rigging part done by the Job, but they ask such an inormous price that I cant agree with them, the lowest that they will do it for is $260.. and if I have to hire men by the day it will cost me about as much so I think that I will keep On loading til the Bark arrives, and then go to rigging whilst they make the rudder, and then finish loading, it will make some delay, but I dont like to indulge them to give them such a price thinking of nothing more at preasant, hoping to be able to make good dispatch and finely wind up to the satisfaction of all concerned. . . .[16]

Key West Octr 11th 1851

I wrote you a few days since informing you of Our progress, &c the Bark arrived night before last with the spars &c, it took us the best part of yesterday to git them On board, and to day we shall Step the mast, I Shall go on with the rigging now til the rudder is made and hung by that time will be about rigged. and we shall then go On with loading, we have unhung the rudder to day and found it broken more then half off much worse then we first thought it was, it will probably take a week to make the rudder and git it hung again, the carpenter thinks that he can do it in four days, but I doubt it. I think we have got a verry good pice of wood for a stock and I hope it will stand longer then the Other two did,—I have given the Capt. of the Bark a draft On Messrs Callender & Co for $383.00 the amount of the freight On the spars and Other materials agreable to Mr Callenders instructions,—as the Juge has not yet arrived nothing has ben done about the settlement of the Salvage, we dont Expect him til the 25 Inst, I can form no Idear what my Expense will be here yet, but I dread the result, I shall do all that I can to lessen the Expenses but, I cant do much, Capt. Hoyt the underwriters agent is here and we git along verry well togeather I am verry glad he is here for he is an intelegent man, and seams well disposed,—I shall keep you advised of my proceedings, Everry Oppertunity. and that is not verry Often, I Send this by the way of St. Marks by the Lluallyn which sails tomorrow. . . .[17]

Key West Octr 24th 1851

I take this Oppertunity of Writing you a few lines by the Steamer Winfield Scott which passes here to day for New York I wrote you some Eight days since by the way of St Marks which is the Only chance I have had Since that we have ben gitting On as fast as possable the Ship is now rigged & the rudder made and hung, & works first rate, and the stick prooved to be a verry good One, we have taken in about half of the Staves that where Out, about 65 tons, it is verry slow Work Stowing Staves here as there is no One understands it. I have to make a

Stevedore of the second mate, I have Only about half my crew by me now, and I have to divide them part on the rigging and part in the hold stowing, I have to hire a large gang to work on the Staves and it will be very Expensive loading as Wages is high the ship is perfectly tight now, and I am in hopes that she will continue so.—the Isabel is due here to night from Charleston, and the Juge is Expected Out in her, and as soon as he arrives I supose then the Salvage will be Settled, and I am in hopes by the last of next week the ship will be ready for sea, and I shall be glad when I git Out of this scrape, I am in hopes to be able to make up a crew here,—I am in hopes to git some letters by the Isabel, and I shall write you again by her On her return from Havana I cannot tel yet what the Expenses will be here, but I fear high, as wages is high and they work slow, you may possably have time to answer this by the steamer for New Orleans, as they Often board them in pilot boats here please to give me all the Instructions that you can, respecting the Settlement of the General Average &c, and provided that there should be any Obstacle in the way of coppering the ship at Bordeaux, if the underwriters will Extend the time to a more convenient place &c that is if the ship prooves tight and there is no risk in so doing,—I dont know that I have any thing more to say at preasant of any importance, but I will write you by the next conveyance and keep you informed of my proceadings. . . .[18]

Key West Octr 26 1851
as the Government Steamer leaves here to day for Charleston, I avail my self of the Oppertunity of writing you a few lines by her, your letters of the 8th & 16—Inst come to hand On the 24 Inst, and contents noted with pleasure I am happy to inform you that I am now nearly loaded shall finish by the last of this week and shall with Out doubt git all the Staves in & have spare room,—the rudder is made and hung and works well, the stick prooved to be a verry good one, the ship is about rigged, and will in all probability be ready for sea by the first of next week about the 6th—of November, the Judge came Out in the Isabel the last mail Boat, and tomorrow we shall commense operations on the Settlement of the Salvage, as it was the wish of the underwriters it should be settled by the Judge nothing could be done in his absants, and I mentioned in my last letter to that Effect, I shall write you by the return of the Isabel which will be On the 1st of November, by that time I am in hopes to be able to ascertain about what the Expenses will be, and I dread the result, but hope for the best, I hope in the winding up it may turn Out better then I first anticipated. I think it can be managed in a way that they cannot git off at Bordeaux, paying up all that we are intitled to, and without delay, the ship is tight as yet and I am in hopes she will remain so—I got a letter from Tobias Lord Esqre. New York saying that he should send Out the Bills certified by the French Counsal, I think that it will be best to send Out two sets for fear one may miscarry, which mite put me in the back ground. I notice the improvements in freights at Orleans, and it cuts me to the quick, I Wish the staves had ben in Kentucky before I had seen them, if I could have fore seen Events it would have ben better for me to have laid there two months longer it would have ben to the Owners Intrest, and saved me much anxsiaty and trouble, but we cannot alwais see far anough a head,—in hast as the steamer is Just shuving off—[19]

The salvage trial began on 29 October 1851 before Judge William Marvin. A libel had been filed by prominent Key West wrecker John H. Geiger, stating that he had come upon the *Mount Washington* on 24 August and that she was stranded at the west end of the quicksands near the Rebecca Shoal. He claimed that he had been on board the *Champion*, and with her consorts the *Louisa*, *Lafayette*, and *Euphemia* took the *Mount Washington* off the shoal and towed her to Key West. Consorting was a practice employed by wreckers whereby several vessels collaborated and stationed themselves at different points along the reef. When one of them came upon a wreck the others were called to aid her and shared in the proceeds.

For his defense, Captain Blaisdell had engaged Stephen R. Mallory, who had studied salvage law under Judge Marvin. Mallory also served as Key West collector of customs, and was about to be elected U.S. Senator from Florida. Mallory counseled Blaisdell to countercharge that he had been in no great danger and had merely wanted a pilot to get him to Key West. The Judge's decision upheld the captain's contention, and Geiger was only awarded $1,500 in pilot's fees.[20]

Any pleasure Captain Blaisdell might have taken in the court's decision was overshadowed by a break with his first mate, Adam McCulloch, Jr. In his last letter written from Key West, the captain informed William Lord of all that had transpired.

> Key West Novr 6 1851
>
> I take this Oppertunity by the Bark [   ] for New York, to write you a few lines, to inform you that I am now about ready for sea,—the staves is all in with some spare room, and the sd mate stood stevedore, and I have alowed him some thing Extra Over and above his wages as well as the crew that worked On the cargo as is the custom here and it is charged as wages which will be brought into Genrl average—the salvage has ben awarded $1,500, which was less then we at first anticipated, the accounts is not quite made up there is some few bills Out yet, but as near as we can come at it the whole Expense here will be about,—$8000. including salvage, and Expenses there On—
>
> I have had some difficulty in gitting a crew here as part of the Old crew had ran away, and I have not got them all yet. Mr. McCulloch has left me, and prooved his gratitude towards me, I find now that I misplaced any confidence and shall be a little more caucious in future in recommending so hastly. I have taken the second mate as mate as there is no one Else here to git, and I shall have to take One of the crew for Sd mate. Capt. Hoyt, the underwriters agent here is a fine man I think, he tells me that as the salvage is so much less then was anticipated he thinks that the underwriters will not hesitate to pay the whole of the bills with Out deducting the customary One Third for New, he sais that he shall do all he can to that Effect, that is after the General average is settled he sais he has no doubt but they anticipated a much higher salvage and the agreable disapointment and I hope it may be the cause of there being liberal, the case has ben so ably defended, that it has ben the means of saving the underwriters probably four or six thousand dollers, although it was found that the ship was cloast on to the

quick sands, her fore masts gone, gib boom & no head sails, the rudder broken, yet our able lawyer Mr. Malery made it Out to be a case of Pilotage, in stead of salvage, and it was the circumstances of the Jury fore mast, and the sails that I had rigged which saved it. I stated that it was my intentions as soon as the wind came round to the N.E. or any favorable quarter, to git the ship underway, and git her into the gulf. and with the asistance of the currant, I had no doubt that I could have reached Eather Havana Or Key west in safety, and it apears that the Juge thought so too, and now as the ships Expenses is high which falls heavy on the Owners, and the salvage verry light, which they cannot deny was brought about by an able defence, and cheafly by my Own testimony, as I Was the Only whitness in the case, as Mr. McCulloch was taken sick whilst in court, and had to leave before he was called, and the Other was not called, I think that by saving such a large amount of salvage they should be considerate and pay the whole amount as the ship is new, and has not ben benafitted by replacing new for old as an Old ship would be,—I shall probably git the accounts tomorrow, and all the nessacery documents & certificates to inable me to settle the General average at Bordeaux, which I hope I shall be able to do to your sattesfaction, I shall send messrs Callender & Co a coppy of the Whole, I am aware that my Expenses here is very high, but you will make allowance for this place is a verry Expensive place and that you are aware no doubt, wages is high, four dollers per day for Carpenter, & three a half for calkers, and work slow at that. but a good deal has ben done and nothing but was really nessacery, and I have got the character since I have been here of being the meanest man that Ever was in Key west, I feel proud of the name here Which I should not in any Other place,—three ships has ben On the reef with in a week, in sight of Key west, the last One the John & Albert (of Bath Capt. Harwood) was On two days and got off badly Injured and brought in here, the other two got off with out much damage, and Went on there voyage for New Orleans, I shall write you again by the regular mail, and give you all the particulars—

I wrote you a week since by a government Steamer bound for Norfolk, but she had to put back, consequently the letter did not reach you, I mentioned in it that I had received a letter from Tobias Lord Esqre. N York stating that he had or should forward the bills to Bordeaux, &c—I think it would be well to send two coppies, I also named that the Rudder stock proved to be a good stick and fitted first rate. . . .

P.S. I have had a trying time of it here, and I think that an other such would be too much for me, but I hope that the other will never hapen—Every thing has combined to perplex me, the case of McCullochs leaving one, his ingratitude after what I have tryed to do for him fairly disgusts me, not only of this place but of the world—I consider the Obligations that I Owed his father is now canseled—for further Information respecting it Or to whom it interests I will refer to Mr. Hoyet underwriters agent, but that I presume will not be nessacery—in confidense—[21]

The *Mount Washington* was ready to sail at last, and the meanest man in Key West with her. Before he left the island, the captain sent a full accounting to George Callender in Boston, who in turn relayed a report on to William Lord in Kennebunk.

We have received a letter from Captain Blaisdell with all the papers—viz.—
Protests, Surveys & Bills & proceedings of Court—We have accepted his draft at 5
days sight for $8,577.76 and we have effected insurance on $12,000.00 to cover
that and the materials sent from New York in case she should be lost going out—
The underwriters will probably advance us enough to pay the draft when due—
They got off very well as to the salvage but the other charges are high, still the
whole amount is less than we anticipated. Capt. Hoyt has written to the underwriters speaking highly of Captain Blaisdell.[22]

Captain Blaisdell himself, meanwhile, was making a rough crossing to Bordeaux, where he arrived in late December. The voyage, which had already
been prolonged due to the vagaries of nature, was further delayed by the low
level of the water in the Garonne River. After all the adversity that he had
encountered following the ship's departure from New Orleans five months
earlier, the captain was stranded thirty miles from his destination at the port of
Pauillac.

Bordeaux
1852

BORDEAUX as Captain Blaisdell saw it in 1852 was a beautiful city of one hundred and ten thousand people. Situated sixty miles upriver from the Bay of Biscay, it occupied a sweeping curve on the west bank of the Garrone River. Long an important port specializing in the shipping of the region's fine wines, Bordeaux was also the administrative and cultural center for the surrounding district. The Languedoc Canal gave the city access to the Mediterranean and a resulting trade with the south of France that rivaled that of Marseilles. Tall warehouses, honeycombed with wine cellars and fronted by wide stone quays, lined the river's bank for five miles. A single bridge, the Pont de Bordeaux, spanned the river with seventeen arches, connecting the city proper with its suburbs. Behind the hedge of warehouses spread the town. To the east lay the old city of narrow winding streets that were flanked by characteristic low white houses. Stretching westward was the newer and more fashionable section of the city with its carefully planned streets and squares. In addition to the city's pleasing architecture, there were parks and public gardens graced by statues and memorials to cultural and revolutionary heroes.[1]

In 1848, when the captain had last been in Bordeaux under happier circumstances and with his wife, he had probably passed some pleasant moments taking in the sights of the city, but on this occasion he would have had little time and even less inclination for admiring his surroundings. Unable to get the *Mount Washington* up the river without delay, he left her and traveled on to the city alone. Three major concerns faced him on his arrival: the settlement of the general average, the coppering of the ship, and the chartering of a return cargo. Whereas his usual practice in obtaining a cargo was to remain flexible on the destination and seek the best rate with a prospect of a return cargo, at Bordeaux he knew he wished to return to New Orleans. Therefore he laid on, or advertised, the ship for New Orleans and let prospective shippers approach him. On 30 December 1851 he notified Lord of his arrival.

I take this Opertunity of informing you of my arrival at this port, Or rather at Poliac On the 23, Inst. but there not being water anough the Ship is yet at Poliac, and will have to remain there till the 6th or 7th of next month, til the next Spring tides, I had Jest 42 days to the Bar, a verry Boasterous passage, but lost nothing. a heavy Sea Struck the Ships stern whilst scudding in a heavy gale from the west-ward, and stove off the curtain rail, but we saved it,—I received your two letters, and One from Mr. Callender, and the Documents, I have got all the information respecting the Settlement of the General average that I was able, and feel in hopes that I Shall be able to git it Settled to the Sattesfaction of all concearned, I have asertained that the wages & victualing is alowed here, which is different from my Expectation, I have Inquired the price of copper &c. french Copper is 24 1/2 sous and yellow mettle 20 sues, and they will alow me 13 sous for the Old, I have not yet decided which I Shall take, there is a good floating dry dock & rail ways, the Expence Coppering will probably be about the same as in Boston, and I believe prety good dispatch, I think that the prospect is prety good for a return freight for New Orleans, at preasant freight is from 5 to 6 dollers per ton, and Should there not be many arrivals I think the above rates will be maintained, if not some improvement, I have ben Offered $3,500 for the Ship, but prefer taking my chances by laying On, but I fear shall be detained here at least two months, and in the meantime if I can git something near $5000, Offered me I think I Shall take it, rather then run any risk, I notice by the last accounts from New Orleans freights was down to 3/8 again, but I hope I shall git down there in time to git something better then stave freights, for I am about sick of them, I shall keep you advised of my proceedings here, by Everry conveyance, . . .

P.S. the Orlando is here, Jest commenced discharging, is up for New York, the wind has ben to the Eastward for ten or fifteen days here.[2]

The captain's principal priority was the settling of the general average. In maritime law the term average refers to any loss or damage to a ship or its cargo that is less than total. There are two kinds of average: particular and general. In the case of particular average the amount of any loss is borne by the owner of the damaged property. In a general average all parties involved in the voyage assume a common responsibility. The idea is an old one, established in Roman law at the time of Justinian in an attempt to equalize any losses. The reasoning was that when some part of a ship or cargo was sacrificed in order to prevent the total loss of either, the owners of the property saved should contribute to make good the loss suffered by those who owned the sacrificed goods.[3]

In the case of the *Mount Washington*, the mast had been cut away to right the ship. She had then had to put in to Key West and be refitted at considera-ble expense. Under general average the expense would be shared among all concerned parties, the amount of their responsibility being in proportion to the value of their cargo or, in the case of the vessel's owners, the value of the ship. Some expenses would be allowed to come into the general average and others would not. There were no uniform international rules governing what was allowed; each country had its own procedure.

Captain Blaisdell's initial act on his arrival in Bordeaux was to file a protest through the customary channels. The protest was followed by his sworn statement that the damages suffered by the *Mount Washington* had been incurred for the sole purpose of saving the ship and her cargo. The information contained in the statement had to be corroborated by members of the *Mount Washington*'s crew.[4] As all maritime and customhouse activities in France had to be conducted through the medium of brokers, the captain was handed an additional responsibility. He was required to select from among the many brokers of the city an individual who could represent to their best advantage the interests of the ship and her owners.

Running parallel to the settling of the general average were his concerns over coppering the ship and his efforts to secure a return freight. He reported the situation to Lord on 5 January 1852.

> yours of the 15 Ult. has Jest come to hand, and the contents noticed. I wrote you by the last steamer informing you of my arrival since which the ship has ben detained at Poliac thirty miles below the city, on account of the tides, but I am in hopes that I shall git up to morrow I have taken the precaution that you named Viz. to have her average bond Signed by the consignees and have got the General average agustment in Progress by a compinant Broker that has ben long in practice and hope to be able to settle it to the Sattisfaction of all parties, I mentioned in my last letter that in this case the wages & vicutaling was alowed and came into General average, &c—I have learnt since that on the aprisal of the Ship and freight One half is deducted, and that the valuation of the cargo is taken here, what it will sell for here which is in our favor, but then it has all to be submited to the tribunal of commerce which has the power to Object to any thing that they think proper—so after all we are compleatly at there mearcy—
>
> so I cannot give you much incouragement til I know the final result—I have decided to put on the yellow mettle again as it is the same that was on before as they mite make us pay the differance if we put on copper, the Copper is 24 1/2 sous per pound, and the Yellow mettle, 20 sous, which taking in to consideration the differance of weight, & Curantsy makes it 17 cents per lbs the Old will sell for 13 Sous per lb—the Expence in putting it On &c will be something more then it would be in Boston, but they tell me they can do it in four days there is a dry dock, and Rail way, both here—about the same price,—I am in hopes that I shall Git a fair freight from here, if there is not too many arrivals, there is but One american ship here at preasant besides my self, she is also bound to New Orleans and will be On with me, consequently will be in my way, but there is a good deal of produce here to go forward, freight at preasant is about $5- per ton for New Orleans—I received Mr. Callenders Letter of advice, and shall be guided by it, &c—
>
> this detention apears unfortunate but it may prove for the best, in the End, hoping that in my next I shall be able to give you some more incouraging news. . . .[5]

As instructed by Lord, the captain had seen that the average bonds were signed by those Bordeaux merchants who were consignees of the *Mount Washington*'s cargo. Such a precaution would expedite their payment upon the final settlement of the general average, as a merchant's signature became his surety. Technically, the ultimate responsibility for payment rested with the actual owner of the goods on board the ship, and the individual to whom the goods were consigned could refuse to sign a bond. The vessel's master could then attempt to coerce the noncomplying merchant into making payment by refusing to off-load the goods as the ship and her owners had a lien on them.[6] When that strategy failed the master's only recourse was to turn to the cargo's owner for restitution, which because of time and distance often caused further delays and difficulties. Of course, in the final reckoning the costs of the general average would be passed on to the insurers of the individual parties.

The *Mount Washington's* owners hoped that the cost of coppering her in Bordeaux would be considered in the general average. Normally there was a very narrow interpretation of what was admissible, and the burden of proof lay with the captain. For inclusion, the damage had to be a direct result of trying to save the ship. For example, if the *Mount Washington* had been dismasted by the hurricane, and being held by its rigging, the wrecked mast was pummeling the ship's side or otherwise endangering her, the cutting away of the wreckage and the damage caused would not be a case of general average. Because in the actual event the mast was not damaged and was purposefully sacrificed to save the ship, it was included. Injury to the copper because of the cutting away might come into the general average, but if the captain could not prove that the sacrificed spars and mast did the damage it would not.

As he wrote to Lord on 14 January, the captain was still weighing the matter of coppering the ship and had his eye on possible business for her. On his arrival he had estimated that it would take about two months to clear up the *Mount Washington's* affairs in Bordeaux. However, he soon realized that he was at the mercy of a creaking, and in his eyes arbitrary, bureaucracy, and the original estimate began to look overly optimistic.

I wrote you by the last steamer Giving you all the Information respecting my affairs here that I was able, Since that nothing new has accured but as far as I can learn the coppering of the Ship here and Other repairs made here will not come into General average unless I can prove that any of the Copper was stove off by the spars that was cut away—I Stated in my last letter that I had ben detained On the river on account of tides, I arrived in the river On the 24th Ult and did not git up to town til the 7th Inst. and have ben Ever since going through with these french customry formalities with the tribunal of commerce &c. so that I have not yet discharged a stave, but Expect to begin tomorrow,—I have Jest had a proposal from one of the Ship Wrights to Copper the ship, that is he is to strip off the Old copper, Calk the Ships Bottom, to the upper part of the copper, find Copper, & pich, & tar, and put On the Copper to pay the Expence of rail way, to find all, Except the Copper & nails for eight hundred french dollers, or 4000 francs, there is another party which has a floating dock which I am to have a price from to day, the price of the Copper is 25 1/2 sues, per lb french weight which will be in Our curantcy after alowing difference of weight and curantcy a little over 21 1/2 cts— yellow mettle is 21 sous per lb But as far as I can learn the french yellow mettle is not as good as the English, and I think I shall put on Copper—the old mettle will bring about 13 sous per lb.—

Bordeaux   115

I can give you no idear as yet how much I am likely to git of General average,
but we have taken Everry nessacery precaution, and shall git what the french law
alows in similar cases, it is the custom here to take half the value of the ship and
half the freight but the whole value of the cargo contributes, and I beleave that
wages & provitions is alowed, but after all I have not much confidence in them
they can do about as they like and strangers are compleatly at there mearcy, but no
Exertion shall be wanting on my part, to bring it to as favorable Issue as possable.—Respecting a return freight. I am guarenteed $3.560, by the Brokers to
have all I can make over and he is to make up the deficientcy if there is any, but I
think I shall be able to Git a charter Offered, if I can git $4.500 offered I think I
shall Except it rather to run the risk of laying On—I doubt if I git away before the
first of march,—the Orlando is not discharged yet, but I doubt if he gits away in
less then 25 days She is bound for New York, the parties chartered her for $3000-
before She arrived,—a ship of about 500 tons has ben chartered at Havre to come
here to load, for $4000- she was chartered By a passenger Broker, here named
Depass I think not verry Responsable, the same man wanted to charter my ship
and Offered a verry good charter Viz. $4,400- but I was afraid of him, I think
however that my chance is worth that now, I shall keep you advised of my
proceadings by Everry Mail.[7]

As January drew to its close Captain Blaisdell had already been in France for a
month. His impatience was beginning to grow. The ship was still not
coppered, nor even completely unloaded, and the settlement of the general
average continued at a snail's pace. On 4 January William Lord had written to
the captain and raised once again the matter of the *Mount Washington's*
command. During the previous September, when the captain had so desper-
ately wanted to leave the ship, he had on his own initiative contacted Captain
Moses Maling. At the same time that Captain Blaisdell was writing to Captain
Maling about taking the ship, he was putting Maling forward in his letters to
Lord as a viable replacement. One of the most important prerogatives of a
principal owner was the naming of his vessel's master, and Lord appears to
have been a man who jealously guarded the privileges of his position. Captain
Maling was not employed at that time and upon receiving Captain Blaisdell's
apparent offer had gone somewhat puzzled to see Hartley Lord. Hartley in
turn had written of the matter to his father, and William Lord would have had
no compuction about reminding Captain Blaisdell of where and when his
authority began and ended. That something of the kind happened is evident
from Captain Blaisdell's response to Lord's letter.

It seems that a Kennebunk master, Captain John Hill, had gotten wind of
the situation on the *Mount Washington* and had applied to Lord for her
command. Captain Blaisdell denied any involvement in the matter. Evidently fearing he may have overplayed his hand and sorely tried Lord's patience on the subject, he expressed the desire to stay by the ship if his health
allowed. He went on to make a perfunctory offer to resign if asked, but was
well aware of how dependent he was on Lord's friendship and patronage. A

master could lose his position when a majority of a vessel's owners called for his dismissal, but Captain Blaisdell being a part owner himself could only be removed for a serious breach of conduct, and there was small chance of that.

your letter of the 4th Inst was duly received as well as your three previous Ones, I have written you three. Since my last nothing has transpired of consequence, I am going On discharging as fast as I can git lighters have got out about 2/3 of the cargo—Shall not git the average settled before the ship is unloaded & coppered, this is a slow place to git business done but I hope by all appearances it will result favorable for us when it is done, I am ancious to git through with it and git my mind relieved,—freights remain about the same as when I wrote you last, but the news from the States is nothing Incouraging to the shipper of wines—I feel heart Sick when I think how long I am likely to be detained here I fear I Shall not git away from this before the first of march I notice what you Say respecting Capt. Hill applying to you for the ship, I have never given Capt Hill any encouragement nor had I any right to, I had much rather that you would make your Own selection, I have had reason to repent Once for recommending a master, but I never shall again, there is some that I should give the preferance over Others and of course you would do the same,—if my health does not improve On my arrival at New Orleans I will telegraph ameadintly so that you will have sufficient time to send a master On and One of your own Choice, but if I am able I shall want to remain by the ship for I supose I shall have to go to sea as long as I do live, that is if it is agreable to you and the Other Owners but alwais ready & willing to leave at a minutes warning—the mate that I have now is the One that shipped second mate in New Orleans, and he does verry well so that I have felt no inconvenience by Adam leaving me, I feel some uneasy for fear the staves may fall short, and I am splitting as many as I can to make them hold Out, I am confident that they will take Everry advantage of me, and I dont concieve it to be any harm to guard against it as much as I can—

I did not answer Mr Callenders letter but you can tell him that his instructions to me respecting the commissions &c—has ben attended to and all brought in, and has ben Explained Everry precausion has ben taken to make it as favorable to Underwrighters & Owners as possable—and I hope that all parties will be sattesfied with the final result,—I shall probably finish discharging this week and then it will take about a week to copper before I shall be ready to receive cargo—the Orlando will be ready about the 10th Feb,y—8

Fearful that some of the staves had been lost when they were unloaded in Key West, and that as a result the ship would be liable for goods short, the captain went on splitting them to increase their number. Two weeks later he reported with relief that there had been no problem. However, the continuing saga of the copper was another matter. With the staves unloaded, the ship was taken to a dry dock for recoppering. Before work began though, the damage was surveyed to ascertain whether the expense would be allowed into the general average. The shipwright contracted to do the work supported Captain Blaisdell. In his opinion the damage caused by the cutaway masts and spars required the ship's bottom to be stripped, caulked, and recoppered. The agent for the insurers, who would have to pay the claims presented when the general average was finally settled, took the view that the damage inflicted by the masts and spars did not call for such extensive repairs. The two parties found themselves deadlocked, but a third party was present for just such a contingency. When this individual sided with the insurers' agent he earned Captain Blaisdell's profound contempt. Blaisdell reported to Lord on 10 February.

yours of the 19th was duly received, you will no doubt be disapointed When you learn the slow progres that I have made since my last letter to you. I Only finished discharging On the 4th Inst. could not git lighters I am happy to say that the staves came Out right I was fearful that some of them was lost at Key West—I have got the Ship into the dry floating dock and shall probably be finished and out again in about four days when I shall commence loading for New Orleans, I had a survay On the ship yesterday and I am sorry to say the report was not favorable for me for giting General arverage, the ship Wright Contended that the ship had ben strained and some of the Copper was stove off by the masts & spars and that it was nessacery to strip off the the copper in Order to calk the Bottom, but he was Over ruled by the underwriters agent and seconded by the third party who was a cunspiring Old broken down ship master who is looking Up to the underwriters for an appointment, so I am afraid it will not be brought into General average Except what had ben stove off by the mast—I have bought the sheathing yellow mettle. Paid 19 sous per lb. which by calculating the difference of weight 10% and Exchange 5% would make it about 16 70/100 cts per lb.—the old copper sells for 12 1/2 sous per lb free of duties & the nails is 21 sous per lb. the Expence of coppering will Be more then in the States notwithstanding the wages is higher it takes them four times as long to do it which brings the dockage up high,— respecting the prospect for freight it is not quite as good as it was when I wrote you last, there is two large ships on for New Orleans at preasant and they have put freights down from $5- & $6- to $4- 5$ per ton, but they are nearly full and I hope that freights will recover after they are full, I have some already Ingaged at five & six dollars per ton.—the Orlando went Down the river yesterday bound for New York her Freight List is about $4.300- I fear that I shall not git my average settled short of two or three weeks, I shall forward them as soon as I Git them. the Bark Byron arrived here a few days since lost her capt. On the Passage a sea came in Over her stern Whilst he was at the Wheel & struck the round house and washed him against the Other house & killed him Instantly his name was Stackpole belonging to maine—we had quite a heavy Shock of an Earth quake here a few days Since, thinking of nothing more at preasant of Intrest. . . .[9]

Since virtually none of the cost of replacing the *Mount Washington*'s copper would be defrayed by the general average, Captain Blaisdell chose to put on the less expensive yellow metal. He seemed well pleased with the work and could only have felt relief that he had one less dilemma to contend with.

The general average was a continuing vexation, but the ship's freight prospects were looking up, as he noted on 16 February.

> I have Jest got the ship coppered and got Out of dock after remaining in Eight Days, it is verry well done, I wrote you last week stating what I paid for the copper &c it took about 1300 sheats weight of copper 8801 lbs.
> Nails 840 lbs. Whole cost of copper & nails 9644.25
> Old copper 5474 lbs. @ 12 1/2 cts- 3421.21
>
> Differance —   fr 6223.04
>
> the copper that I have put On now is some heavyer then the Other Viz. 500 sheats of 30 Ounce 400 do 28 Ounce and 400 do of 24 ounce I have not yet got the ship wrights Bill so I dont know Exactly what it is, I have cargo along side and shall commence aloading to day, I have about 400 tons ingaged part at $5- and some at 6$- per ton, there is two large ships now On for New Orleans but One is all filled Or ingaged full and the Other is an Old prussian ship which will not be much in my way, but the bad accounts from New Orleans has a bad affect On freights shipers are afraid to ship, but I think I shall make $5000- my average Broker tells me that my prospect is pretty Good for the Settlement of the average, but I have not much Confidence in a french man. I dont See as I am Ever going to git to a final Settlement for they have ben at it Ever since I first arrived and not half through yet they have got the best part of a reem of paper written Up already, and if I have to send it all by the steamer the postage will be more then the General average for a single is 30 cts. and with invelupe 60 cts.—the postage On the a/c from Boston & New York was about 60 franks—Capt Gould the Orlando went to sea On the 13th Inst. and had a fair wind, at least there has ben a fine Breese here from N.E. for three days after he left. so he must of had a good run Out of the bay of biscay, but to day it is blowing a gale from N.W. there has only ben two or three light frosts since I have ben here, and no snow this winter it seams that you have had all the snow on your side of the Water, if the weather was so severe here as it has ben at home this Winter there would be nothing done, for they complain bitterly of a little frost, I hope this will be my last voyage to this place Espeacialy under preasant circumsances, for it is the most trying place to git any thing done that I was ever in—I am in hopes to git my average business settled up in the cource of ten days so that I can forward the document and make a remitance I dont think of any thing more at preasant of importance. I Will keep you advised with my proceedings by Everry mail. . . .[10]

Eight days later, though the general average itself had still not been settled, the captain was able to report that the valuation process had been completed. The valuation process assigned a monetary value to all the goods and property contributing to the payment of the general average. The formula used in France to arrive at their combined worth differed slightly from that employed in the United States. In America the value of a ship was reckoned at the end of her voyage. If she had undergone repairs, one third would be deducted from the price of any new materials. To the adjusted value of the vessel would be

Though lying sixty miles up the Garrone River from
the Bay of Biscay, Bordeaux was
France's principal west coast port. Seagoing traffic
halted at the Pont de Bordeaux, which led to the
city and its facade of warehouses on the west bank.
Aquatint, drawn by Ambroise-Louis Garneray,
printed by Basset, Paris, ca. 1850.
(Courtesy Mariners' Museum, Newport News, Virginia)

added the amount of her freight and the actual value of the entire cargo.[11] Under French custom, however, the vessel and her freight were allowed to contribute only half their value toward the total valuation. The cargo was appraised according to the price it would command at its destination.

Once the value of the contributing goods and property had been officially determined, the total amount of the losses and expenses to be shared proportionately among them had to be figured. The party suffering the loss and hoping to benefit from the general average would naturally strive to have as many of the accompanying expenses as possible taken into consideration in order to alleviate their own burden of payment. The agents or insurers of the other concerned parties would just as diligently work to limit the number of admissible costs for the very same reason. In the *Mount Washington*'s case there was the expense of her court settlement in Key West. New rigging, spars, and masts had been purchased in New York, shipped to Key West, and installed there. The cargo of staves had been unloaded, a new rudder made and hung, and the staves returned to the ship's hold. There was the caulking and various other necessary repairs, as well as the needed replacement of the ship's copper. Some of these expenses would be accepted into the general average, and others, like the coppering of the ship, would be denied.

When the total value of the contributing property and the full amount of the expenses were both known, the general average could be computed by setting up two ratios: the amount of the contributing goods is to the total expenses as one hundred is to what number? By dividing the expenses into the amount of the contributing goods, and then dividing that quotient into one hundred, a figure of percent was obtained. The resulting figure could then be used by each of the contributing parties to calculate what percentage of their property's value was due as their payment into the general average.[12]

Captain Blaisdell had his own ideas on what the percentage should be in the case of the *Mount Washington*'s general average. He also fully expected that the figure handed down by the Tribunal of Commerce would be substantially lower than his own. That is, if they ever handed one down, which he was beginning to doubt. On 24 February he wrote to Lord again.

Since I wrote you last another Week has passed away with Out any good result, I am going On Slowly loadin but verry Slow, have considerable cargo ingaged about 450 tons at $5- & $6 per ton. and I have not much doubt but I Shall be able to fill up at the same Rate, but Everry One wants there Wine on top, and One is holding back for the other, the average is not yet settled—they tell me that they are going on with it as fast as possable but it takes them for Ever here to do nothing—Some times I think that they are puting it off on purpose till I am loaded and ready for sea and then refuse to pay it thinking that I will not detain the ship to bring on a suit, but they are mistaken if that is there intentions for I would stop six months sooner then to be defrauded, unles I had orders from you to the contrary, some times I think that there is bribery in the way. the valuation has ben made on the ship and cargo, as follows,

Ship fr 95.000 half of which is 47500
freight fr 37 800 half of which is 18900
On the staves .... 90.000 all contribute 90000
On the Speacie .... 47250 all contribute 47250
                                                              fr 203650

Which is worked thus, as follows there is about $14,000 the princible part of which should come into General average Which is fr 73 500
the whole Valuation of ship, freight & Cargo & Speacie is fr 203.650—the whole amount of bills brought into General average is $14,000 or fr 73.500—
if 203.650 contribute to 73.500—what will 100 which results in about 36 1/2 pr—which if I git my rights would result as follows—

fr 90.000 @ 36 1/2 would pay @ 36 1/2 p/c .... fr 32.850
Speacie $9,000 fr 47.250—@ do .... fr 17.246
Total amount which I Should receive if paid   50.096

but I doubt if I git half of the above amount—the result of the last survey on the ship they condemn Eight knees Which was badly sprang, which I have got to take Out and refasten the rest which is started off and for which they alow me together with some copper that was Stove off by the spars and other damage sustained to come into General average—about fr 3000 that is all that they will alow towards repairs here, I hope that I Shall be able to give you the final result by the next steamer, and forward the documents that you may be able to settle with the underwriters in Boston, you may rest asured that no Exertion has or shall be Wanted On my part to bring it to as favorable Isue as possable and as Short, you must make alowance for the slow movements of the french, and Bordeaux in particular, your ancsiety cannot Exceed mine and I trust in God that I never shall have such a trial again, . . .

P.S. the Ship Cleave which arrived here some four weeks since that took off the Crew of an English Brig on her passage here has ben awarded by the british Government with a Gold meddle and sexton, and fifty pounds, besides there thanks, I think that they have behaved honorable but I think he is desiring of it.—the wind has ben to the N Eastward Ever since capt. Gould left and I think that he must have had a good chance—it has ben verry cold here of late, all is quiet in france at presant, but I think by appearances a storm is geathering, they are not satisfied in this place With L.N. proceedings but have to submit to the yoke—13

The L.N. in the captain's postscript was the president of France, Louis Napoleon. During the captain's stay in Bordeaux there was a flurry of political turmoil. Louis Napoleon, who was the nephew of the original Bonaparte, had been elected president of the Second French Republic following the Revolution of 1848, which had driven out the Bourbons for a second time. In December of 1851 an attempted coup d'etat took place. Just before Captain Blaisdell's arrival, Paris had been occupied by troops and a valiant but weak Republican uprising was bloodily put down. Napoleon then pushed through a new constitution, making himself president for a term of ten years with sweeping autocratic powers. Captain Blaisdell wrote of a storm gathering in France, but, if it was, it was slow in breaking. In December of 1852 Napoleon went on to become Emperor Napoleon III, and he ruled France until he was overthrown in 1870.[14]

Regardless of political upheaval or bureaucratic foot-dragging, the captain finally concluded his business in March and made ready to leave France for America. The "better part of a ream of Paper" written up by the Tribunal of Commerce is not to be found in William Lord's surviving correspondence, so the details of the final settlement of the *Mount Washington*'s general average are not known. Evidently he came out with a balance in his favor, for he was able to send a remittance of £1,100 from Bordeaux to the London banking firm of Baring Brothers before he left.[15] Perhaps the final word on the matter best belongs to the man who handled all the details: Captain Blaisdell's French broker H. Constantine.

Bordeaux, 6 April 1852

William Lord Esqre.
Ship owner
Kennebunk, Maine
Sir,

In conformity to my promise to our mutual friend Capt. Blaisdell of your ship Mount Washington I herewith enclose a faithful copy of his general accounts and financial affairs from the day of her arrival to her day of sailing, resulting from both her freights carried and average settlement, which as you were aware are of some importance, on the whole I believe Capt. B- and successively your good self must be satisfied, as the matter was legally conducted, without loss of time or extra sacrifice. Ere this you must have received the English copy of the arrangements which precludes my entering into any further details—the cause bearing its own defense. From the very constant aid & attention I have paid to the affair (although generally granted to all my clients yet more special for my worthy friend Capt. Blaisdell) I should be pleased to learn sooner or later that the settlement at home has been made without observations or difficulties with your insurer, for what relates to partial average falling on them or it may be a guide for cases of similar nature when called to defend & represent American interest.

Our friend had left us on the 27th ult. to join the ship at Pouillac and tried to get to sea with the last Easterly breeze that had been leighing here for six weeks. Unfortunately in a change of weather due to the Equinoctial Season, he lost his anchors at Verdon Roads and although he had replaced one on the near spot he never-the-less was compelled to call and anchor in the Rochelle Roads where he provided himself with other anchors and put lastly to sea on the 1st inst. Since the weather has continued very fine, winds favorable from the N.E. and I dare say his is now far off on the Gulf. You'll read on the annexed Copy of his last letter the more explicit recital of this last misfortune which I write him may be legally repaired at New Orleans in a supplementary average, loss of anchors & claims. Reimplacing them and putting into port being a forced Fortuitous Accident brought on for the general salvation & safety.

Although our friend has given you the state of the freight he took out. I'll again repeat that he has on board 902 tons of assorted cargo making as per manifest $4,966.00 freight & primage with a few passengers in the steerage that went down to join him at Pouillac.

With hopes of meeting after occasions to promote your ship interest and claiming your patronage under consideration in the case of some of your vessels coming this way I beg to suscribe myself, . . .[16]

After sailing down the Garonne River, Captain Blaisdell had taken the ship up the coast of France to Verdon Road, there to await a fair wind. As reported by the broker Constantine, while at anchor in the roads the ill-fortune that seemed to stalk the voyage struck again. In a sudden squall the ship lost both her anchors, requiring the captain to return to shore and obtain replacements. A very ill and weary Captain Blaisdell wrote to William Lord before finally quitting the coast of France.

Off the Isle of Ree—March 31—1852

I am now about discharging my Pilot for the second time with a fine breeze from the Northward, and I hope that this time I shall Succead in gitting to Sea, sence I wrote you last I have ben laying two days in the Roads of Palsse When I Entered the roads as I informed you before I had but One anchor which I had purchased at Reyon Weighing about 1100 lb. and One of my Old anchors with one fluke, I went on shore at Rochelle distance from where the ship lay six miles, and purchesed an Old anchor Weighing 1660 lbs. and had a stock put to it, which cost me altogeather including gitting it Onboard about fr 400. my whole Extra Expence since I left Bordeaux for anchors, Pilotage and all is something Over fr 1000. sence I have ben laying in the roads the Weather has ben Bad, blowing a gale from WSW.—I hope now the Worst of trouble is Over for Heaven knows I have had anough since I left New Orleans, my ancsiaty has ben so great of late it has contributed to impair my health, and I and my health at preasant is verry poor—fortunately I took money anough with me from Bordeaux to defray my Expenses, so I did not have to draw.—the anchors that I have bought are not suitable for the ship shall have to git Others when I git where they are to be had, but they were the best I could git—in hast, I remain sir your Obedient Servent.[17]

ELEVEN

A Change for Luck's Sake
1852

TWO MONTHS after finally turning his back on Bordeaux and her attendant trials, Captain Blaisdell arrived in New Orleans. An entire year had passed since the *Mount Washington* had last made her way up the Mississippi, a year that had been kind to neither the ship nor her master. On more than one occasion during that period the strain of service had caused the captain's resolve to weaken. Not long after his arrival in New Orleans it finally broke, and he gave himself over to momentary despair. He poured out his discouragement to Lord on 6 June.

I take this Oppertunity to inform you of my safe arrival after a teagous Passage of Sixty days. I was three days Out side of the bar at Anchor before a tow boat came near me, the Excuse that they made that there was not Water anough On the Bar to take me Over, as I drew nearly 18- feet, but I was fortunate in gitting over and in with Out stoping On the Bar, or with Out acsident. I have had the winds verry light all the passage and the ship being deep She sails oncoman dull on light Winds,—I have come to a bad market again bad luck has seamed to follow me all the way round this year, I am about discouraged, it would have ben better for the Owners I think to have let the General average gone, then to have detained the Ship there two or three months and got hove out of a good freight here,—I believe it never was worse then it is here at preasant, and a prospect of its being still worse—

I telegraphed from the Balize to let you know of my arrival thinking you mite give me some Instructions for realy I am at a loss what to do my self, it will probably take me nearly twenty days to git my cargo Out, by that time I can git an answer to this, dont you think it would be better to take what I can git and come north then to go to Liverpool for 1/4- Or to lay the ship up here, if the Ship has got to lay up here all Summer, and if you can find any One that suits you to take charge of her with Out Inconvenience I Should like to leave and go home, as the mate that I have got now in a Stanger I Should not like to leave him in charge,—as I did not arrive in time to mail this as per date, I have Since received your three letters of the 4th 19th & 29th Inst. and noticed there contents, and I feel much greaved to find business or the prosect so much changed here from what you anticipated when your first letter was written, I dont know that I Ever felt more discouraged then at preasant, after so many misfortunes I was in hopes all the time On the passage hear to find busines good that I Should be able to make up

123

for some of the loss, but I have got disapointed, I have here to fore had prety good fortitude, and born up against misfortune & hard luck with Out avail but now I can hold On no longer my fortitude begins to give way, I was born a beggar and I shall die One it is useless to Strive against fate, I will stick by the Ship if you wish it but at preasant I am at a loss what to do, for the prospects looks worse then I Ever knew it, I shall probably be fifteen days discharging, and then I Should like to git some Instructions from you what to do, at any ordinary time I would not ask it, but when freights gits down to 1/4- for Liverpool and $1.00 per bale for Boston, and hard to git at that I think it is nessacery to cunsult the Owners, as to a bordeaux freight I never will take another unless I have Orders from you to that Effect. as you hear from this about Every day by telegraph you of course know What is doing, and will advise me acordingly, I saw capt. Paine to night, and Capt. Wm Lord, Son, the latter takes passage in the Ship Enternational, left to night, Capt. Pain told me he had Telegraphed home for instructions, &c—it seems to be my lot of late to give you nothing but bad newes, and I begin to dispair of Ever being able to give you different, as my luck is so bad perhaps it would be well to change masters, if you can find One that suits you, I am willing to give up to any One that you think proper to apoint all is I dont like to put you to so much trouble you have had so much already,—I was some surprised to day when I read my wifes letter that you had sent Adam McCulloch on to take charge of the Ship til I read your letter, it is strange how these reports git started, I would give the ship up to any One that you saw fit to send Even him, but I would sell Out my part if I did not git fifty dollers for it, if you sent him after serving me as he did, I have herd that he has ben telling some hard storys about me, at home. he told a gentleman here after he left the ship that he came Out in that he rued the day that he Ever left me, I care not what he sais about me Or any One Els if they tell the truth, I felt an obligation to his father for promoting me, and thank God it is Paid, or I have tried to pay it—I dont Expect that this will be Verry Enteresting to you, but I had it On my mind and so I have let it Out, not having any thing better to write,—I hope that your Other Ships have done better this year then this one and I hope that I Shall be able to give you something more incouraging in my next, . . .[1]

In addition to the vicissitudes of the *Mount Washington*, 1851 had brought other, graver concerns to William Lord. Captain Blaisdell's sensibilities caused him to allude to Lord's troubles and to apologize for compounding them. Probably foremost in his thoughts as he wrote was the year's greatest calamity, which had brought both financial and personal loss to the Lord family. In 1849 a ship of 743 tons had been built and launched for Lord. Christened the *William Lord*, she was entrusted to her owner's son-in-law, Captain Charles Barry. In December of 1850, Captain Barry and a recalcitrant crew sailed her from Savannah, bound for Liverpool. The ship never arrived in England, and as the months passed hopes that she might turn up safe at some other port evaporated. The fate of the ship, her master, and crew was never discovered and is still unknown.[2]

Though appreciative of Lord's problems, Captain Blaisdell was over-whelmed by his own. The fact that his falling out with Adam McCulloch was providing grist for the rumor mill at home evidently stung his pride. McCulloch never did assume command of the *Mount Washington*, and Captain Blaisdell's outburst is the last mention of the matter in his surviving letters. Young McCulloch himself probably continued in the merchant marine until the outbreak of the Civil War, when he volunteered for military duty. In 1864 he was serving on a sloop of war. In December of that year he fell ill and died at the age of thirty-four.[3]

The captain may have been vexed by the McCulloch affair, but he was in a genuine quandary over what to do about a freight for the ship. In order to do what was considered a fair business, cotton freights for Liverpool had to be at least one half cent per pound. One half cent would pay for the depreciation of the ship, provisions, sailing the vessel, insurance, and incidental expenses such as port charges, while still leaving a small profit to be divided among the owners. As a general rule, anything over one half cent could be counted as net gain; conversely, rates under that mark would result in a loss.[4] In addition to half-penny freights, another figure served as a bellwether of business for Captain Blaisdell. The amount was five thousand dollars. While in New Orleans the *Mount Washington* could be expected to run up expenses and disbursements totaling anywhere from four to six thousand dollars. Consequently, before a profit could even be contemplated the ship's freight and primage had to be at least in the five thousand dollar range. Continuously reviewing his chances with those figures in mind, the captain watched the fluctuating rates and wrote to Lord on 23 June.

I Expected a letter from you to day in answer to Mine but got disapointed. I have done nothing yet in the way of Freights, I thought I would wait til the cargo is Out which will be tomorrow before I done any thing, in fact I have had no offer Worth taking, as it is so late in the season I thought I would take a coastwais freight if there was any Offered worth taking, I think by going to Europe it would throw the ship Out of the way for a fall freight, by coming coastwais you could chuse your Own time & place when & where to send the ship   it so hapened for the last two years she has alwais ben Out of the way of the best Freights—at preasant There is little Or nothing going to Boston and six or Eight Ships Laid on, the best chance at preasant is for New York, but low rates is given to all northern ports, I mite posably make about $3000 to New york, to Boston I could not make $2000 they are paying for Liverpool for parts of cargo for consignment 3/8—the Nat. Thompson & Osburn was taken yesterday 2900 Bales divided between them, Stave freights are low about $35- per mm for Marsielles & Bordeaux, 36 shillings for Tobacco for Liverpool, & 35- s- for London, I doubt if the Ships that are taken for Liverpool will be able to fill up at 3/8- as there is a good many On at preasant, and I fear that Return freights from that port will be low as there will be so meny ships there togeather, so unless I can make sure of nearly a full cargo of cotton at 3/8 for Liverpool, I think I Shall take the best I can git and come coastwais Unless I hear from you again as to Stave freights at the preasant rates I will not take.[5]

When the captain wrote that it was late in the season he was referring to the freighting season. In the cotton trade the freighting season was calculated to run from September of one year to August of the next. The first bales of a new cotton crop began arriving in New Orleans as early as late July, although the receipts through the end of August were generally fairly modest. From an initial trickle, the volume would increase in proportion to the abundance of the season's crop and the duration of the harvest, which was usually terminated by killing frosts during October or November.[6]

Some planters sold their crops outright to one of the many cotton factors or brokers who resided in the major southern ports. Others preferred to employ agents on a commission basis. In either case, the individuals holding the cotton hoped to sell it for the best possible return.

The level to which freighting rates rose or fell was determined by several interdependent variables. Of prime consideration was the size of the year's crop. If the amount of cotton brought down to the ports for shipment was large in relation to the number of vessels available to carry it, the positive effect on freights is evident. On average, the years prior to the Civil War saw the overall production of cotton continually increase. Northern shipowners and merchants watched the trend, and in optimistic expectation steadily launched more vessels into the trade. In the early 1850s the cotton port of New Orleans alone received about 1,000 arrivals of ships and barks annually. However, in reality the growth of cotton production did not result in ever larger annual crops, and when a season's harvest fell short of expectations, as it sometimes did, the increased supply of vessels had to scramble to gain a smaller share of the reduced stock of cotton.

Of equal importance was the demand for cotton on the world market. When the needs of the textile mills of Europe and America were low, so was the price cotton buyers were willing to pay. In turn, shipping would decline as factors and brokers held on to their cotton in the hope that demand would rise, and with it the price.[7]

Shipowners and their masters tried to anticipate business by studying newspapers and publications such as the *New Orleans Price-Current*. They looked for trends of rising or falling prices; they made careful note of the stock of cotton in southern ports versus the stocks in Liverpool and Havre; they read the predictions for the next year's crop and contemplated the projected demands of the mills.

In order to receive the highest freighting rates, a ship had to be in port at a time when the number of waiting vessels was small. At the same time, cotton prices had to advance to a level that was deemed to be their peak for the season, causing the market to become flooded with cotton in need of transport as the factors and agents rushed to sell their stocks before the prices fell.[8] Despite the efforts of those involved in the shipping trade, a formula to accurately predict when and where to find this magic combination remained elusive.

In many respects whether or not a vessel received optimum freights was a matter of chance, but the prospects for business were definitely better at certain times of the year than they were at others. The months from November through May saw the most activity, and monthly arrivals in the port of New Orleans would peak during that time. Over 300 ships and barks arrived at New Orleans in November and December 1851; only 88 came in with Blaisdell in June 1852.[9]

By December the cotton harvest had been completed and a large portion of the crop had already found its way to the seaports. Vessels making port early in the calendar year would at least have the advantage of an ample and growing supply. Late spring would find the new crop in the ground and virtually all the previous fall's harvest in the hands of the brokers. With the approach of summer, activity in the freighting business declined as each shipment of cotton further reduced the supply on hand.

In both 1850 and 1851 the *Mount Washington* had arrived in New Orleans at this time of the season, to find a waning market. On each occasion, conditions had forced her to take staves for France rather than cotton. Then the hurricane of August 1851 had thrown her out of the trade for a year, and once more in 1852 she returned to New Orleans in June to find low freights and a depleted stock of cotton. In seeking business for the ship, Captain Blaisdell was trying to balance the financial considerations with the necessity of putting the ship back into a sailing routine that would bring her to New Orleans at more opportune and lucrative times. He discussed the scheduling in a letter to Lord on 25 June.

your favor of the 15th Inst has Jest come to hand, the mail has failed three days in succession, you are in receipt of my letter of the 4 Inst. I wrote you two days since stating that I thought there was a prospect to make something like $3000- for New york, but a ship laid On and took under the former rates, and cut freight down, and have me out of that, so I see no prosepct of coming north I have had several stave & Tobacco freights offered. at such low rates that I could not take them, I may be able to git a freight of cotton & Tobacco, for Liverpool @ 3/8 cotton & 30 shillings tobacco, or 35 shillings for London for Tobacco there has ben more inquiryes for ships of late then since I have ben here, and if there is no more arrivals for some days freights of tobacco may improve a little, but as the stock of Cotton has got reduced so much I doubt if there is any improvements in cotton freights, Espeacealy as there is a large number of ships to fill up on the berth, I shall get the best freight I can for Liverpool, if I find no chance, or see no prospects for improvement, and git the ship off as soon as possable, so that she can git back in time for Early business and be able to make two freights next year, and Escept your Generous Offer of sending you a dispatch for another master as soon as I ingage a freight for the ship, I am sorry to give you so much trouble, but I think it is nessacery that I should be at home Onse in a while—my cargo is all Out, but I have not yet Settled the freight, I shall do so as soon as possable I shall probably decide On something with in a few days, unless I see a better prospect then there is at preasant, and as soon as I do so I shall ameadently advise you of it.[10]

Within four days of having heard from Lord the captain acted and took a charter to Liverpool. As Lord had agreed to allow him to leave the ship if she were chartered to a foreign port, the captain telegraphed the necessary information to Hartley Lord in Boston, who in turn relayed the message on to his father in Kennebunk. "We have just received the following dispatch from Capt. Blaisdell dated N. Orleans, June 29—'Ship Mount Washington is chartered for Liverpool—send master' It does not mention the rate but we presume it is 3/8- which is—we should think—as good or better than coming coastwise @ $1.25 or @ $1.50 per bale."[11]

Two weeks later the captain had received no response to his dispatch and as a result had grown somewhat uneasy. In a letter to Lord he noted how the low stock of cotton had affected the rates and the make-up of his cargo. He also attempted to justify his desire to leave the ship, but at the same time reaffirmed his loyalty to Lord by promising to take the *Mount Washington* to sea when she was ready if his replacement had not arrived.

I have Omited writing to you for Some days for the reason that I had nothing of intrest to Write, I stated in my last letter to you that I had taken a low freight of 3/8 for Liverpool, given away the consignment for 1560 Bales, but as the Brokers could not git but 1229 Bales of cotton I took Tobacco at 30 shillings which is Estimated Equivalent to 3/8 for Cotton, I have now about Equal to 1600 Bales in of Cotton & Tobacco, and 300 Bales more which will be along side to day at 5/16 making Equel to about 1850 or 1900 Bales, and if I cant git any more Tobacco I am afraid that I shall have to take the Balance in Cotton at 1/4- for others are taking it and unless I keep the ship waiting I shall have to take the rates, a British ship took up last Week at 1/4 and ships have ben filling up for the last week past at that rate, as you are in dayly receipt of news from this port it is unessacery for me to Enter into any details—I saw Capt Fairfield yesterday, told me he had ingaged a cargo of Tobacco for Liverpool, a part of a cargo at 30 Shillings and I should think it was as good as could be done for the preasant, and perhaps as good as will be done for some time to come, I think it is about Equal to 3/8 for his ship—she is larger and makes better stowage in Tobacco then this ship would, the Josephas & Osburn sailed Saturday 10th the Nat- Thompson goes today—I sent On a dispatch & wrote you On the 29th of June Presuming On your kindness to send Out a master to Releve me, as you wrote me that if I took a freight for any Foreign Port and wished to come home if I would send On a dispatch that you would be prepared to send One Out. I hope that I have not given you too much trouble by presuming On your Generous nature and I hope that you will find no dificulty in finding a man of your choyse, I would not put you to this trouble if I could reasonaly avoyd it, but my health is not verry Good, and I had set my mind upon coming home and I supose it is nessacery that I should be at home once in a while having a large family, that requires counsal & protection—I am well aware that I am not verry well able to stop at home and I am not verry well able to go to sea, but on some future day if I recover my health and feel able to undertake the task and if I have given you sattisfaction, I may again have to presume on your Goodness for a situation,—it has ben now thirteen days since I sent the dispatch, if you received it I shall Expect an answer soon or now dayly— but if in the meantime I git loaded, and there is no One comes to releive me, I shall not detain the ship One hour, but procead On my voyage with all possable dispatch, unless I am so unwell as not to be able which I hope I shall not,—I Expect it will take Everry cent of my inward freight if not more to git me away, as I have had to buy two anchors &c I have ben rather fortunate in gitting two anchors, One of about 2000 lbs. and the Other 1700- as Good as new, in fact they have never ben used, at 5 cents per lb.—and sold the small one of about 1200- at the same rate, and the old duch anchor that I got at Roschell which was about 1700 and good for nothing but for scrap Iron I have sold for one cent as it is no use to keep it on board the ship I did not lose chain of consequence anough to git Eny more and now the anchors are as good as before—

I have not settled all the Freight yet, the consignees make some claims and I have got to Extend a protest, but after all I should not be surprised but I shall have to submit to some claim of perhaps a hundred dollers or sue them and leave it unsettled for some months Which is not a verry pleasant Operation, as the court does not sit til October, there claims are for casks broken by pressure and verry unjust, and no doubt in the process I should gain the suit, but the Expense would be as much as the claim besides being kept out of the money. . . .

P.S. I like the apearance of your ship *Windemere* and as well Capt. Fairfield Verry much, hoping that you may be as successful in gitting as good a master for this ship.[12]

Captain Blaisdell was favorably impressed by Lord's ship *Windemere* and her master, Captain John W. Fairfield of Saco. The *Windemere* was roughly twice the size of the *Mount Washington*, but even at 1,100 tons she was still slightly below the average for the trade. In the two decades between 1830 and 1850 the average size of vessels employed in the cotton trade had increased in size from 400 tons to 1,400 tons.[13]

Builders on the Kennebunk strove to meet the demand for larger craft, but their efforts were restricted by the river's narrow channel and shallow water. To extend the collective lives of the shipyards on the upper river, the builders banded together and constructed a lock. Completed in 1849, the lock allowed shipbuilding to continue for an additional nineteen years. Even with the lock, to launch and then warp a vessel downstream was no easy feat. The largest vessel ever to use the lock was rated at 1,273 tons.[14] Only 150 tons smaller, the *Windemere* was launched on 25 October 1851. On 27 October she had been caught above the lock in a snowstorm and so missed the high run of tide needed to get her through. Not until 10 November was there a rise of water sufficient to allow her to pass safely.[15]

The increased difficulty encountered in maneuvering the vessels on the river, and the capital used to construct the lock were looked upon as worthwhile investments in the future. Larger vessels had obviously arrived to stay. The amount of freight they earned due to their added carrying capacity more than offset the additional costs of building and sailing them. It was the larger vessels, by Kennebunk standards from 800 to 1,200 tons, that were paying good profits, while smaller ships in the 400 to 500 tons range were often losing money for their owners.[16] A ship's expenses could be expected at best to remain static and at worse to increase. In periods of low freights, such as 1850, when it was reported that few if any Kennebunk vessels ever engaged above the rate of 3/8-cent per pound, the smaller ships could not cram enough cotton into their holds to raise their freight totals enough to cover all their expenses.[17] The larger ships, on the other hand, might see their margin of profit diminish, but it would not disappear quite so quickly. At 547 tons the *Mount Washington*'s size worked to her disadvantage. Captain Blaisdell might attempt to improve the ship's chances by modifying her sailing schedule, but he was powerless to enlarge her hold.

The *Mount Washington*'s freight of $6,748.00 was the lowest of Captain Blaisdell's career, as apparently was his morale. His handling of the consignees' claims for damages is indicative of his frame of mind. Three years earlier, in July of 1849, when a consignee in Boston had refused to pay the freight due on his cargo of iron because of damage, the captain had been prepared to take the case to court on principle alone. However, chastened by the ordeals of the previous twelve months, his will to fight was gone. His only wish was to go home.

In light of Lord's promise to send out another master, Blaisdell must have experienced mounting apprehension as the day of the *Mount Washington*'s sailing neared and no replacement had materialized. On 18 July, two days before his planned departure, the worried captain wrote to Lord.

> your letter of the 8th was Duly received Stating that Capt. Goodwin had Started that day the 8th by mail Rout to Joyn this Ship. letters of that date reached here two days since but no Capt. Goodwin has arrived. I think he must have taken some Other Route, I shall be ready for sea On the 20th and if Capt. Goodwin is not here then I shall not detain the Ship for had he have taken the mail rout he would have ben here two days since.—I wrote you that I had taken up at 3/8 for 1500 Bales,—I have got 1229 Bales @ 3/8- 300 at 5/16- 148 at 1/4- 136 Hhds at 30 shillings & 60 Hhds at 27 1/6- making 1679- Bales of Cotton and 196 Hhd Tobacco,—the poorest Freight that I Ever took—shall make probably Freight & Primage from £1400- to £1450- I dont think that I shall have quite anough of my inward freight to git the ship off—as I have had to alow some $150- claims On damage & leakage Or go to law With the Consignees,—One Ship from Bordeaux this year has paid $500- claims—and all of them more Or less—[18]

The next day, one day before the ship was to sail, Captain Ivory Goodwin arrived in New Orleans, much to Captain Blaisdell's relief. Though unknown at the time, Captain Goodwin's tardy appearance presaged the quality of his tenure as the *Mount Washington*'s master. Captain Blaisdell, confident in Lord's choice, negotiated the terms for handing the ship over to her new master and then on second thought diplomatically left the matter to Lord's discretion. Captain Goodwin wrote:

> Capt Blaisdell settles all bills here therefore I shall have to make no account in regards to disbursements.
>
> My arrangements between Capt. Blaisdell & myself as regards the primage on the cargo to Liverpool is in case he should have to pay my passage out he will allow me one half, but in case the owners should pay it he will allow me two-thirds primage.
>
> I have the cargo all on board and shall go down tonight if the weather permits, while writing it blows & rains very heavy.
>
> P.S. I have shown the letter to Captain Blaisdell—he wished me to leave it for you to decide what my compensation should be on this cargo out to Liverpool.[19]

With the business aspects of the voyage settled as far as possible under the circumstances, all was ready for sea. On 21 July Captain Blaisdell finally saw the *Mount Washington* off. Except for the settling of the damage claims, he was at last free to return to Kennebunk. On 22 July a relieved Captain Blaisdell wrote to Lord.

> I embrace this Oppertunity to inform you that the ship Mt Washington, Capt. Goodwin, sailed last Evening Or went down the river having Onboard 1669 Bales of Cotton & 191 Hds. Tobacco & $24,400 in Speacie, making freight & Primage £1450- I had to draw £83- On the Freight or $400- Over & above my Inward freight, but Out of that I paid Charges On Tobacco, about $172- which will be collected in Liverpool besides some I took my self—I had to alow claims On the Inward freight of about $160 for leakage & breakage Which I could not git with Out going to law, and as Court Dont set til Oct- I thought my chances was small, I have sued One claim for about $56- and had to leave $15 With the Consignee lawyer fees, making $71- this case comes On this week as the amount is under a hundred dollers it is tryed in the petty Court, and I feel prety confident that I shall recover it.—if it is tryed this week I think I shall stop & attend, my Consignee is a very Good man, and I think that I can place confidence in him in attending to it—[20]

Captain Blaisdell did remain in New Orleans long enough to see the law suit settled. However, he was not long in making his way home, and on 17 August, in answer to Captain Goodwin's inquiry, William Lord wrote, "Capt. Blaisdell reached home since in good health."[21]

Captain Blaisdell had hoped that giving up his command would bring a change of luck for both the ship and himself. The five years he had spent as the *Mount Washington*'s master had not been crowned with success. Rates in general were low during those years. Both 1848 and 1849 had seen large crops of cotton and correspondingly high exports, but the price of cotton was low and the rates given reflected that fact.[22] To compound the situation, the

Mount Washington had managed to make only one New Orleans freight during each of those years, instead of the usual two. In 1850 the price of cotton rose, but the harvest was small and the competition among cotton vessels was keen.[23] Captain Blaisdell did manage to secure a respectable freight to Havre, but the delay caused by the loss of the ship's rudder and the settlement of averages in France put her out of the way of the better cotton freights. The harvest of 1850 was of average size, and the ship took a fair freight to Havre early in 1851.[24] Her return to New Orleans late in the season meant another stave freight, and then the hurricane of August 1851 put her out of the trade for a year. The year 1852 was one of notoriously low freights, and it is not surprising that the captain admitted defeat and left the ship.[25] With his return home his prospects began to look up, and it appeared that the longed for change of luck was coming his way.

TWELVE

The Master at Home
1852–1858

CAPTAIN BLAISDELL'S stay in Kennebunk proved to be a lengthy one. In fact, as the weeks turned into months, and the months into years, it became a virtual retirement from the sea. While not actually commanding vessels, his interest in maritime affairs remained keen, and during this time his holdings in the local merchant fleet increased appreciably. His livelihood, as it always had, continued to depend on the sea and shipping. In conjunction with William Lord and other local men, he acquired interests in different vessels as the opportunities arose, and found for the first time in his life that he could support his family on the returns from his investments.

The first vessel in which Captain Blaisdell took a share was under construction in the Kennebunkport yard of Stephen Ward at the time of his return home in August of 1852. Her organizer and principal owner was William Lord.[1] This full-rigged ship of 849.88 tons, named *Neva*, bore the same name as Lord's very first vessel, launched in 1831. Captain Moses C. Maling sailed the new ship to New Orleans in late November of 1852.

By December of 1852 cotton freights had revived. The harvest had yielded a large crop, and the price of cotton had risen.[2] The improvement held throughout the season and rates of 3/4 and 7/8-cent per pound were given for Liverpool.[3] With his interests in the *Mount Washington*, *Ocean Star*, and *Neva*, Captain Blaisdell found he could remain at home with little financial worry. However, the new master of the *Mount Washington*, Captain Ivory Goodwin, was not long in giving the ship's owners cause for worry and concern. That December Captain Goodwin had sailed from New Orleans, bound out to Liverpool. Upon his arrival in England he found a letter from William Lord waiting for him. Lord discussed the options for cargoes, considering freight rates, ports with a likelihood of return freights, the depth of water at such ports, and the problems attendant with various cargoes, such as emigrants.

As to instructions on your arrival at Liverpool I would reccomend returning to N Orleans in preference to coming north—if however there is little or nothing offering for N Orleans or Mobile (giving N Orleans the preference) and you can charter right out for say not less than £1300 or 1250 or more to Boston—perhaps it would be preferable for two or three hundred pounds,—as there will likely be more or less Rail road Iron shipping for N Orleans and Mobile you may succeed in obtaining a charter by going to Cardiff or Newport—If a charter say viz 25/ twenty five shillings, could be had by going to either of these ports N Orleans or Mobile. I should advise you to accept of it—Its my impression Capt Blaisdell loaded at Newport viz Rail road Iron for N Orleans about 800 tons—I should think 16½ feet would be about her draft for that quantity—for Mobile it would not make much difference if the draft was more—if 25/ could not be had I dont know but you might as well accept of 22/C rather than go back and not make over £250 from Liverpool—if however £1300 could be had for Boston, I should think it would be preferable to either of the rates I have named—In taking passengers we have had a good deal of trouble with them here viz when they have become paupers had to support them and should look out and guard against it—I should not care to have you charter the ship for N York. should you load with Rail road Iron, I would recommend to take pains in having it properly stowed. not to much in the middle of the ship you will pay over your remittance to Barring Brothers should like for you to keep me advised by every steamer of your proceedings—

P.S. as the expenses will be a good deal in fitting up for passengers I would not accept of less than £1300.[4]

The *Mount Washington* had made what Captain Goodwin described as "a long and severe passage of 68 days." During the crossing it was discovered that both the mainmast and the mizzenmast were rotten in places. In fact, Captain Goodwin reported he could run a handsaw ten inches into the mainmast in three different places. The ship's carpenter did what he could to "fish," or reinforce, the masts by using spare yards to shore them up. In Liverpool repairs were made to both masts, and Captain Goodwin felt confident that "they will be equally as strong as when they were new." He also repaired and replaced some of the copper on the ship's bottom and had the upper deck caulked. The ship was chartered to carry cargo and thirty passengers for £820.[5] A quick note jotted on 29 March 1853, as the ship departed, mentioned additional repairs and high expenses: "I finished loading last night and shall go to sea to day. My expences has been very high, have had to pay $2 per day for Mechanics. I had to fit my new main yard found the old one to be rotten on the forward part, also a new chamber to one of the pumps. I am in hopes my expences will not be so high in future."[6]

If there were raised eyebrows back in Kennebunk over the expenses incurred by Captain Goodwin, Lord gave no hint of it in the letters he sent off to New Orleans in anticipation of the *Mount Washington*'s arrival. On 11 May he wrote, "your several letters at Liverpool were duly recd—I think you made a very good freight down to New Orleans."[7] Lord's tone belies the fact that there must already have been a move afoot to replace Captain Goodwin. In August, after the dust had settled, Captain Blaisdell wrote to Lord, indicating that the dissatisfaction of the owners was neither sudden nor arbitrary. "As I have not had an Oppertunity of Seeing you lately I thought I would Send you a few lines to inform you that Mr. Bidwell is hear from New Orleans and if you want any further information Respecting Capt. Goodwin's Conduct I think he will give it to you I Should like for you to See him before he goes, he will leave the last of this week, he has told me more then I Ever heard before and I am more convinced then Ever that you did not replace him any to Soon."[8]

The Mr. Bidwell mentioned in the letter was a shipchandler from New Orleans. He routinely serviced many of the vessels in which Lord held an interest, the *Mount Washington* of course being one. It is unclear exactly what tidings Mr. Bidwell bore to Kennebunk, but they undoubtedly concerned any unwise or unorthodox behavior on the part of Captain Goodwin while in New Orleans.

At the end of May, two months after sailing from Liverpool, Captain Goodwin informed William Lord of his safe arrival at New Orleans.

> Yours of 11 & 17th is received. I arrived here this morning. had light winds after leaving the channel for the most of the passage. the second day out from Liverpool I had a very heavy gale was obliged to carry sale to keep the ship off shore and carryed away my jibboom but no other loss this passage.
>
> I have painted the ship inside & out this passage.
>
> Ships are filling up at 9/16 and Masters that have not engaged are asking 5/8 I shall try and get ready for freight as soon as possible.[9]

In his letter of 17 May, Lord reiterated his counsel and advice on freights. There was still no indication that anything was amiss.

> I wrote you on the 11th—I notice by accounts from N Orleans as late as the 13th freights had not improvd much—viz 7/16. I beleive they have been quoted as low as 3/8- I think I reccommend rather than accept of 3/8 you had better come coastwise even if you could not get over 1/2 ct for cotton and heavy freight in proportion. I am in hopes you will find no difficulty in getting 1/2 or equivalent to that. as I mentioned before I would be guarded against a Stave freight and tobacco freight to go into the Mcditcrainean and esspecially to more than one port—why I am prejudicd against going into the Medeterainean with Tobacco & Staves that you are liable to get deceivd in the quantity of Staves that the ship will carry and the voyages are generally made longer than first calculated upon—I dont wholly (object) to one of these voyages but I would give other business the preference—I can not but think by the time you are ready for business freights will improve some at any rate and equal 1/2.
>
> In case you should come coastwise I would give Boston the preference—[10]

The lateness of the season was once again working to the disadvantage of the *Mount Washington*. As the cotton stocks declined and the number of vessels in port increased, the high rates given earlier in the season were not sustained. In spite of Lord's letters deprecating stave freights, Captain Goodwin proceeded to charter the ship to carry staves to Bordeaux, as he informed Lord on 9 June.

Since writing my last there has been so many vessels arrived it has frightened ship masters and some has taken 7/16 to fill up, and others has taken 1/2 and given there consignment for a thousand bales, and one Master has taken 15/32 to day, Shippers is offering 7/16- & 3/8, and four large ships arrived

I have chartered the Ship to take a cargo of Staves to Bordeaux for $8000 and 5% primage to Mr. T.C.Jenkins. I think it is equel to 9/16 to Liverpool considering compressing, stowing, and the three months intrest and loss in weight in Liverpool.

I saw a letter from Bordeaux stating they were paying $12 per ton. I think I may get as good freight from there as from Liverpool as there will be a large fleet at Liverpool about the time I should arrive. I shall finish discharging about the middle of next week. and my cargo is all ready when I am to receive it.[11]

Captain Goodwin was not relieved of his command for taking the stave freight. The decision to replace him had been reached in Kennebunk more than a week before he chartered the ship in New Orleans. Not long after accepting the Bordeaux cargo, Captain Goodwin was hand-delivered a letter from Lord dated 31 May.

I hope before this you have arrivd safe—I notice by late telegraph accounts freights had inprovd and masters were asking 5/8, but I am afraid they will not obtain it—I wrote you on the 11th & 17 inst advising your holding on awhile rather than take less than 1/2 c—Capt Davis the bearer of this goes out to take charge of the ship Mt. Washington by request of all the owners, and you will therefore give up the command of the ship to him and every thing in relation to the ship any assistance or information that you may render him will no doubt be kindly recd—The balance of wages for your service that may be due I will settle on your arrival home—hoping soon to hear of your safe arrival at New Orleans— I remain very Respectfully yours. . . .[12]

That the *Mount Washington's* owners found Captain Goodwin's conduct as master lacking is evident from Captain Blaisdell's letter of August. Exactly what his faults were is not clear. Did the owners view him as a spendthrift? The repairs made in Liverpool certainly appear to have been justified, and they apparently warranted no comment from Lord at the time. Perhaps they found Captain Goodwin lacking in business sense, or maybe he had only been Lord's second choice from the start. The decision to replace him had been reached before he had arrived in New Orleans or even considered taking the stave freight; yet in that stave freight there may be a clue to his dismissal. Lord had advised him to hold off on chartering the ship until he had carefully considered his options. However, a week after his arrival he had taken a freight for Bordeaux, even though in his two letters Lord had indicated that stave freights were to be taken as a last resort. It would seem that in the owners' eyes Captain Goodwin fell short in two things, one being that he was not cautious or careful enough in considering his business options. The other, perhaps the more damaging to his position, was that he does not appear to have been as attentive to William Lord's views and opinions as was expected.

For whatever reasons, ineptitude or misconduct, the owners had serious doubts about Captain Goodwins's business ability. That spring William Lord, his daughter Sarah as Captain Barry's widow, Captain Blaisdell, and Robert Smith had come to another decision concerning the *Mount Washington*, which probably preceded the matter of Captain Goodwin's replacement, but was closely connected with it. The *Mount Washington* was to be sold. The owners naturally wanted a man in charge of the ship who could carry out the business to their best advantage. They had placed their confidence in Captain William Davis, who arrived in New Orleans with Lord's letter and assumed command of the ship.

In the fall of 1853 Captain Blaisdell was keeping abreast of the news concerning the *Mount Washington* and the *Neva*. He was also following the construction of a new vessel very closely. The good business of the 1852-53 freighting season had brought a boom to the yards on the river as the demand for new vessels grew.[13] For their part William Lord and Captain Blaisdell had jointly purchased a quarter interest in a small ship being built at the yard of Clement Littlefield in Kennebunk Lower Village. In October Blaisdell assessed the *Mount Washington*'s prospects in a letter to Lord, and noted the progress on the new vessel.

> I received your letter of the 4th relative to Capt. Davis &c am much obliged to you, I received one from him a day or two since which I will send you, it apears that the prospect for a return freight from Bordeaux was rather poor when he wrote me. If he lays the Ship On there I think he will have to lay some time to git a little, I hope that he will not lay long, for I think that business will be good at [New] Orleans the first of the Season, I think that Capt. Maling will be down in good time if nothing hapens,—the Brig arrived yesterday with the planks for Emmons & Littlefields Ship, and I hope now they will go ahead, they say they will have her all planked up in three weeks and I see nothing to prevent them gitting her off in all next month,—My third payment is now due and I Shall have to pay up this week, will you please to accomitate me with $600 by so doing you will much Oblige. . . .[14]

Again, a month later, the captain wrote to Lord requesting another draft on his account to meet the payment due on the new ship. "The fourth & last monthly Payment has become due to Emmons & Littlefield they want money to pay Off there men tomorrow and if you will please to accomedate me With Six hundred dollers & send it down with Bryant, you will much Oblige. . . [15]

William Lord and his son Hartley, in Boston, kept the accounts for the ships in which Captain Blaisdell held an interest. Whenever he needed a sum of money, the captain would draw on his account through William Lord in Kennebunk. From Boston, Hartley would send him periodic statements as to his account's balance.

By the end of November, Captain Blaisdell had obtained information about the *Mount Washington*, which he was quick to pass on to William Lord, along with a brief report on the progress on the new ship.

I Saw Capt. Davis's Son last Saturday, and he told me that his mother had got a letter from Bordeaux from her husband dated the 2d Inst. Saying he was ready for Sea and Should drop down the river on the 3d Inst. and Should write you as soon as he had settled up with Broker, he wrote that he had Onboard 800 tons of wine & Goods and about 70 passengers, but did not Say how much freight he makes,—I thought I would tell you this thinking that you had not got any letters from Capt. Davis by the last Steamer, you will probably git One by the next,—we are gitting along pretty well with the Ship now, but as they will not be able to Launch On this run of tides we think some of Rigging her On the stocks, do you not think it will be advisable. . . .[16]

The new 467-ton ship, christened *Abby Brown*, was registered on 11 January 1854.[17] Her master, Sylvester Brown, would eventually take her to New Orleans, but when Captain Blaisdell wrote to William Lord with a final reckoning of their expenses on 16 January 1854, she had not yet sailed.

Cost of Hull of Ship Abby Brown
482.61/95 Tons at $38.50 per ton $18,581.72
        One quarter of which is . . . . $ 4,645.43
By Cash Paid by William Lord Esqre $1800.00
    "   "   "   My self . . . . 1200.00 . . . . 3000.00

Balance due Emmons & Littlefield . . . . $ 1645.43

    The above is the cost of the Ships Hull and the balance due Emmons & Littlefield on Our quarter of the Ship Emmons told me Saturday that he should like to have the balance as soon as we could make it convenient to pay it—we have made three tryals to git the ship to sea but have failed she is now at government wharf all ready for the first chance. Capt. Perkins is gitting in her Bills of Out fits and we shall soon know the result—[18]

The principal owner of the *Abby Brown* was Eliphalet Perkins of Kennebunkport. His firm, which transported sugar from Cuba and Puerto Rico to Philadelphia, New York, or Boston, was the last vestige of the West India trade in the Kennebunks. The *Abby Brown*'s small size was against her being truly competitive in the cotton trade, and there is every indication that she was built to carry sugar. However, during her career her cargoes would be extremely varied, ranging from sugar to guano. As an investment, Captain Blaisdell's share in the *Abby Brown* made his income slightly less dependent on cotton freights.

    The expense of building a vessel in Kennebunk had risen over the years. In 1830 the cost had averaged $23.00 per ton.[19] In 1846 the hull of the *Francis Watts* had been built for $26.00 per ton. For the *Abby Brown* in 1853 the cost stood at $38.50. The local stands of timber had been depleted, and as a result many of the materials needed for construction, such as southern pine, had to be imported. The higher cost of building a vessel meant that more investors clubbed together. Where earlier vessels in which Captain Blaisdell held a share had had only three or four owners, the shares of the *Abby Brown* were divided among nine people. Eliphalet Perkins and Warren Brown of Kennebunkport each held 3/16 and were the largest single investors. Holding shares that ranged from 1/12 to 1/16 were Captain Charles C. Perkins, Dr. Nicholas E. Smart, Horace Davis, and Mary E. Brown, all of Kennebunkport, and Jefferson Cram of Unity, New Hampshire. William Lord and Captain Blaisdell, alone from Kennebunk, jointly controlled 1/4 of the ship.[20]

Captain Blaisdell and William Lord had no difficulty in meeting their remaining financial obligations to the builders of the *Abby Brown*, if for no other reason than that the *Mount Washington* had been sold. The decision to sell her had been reached during the previous spring, and Captain Davis had gone out to New Orleans with instructions to that effect. Once in control of the *Mount Washington*, Captain Davis had quickly concluded her remaining business and then sailed to France. He tried his luck in Bordeuax, but as he reported to Lord, "I have made enquiry about selling the Ship the best offer I had was Seventeen thousand dollars they want the Ship much but it is to dull at this port at present to find a sale for her." Captain Davis then loaded wine and took on passengers and returned to New Orleans.[21]

Upon his arrival in December he once again sought out buyers for the ship. In early January of 1854 a group of investors made a serious offer. On 25 January 1854, in consideration of $27,000, the *Mount Washington*'s papers were transferred to the new owners.[22] They retained the services of Captain Davis as commander.

Even without the *Mount Washington*, following the movements and business of the *Ocean Star*, *Neva*, and *Abby Brown* kept Captain Blaisdell occupied. He and Lord shared the correspondence they each received from their vessels' masters. In his new role as land-based owner, the captain could draw on his long experience as a master mariner to make relevent comments and observations. In mid-February he commented to Lord on freights.

> Capt. E. Perkins received a dispatch yesterday Saying the Abby Brown had arrived at the SW pass on the 11th Inst—all Well freight 3/4- George Davis got a letter from his brother Wm Saying the Mt. Washingtons Freight List told up to the sum of $19,400 Which is a tall freight—I hope that Capt Brown Will succeed in gitting a good freight—I send you back Capt. Malings letters and am much Obliged to you for your kindness in sending it down it seems that Capt. Maling is well sattisfied with his freight if the Other Owners are not. I think my self it is Equel to 3/4 but wether the Ship will be placed in as good a port for a return freight is an Other Consideration. . . .[23]

Well might Captain Blaisdell wish the master of the *Abby Brown* business equal to the *Mount Washington*'s. His feelings could easily have bordered on incredulity as he compared her purported freight with the business she had done under his command. Captain Maling of the *Neva* had chartered his ship in January to carry 1,200 bales of cotton and 6000 barrels of flour from New Orleans to Havre.[24] The *Abby Brown* was chartered in February, and Captain Blaisdell was already looking to the future and a Cuban sugar freight, as he commented to Lord on 18 March.

> Capt. Perkins got a letter from Capt. Brown to day dated the 9 Saying he was loaded and Should go down that Evening—he makes something Over Eight thousand dollers freight his Expences about $2,530- had drawn On the freight for $2400 & said he had written to the Consignee at New York to effect Insurance on $8500. but as Capt. Perkins had previously Effected Insurance on the freight at Boston he has written to New York to advise them of it and to stop them from Effecting Insurance, it may be that the parties at N Orleans required it for there own security, he writes that the ship is verry Crank has got heavy weight between decks I think he has done verry well, his Expences lighter then we Expected, I hope he will have a short passage and be in time to secure One of the great Havanna freights. . . .[25]

In the summer of 1854, Captain Blaisdell was offered the opportunity to go back to sea. He did not give a definite answer, preferring first to consider his options. George Callender wrote to William Lord in August asking that a decision be made.

> Capt. Morrill said yesterday if we wanted a master for the Ocean Star he should like to go in her—He says he is not dissatisfied with going in the Hartley, but should like the O. Star as being a larger ship, but should not get so good a one as he has now. We told him that you had talked with Capt. Blaisdell about going, but if Capt. B- did not want to go we should be glad to give her to him. So as Capt. Lord has decided not to go, you will please ascertain about Capt. Blaisdell & if he does not calculate to go in her we will engage Capt. Morrill if agreeable to you.[26]

Captain Blaisdell declined the offered command and Lord consented to Captain Morrill taking the ship. Captain Morrill's observation that he should not get a better ship than the *Hartley* by taking the *Ocean Star* proved to be prophetic. In the spring of 1855 he was forced to have repairs made in New York. The ship's metal sheathing kept working loose because the hull was not rigid enough to prevent distortion, or working, in a seaway. While repairs were being made, Captain Morrill requested to leave the ship, and another search began for a new master.[27] Again Captain Blaisdell was consulted, and he replied to Lord early in June 1855.

> As respects a master for the Ocean Star you asked me to try and think of some One, I mentioned Capt. Mason, I did think of another that would probably like to have the ship if you have no Objections to him that is Capt. Curtis, that is, if he can git off honorably from the Mary Ward, for he told me that he did not like to go to New Orleans at this season of the year nor would not go if he had any

prospect of gitting another ship he feels himself under an Obligation to the
Owners for giving him Charge of the ship, but if he can better him self I dont
think that they will have any Objections, I believe that he has given Entire
sattisfaction so far, if you have no Objections I will write him tomorrow if you
think favorable of it please write me by return of mail. . . .[28]

Captain Blaisdell seems to have forgotten the promise he made to himself
after the Adam McCulloch episode.   There were, however, extenuating circumstances in Captain Curtis's case and even shades of nepotism.   Captain
Isaac Curtis was Captain Blaisdell's son-in-law. He had married the captain's
eldest daughter, Elizabeth, in 1853. He was twenty-five years old, and the
Mary Ward appears to have been his first command. Captain Curtis did not
get the command of the *Ocean Star*, it went instead to Captain William
Symonds. It may be that Captain Curtis was unable to arrange to leave the
Mary Ward, but it is more likely that William Lord declined to entrust his
interests to a neophyte master.

The spring of 1855 found freighting rates low, and many ships were having
difficulty covering their expenses. In the fall there was an unexpected rise to
7/8 of a cent, but by the spring of 1856 rates were down again.[29]

During that period, world demand for cotton grew, and the price of cotton
remained high. The American crop of 1854-55 was slightly smaller than the
previous season's harvest, but the crop of 1855-56 was a record 3.5 million
bales. The explanation for the soft cotton freights must be the glut of vessels
in the trade: 1,249 barks and ships entered at New Orleans that year, 263
more than the previous year.[30] The good freights given between 1852 and
1854 had stimulated shipbuilding to the saturation point. The consensus in
Kennebunk in May of 1856 was that the prospects for new ships were not at all
promising.

Despite the bleak outlook, builders had to make a living, and Stephen and
Charles Ward had a new bark under construction in their yard at Kennebunkport. Captain Blaisdell held an eighth share in the new vessel, and his
son-in-law, Captain Curtis, was to be her master. The 604.30-ton bark,
registered on 29 March 1856, was named the *Waverly*.[31] That summer Captain Blaisdell still owed money on her account, and requested Lord to draw on
his account for the payment. "The last payment of the Out fits of Bark
Waverly becomes due the 15th Inst. my eighth part of which is $600- will you
have the kindness to accomidate me with that amount in any way that suits
your convenience either through the Bank or by an order on Messrs. Callender
& Co. If you can accomidate me will you have the goodness to drop me a line
by the return of mail, by so doing you will much Oblige. . . ."[32]

Evidently the returns from the construction of the *Waverly* were insufficient,
for in the fall of 1856 the Ward shipyard failed. Across the river in Kennebunk, the yard of Emmons and Littlefield had to assign their property in order
to prevent going under. The poor state of cotton freights was not the only

factor working to the detriment of the builders. Construction costs had continued to go up until, in 1856, it was estimated that a large vessel would cost at least $57.00 per ton, and smaller vessels cost more in proportion to their tonnage than the larger vessels did.[33]

By the spring of 1857 it was apparent that it was another season of "uncommon low freights." Few Kennebunk vessels were earning enough to meet the cost of their insurance or the expense of sailing them, leaving nothing for depreciation or dividends.[34] Investments in shipping had never been secure, being at the mercy of nature, unpredictable market conditions, and the dishonesty and incompetency of men. The lot of the individuals who made the investments, many of whom sat far from the action, dependent on letter and telegraph for their information, was far from placid. In March 1857 Captain Blaisdell voiced his concerns to Lord about the expenses of the *Ocean Star*, the whereabouts of the *Waverly*, and the command of the *Abby Brown*.

> I received your note yesterday Relative to the Ocean Star. am much Obliged to you for the information, her freight list tells up pritty well, but her Expences I think is verry high. as you say it takes about all of the freight to pay Expences now a days. I think he was fortunate in taking up when he did for freights has been graduly declining Ever since, Capt. Brown received a letter from Fostick the Broker at New Orleans a few days since, dated Feb,y 14—saying that he was much surprised by the appearance of capt. Briggs in his Office the day before, which was the 13 ult. Saying that his Chronometer had given Out and that he did not feel himself Justified in proceeding on the Voyage with out One, so he put back after being out 11 days to git another, that he had procured One and had gone down again On the 14 to joine the ship again which he had left at anchor Out side of the Bar, since that we have heard nothing more from him but supose he got to sea again on the 15 Ult. which leaves him Out 18 days, I should call that a great piece of Prudence or folly I dont know which he must have been born in the Chronometer age—the Waverly has now been Out 31 days for Boston and no news of her I begin to fear something has hapened to her. . . .
>
> P.S. I was looking over my accounts and found my expences at New Orleans when I load for Russia was $4036 or less then half what the Ocean Star is and I had part of a cargo of hay to discharge too, the whole of my stores & Chandler Bills was $322.00.[35]

Three weeks later he wrote to complain of Captain Brown's apparent presumption in turning over command of the *Abby Brown* to another master without consulting all the owners. Although he had declined the offer of a command in 1854, Blaisdell now hinted that he would be willing to return to sea.

> You no doubt are advised of the arrival of the Abby Brown, Capt. Brown is at Boston superentending I have been lead to supose all the time by the Conversation that I have had with Capt. Brown that he intended to go in the Ship next Voyage and never learnt to the Contrary til yesterday, it seams that he has ingaged Capt. Bearse to take Charge, I mean the Bearse that was in the Sealea, wether he has done this on his Own responsibility or not I am not able to say he may have

Capt. E. Perkins santion, but some of the Owners was as Egnorant of it as I was til yesterday, I think if Capt. Brown dont make a better selection then he did last voyage he had better Consult some of the Other Owners, I am inclined to think that he has sold his Intrest Out to Capt. Bearse but dont know for ceartin I dont know but Capt. Bearse may do as well as any one, but I have my Pregidices as well as Others, had I known that Capt. Brown was not a going I would have made arrangements so as to have gone my self, but now it is too late—I Expect that the Credit will be on the wrong page this time, they have got to git sails & mend the copper &c which will swell her Expences up high. they have brought the duck down here to have the sails made. they think of sending her to Cuba to git a Charter before they start if they can, I think that will be the best movement if they Can succead in gitting a good one—[36]

In 1857 the country suffered a financial panic. Half a world away the Crimean War had ended. The peace brought Russian wheat into the world market, causing prices to fall. The American agricultural expansion suffered a serious setback that had a ripple effect throughout the economy. While cotton prices remained stable, the demand for other agricultural commodities dropped markedly. The farms in the upper Mississippi Valley were hit especially hard.[37] The amount of produce brought down the river to New Orleans declined.

Vessels that had formerly carried farm commodities entered into competition for whatever business was available, especially cotton. By early 1858 the pinch was being felt in Kennebunk, and in February Captain Blaisdell had to seek a bank loan from Lord to meet the operating expenses of the *Waverly* and *Abby Brown*. "I have to make Out about Eight hundred dollers the last of this week to pay my Eighth part of Out fits of Bark Waverly & Insurance on the Abby Brown, will you have the kindness to help me git my notes through the Ocean Bank, for that amount for 90 days, by the End of that time I shall be able to take it up, we are in dayly Expectation of receipt of a draft from Capt. Curtis of some $8,000 or $10,000, if you will acomidate me you will Confer a great favor On your Much Obliged Obedient Sert."[38]

The bad news continued as reports came in on the business transacted by the ships. It was a disheartened Captain Blaisdell who returned the *Ocean Star*'s papers to William Lord in March 1858.

I send you the Ocean Stars a/c &c Capt. Williams Letter, we seem to be in luck this year in hitting the highest rates or rather the lowest rates of freights I noticed yesterday accounts from Charleston of the 16 Inst. freights was 7/16 and 5/8 at New Orleans, it is a great pity that Capts. Williams and Moody had not held on a few days longer after waiting so long   at the preasant rates they would have made a good business, but at the Rates they have got they cant pay there Expences, I am much obliged to you for keeping me advised of the proceedings of Ocean Star. . . .[39]

The shipyard of Daniel and Stephen Ward at
Kennebunkport, ca. 1855. Engraving by Sargent, 1856.
(Courtesy Brick Store Museum, Charles S. Morgan Collection)

Captain Blaisdell
purchased this home
in Kennebunk Lower
Village for $400 in the
summer of 1834. It
remained his home
until his death in
1874. *(Photo by
author)*

THIRTEEN

The Final Years
1858–1874

WHEN AN OPPORTUNITY for Captain Blaisdell to return to sea presented itself early in the spring of 1858, he readily accepted. With the income from his investments now less secure, and his faith in his own business judgement perhaps reinforced as he watched the performance of other masters, he could not resist a return to command after six years ashore. His command was the new bark *Jacob Merrill*. The 343.48-ton vessel had been built by George Christenson of the Kennebunk Lower Village for owners Jacob Merrill and Charles Goodwin.[1] She was registered on 19 April 1858 and soon after sailed for Portland, Maine.

In Portland, the *Jacob Merrill* probably loaded the disassembled sugar boxes and hogsheads manufactured there for export to the sugar islands. The bark and her crew left Portland Harbor on 11 May, bound for the Cuban port of Cienfuegos. She arrived at her destination on 9 June, and after conducting her business there she sailed on to Havana. As soon as the bark was fully loaded, Captain Blaisdell quit Havana and set a course for Philadelphia.

The return leg of the passage was marred by the loss of one of the *Jacob Merrill*'s crew. It was an accepted risk that along with warm temperatures and hurricanes, the summer season in the Caribbean brought the peril of yellow fever. Serving in the bark's crew was sixteen-year-old George Pope of Kennebunkport. Not many days out from Havana the boy fell ill. On 12 July he died. To Captain Blaisdell fell the melancholy tasks of committing the body to the deep and writing a gentle letter to break the hard news to the youth's parents. The premature end of young Pope was duly recorded in the town records: "July 12, 1858—George Fuller Pope, aged 16—at Sea on the passage from Havana to Philadelphia on board Barque Jacob Merrill—second son of Samuel Pope."[2]

The family scarcely had time to come to terms with their loss before they were dealt another. On the same page in the town's record book is the terse entry for another death: "Sept. 12, 1858—aged 45—Samuel Pope."[3] A family mourned for a lost parent and a son who would not return from the sea.

The *Jacob Merrill* herself did not return to Kennebunk. She was sold by her owners at Philadelphia in October of 1858. The following year she was sold again to interests in New York City.[4]

Captain Blaisdell returned home in late 1858 fully expecting to remain there. At sixty-five, he had found going to sea a more difficult undertaking than it ever had been before. Nonetheless, a controversy over the command of the *Abby Brown*, which developed in 1859, would compel him to put to sea once more.

While nationally 1859 would show evidence of a moderate economic revival, the effects were slow to be felt in Kennebunk. Shipping was dull. The costs of materials and labor were up, and few new vessels were planned. The local economy languished.[5] For Captain Blaisdell the year began with bad news of the *Ocean Star*. In the fall of 1858, while crossing to Liverpool, the ship had encountered foul weather and rough seas. She managed to limp into port, and her master, Captain George E. Brown, sent word of his predicament to Hartley Lord in Boston. Hartley sent copies of Captain Brown's letters to his father with the observation that "he has had a pretty hard time and a wonder to me how he got there—He is a persevering fellow & used to a leaky ship or he would have been frightened out of her   I think he managed well not to lose sails or spars as most other vessels have."[6]

The *Ocean Star* was sent into drydock to receive much needed attention. She was strengthened, caulked, and coppered. Lord in turn informed Captain Blaisdell in February 1859. "I send you copies of letters from Capt Brown— Ocean Star when I hear from Hartley how he comes out in the settlement with underwriters will let you know—upon the whole we came off as well as could be expected the money laid out upon her was needed, and the ship will be all the better for it—What news do you get from Capt. Moody, Abby Brown I have not heard anything.[7]

When Captain Blaisdell had returned home to Kennebunk from the *Jacob Merrill*, the *Abby Brown* was on the West Coast. If the opinion Captain Blaisdell expressed in his reply to William Lord was commonly held, it would seem that the owners were not pleased with the business conditions of the region.

I return you the 2 Coppies of Capt. Browns letters & am much Obliged to you. I think she got Out of the Scrape as well as could be Expected,—Capt. E. Perkins Got a letter by the last California Mail from Capt. Moody of Abby Brown dated Jan,y 5,—saying he had Chartered his Ship to go to Johnsons Islands to load with guano at $11.00 Eleven dollars per ton for Hamton Rds. Johnsons Islands lais in Lat. 17 N. Long. about 170 W. or about 700 miles W.S.W. from Sandwich Islands a long voyage for so low freight. he said he is to have half of what the guano brings over $19- per ton it is like taking a Cargo of sugar on half profet in former times when the Commission & Expenses Eat up all the profets—he remited

$2000- $400 of which was Capt. Moody's St Francisco is a verry Expensive place, the guano that they git at Johnsons Islands is not worth as much as that at the Chinclois [Chinchas], he sais the last Cargo that shipped from there sold for about $25. per ton, . .[8]

When the *Abby Brown* returned to the East Coast there was a change of masters, either at the owner's request or because Captain Moody wished to leave the ship. Ever looking to advance the career of his son-in-law, Captain Curtis, Captain Blaisdell had arranged what he thought was a firm commitment from the other owners for Captain Curtis to take command of the *Abby Brown* on her arrival. However, when she arrived, principal owner Eliphalet Perkins balked at turning over the ship, which annoyed Captain Blaisdell considerably. Rather than see the ship go to another master, the captain took command of her himself.

The *Abby Brown* sailed to Charleston, South Carolina. Captain Blaisdell did not want to go to sea, but he was determined that the promise made to him would be kept, and he could not rely on another master being willing to relinquish the ship. Feeling that he had been inconvenienced, the captain wrote to William Lord from Charleston in December 1859, explaining the situation and enlisting his help.

Probably you have learnt from Capt. E. Perkins my proceadings but as you are interested and my best friend I thought I would drop you a few lines, I had got all ready for sea with the intentions of going to apalatch[icola], when I had this Charter offered me, viz from this port to Nants with a Cargo of Cotton & Rice, as follows, 200 tierces Rice at [£]2.0.0 per ton, the balance of my Cargo in Square bales of Cotton at one cent per lb. which I thought at the time was as good as any thing I could do, but I notice freights have improved since that in the Gulf ports and I am Sorry now that I had not gone to apalach, but I done then what I thought for the Best—I had a fine passage Out here of less than four days, and am in hopes to git good dispatch, at any rate I Shall do the best that I can—I am gitting Old, too Old to go to sea, and hardly Equal to the task, & I Should not have gone had I not got disapointed in gitting Capt. Curtis in to the Ship, by the Conversation that I had with Capt. E. Perkins last Spring I as much depended on his going, as if I was sure of it, & Curtis Stoped unpurpose to take her when She arrived. Otherwais he would have gone off last Spring, and at the last moment Capt. E. told me that Curtis Could not go in the Ship, and that if I did not take her that he should telegraph for Capt. Symonds, to N. Orleans to come and take her and the Only reason that he gave why Curtis could not have her was, the misunderstanding between him and Walter Littlefield, a poor Excuse is better than none, but I should not think that it was much then none,—if I thought that, there was any reasonable Objection against his going, I should be as much against it as the rest of the Owners, but by all the information that I have been able to git respecting his Character I cant see any thing of so serious a nature as to keep him out of a ship that he is Enterested in, and in which I had the promise, or he had the promise of after Capt. Brown Sailed her One year and how will the promise be fulfilled—

I had no Oppertunity of seeing you before I left, having to start sooner then I
Expected but I beg to request One favor of you that is if you will take the trouble
of making Enquiry of those that are acquainted with Capt. Curtis that have been
in port with him when he was master, & I will refer you to One, viz. Capt.
Willson, he was at Iquque, & Callio, there is the owners of the Mary Ward, Capt.
A. Stone had something to do with him, or any others that may be acquainted
with him, and if cant find any suficiant Objections to him will you do me the
favor of using your influance with Capt. E. Perkins to give him Charge of the Ship
after this preasant voyage is performed I hope you will Excuse [me] for presuming
too much On your kindness but I feel interested for the young man, and wish to
sustain his reputation if there is good cause for it, will you please to write me a few
lines, . . .[9]

Evidently there had been some difficulty about the freight for the guano
brought to Hampton Roads, although it apparently did not delay the sailing
of the ship. Shortly after the arrival of the new year the captain wrote again
from Charleston to Lord. His letter was filled with the news of ill-fated ships,
luckless men, and the effects of bad business.

I Expect you will be some surprised to find me here yet, but there was more than a
week that we done nothing and the cotton stows verry hard, I have had cotton as
fast as I wanted it, but five gangs would not stow more then 60 or 70 bales per day,
I have now got in 1200 bales & 210 turces Rice, and shall probably take from 200
to 250 bales more, it is mostly Georgia cotton large light & Spungy Cotton, I am
in hopes to make $7000 freight & that will be the Extent, but I dont think that
my Expenses will Excead $2300, I am in hopes to git away by the 12th—I have
heard nothing about the Guano freight of late, I hope they will git it, if we lose
that it will take the whole ship to pay Expenses, I understood that she Owes Capt.
Moody $2000, I dont see how that can be possable, for he had sent home to his
brother from Liverpool $400, and from san francisco $400, he will make a much
better voyage then the Owners, this ship & the Waverly has been the Ruination of
me,—I heard that the Windemeer & Golden Eagle had both been condemned,
and the H.M. Hayre was in trouble Capt. dead and crew in Prison—freights here
is 15/32 & 7/16 to Liverpool & 7/8 to Havre, I have got a verry bad cold, have
been in the hold so much amongst the damp Cotton, I am almost sowed up, but
hope I shall be better when I git to sea—when I wrote you last, I forgot to
mention my note in the Ocean Bank for $300-which you had the kindness to go
surity for me, which will become due the 7th of april, which I hope before that
time Expires to be able to meet it, but should I not will you have the Goodness to
protect it for me. by so doing you will have my Everlasting Gratitude,—I find it
much Easeayer to git in debt, then Out of it.—I rec,d a letter from your Son
Hartly with my yearly a/c & find a balance in my favor of $81-which was verry
gratifying, for I was fearful that I had Over drawn on him, the Ocean Star is the
Only ship that I am Enterested in that I git any thing from, and I don't git a
quarter anough from her to make up what the Others brings me in debt. well, I
fear my long preamble will not be verry Enterresting to you, so I will close by
wishing you health & happiness Please drop me a few lines to Nantes to the care
of Monsieur A. Garnier, . . .[10]

The captain's letter of 7 January 1860 is his last to be found among the great volume of papers that once belonged to William Lord. The *Abby Brown* made her way safely to France, and from Nantes sailed on to Cuba. In May she was reported to be loading sugar in Mantanzas, and later that month she set sail for England.

Following Captain Blaisdell's request, William Lord did use his considerable influence to good effect, and arrangements were made to turn the *Abby Brown* over to Captain Curtis. There are conflicting reports as to exactly when Curtis took control of the ship. One source shows him as master of the *Abby Brown* when she arrived out at Bristol, England, from Matanzas in July 1860, but according to the *Boston Shipping List* he did not assume command until the ship had returned to New York from Britain in October. At any rate, it is certain that by the fall of 1860 Captain Blaisdell had the pleasure of seeing the matter resolved to his satisfaction. On his part, Captain Curtis retained his hard won command of the *Abby Brown* until February of 1862, when she was sold in Boston for "something less than $40,000 dollars."[11]

The *Abby Brown* was Captain Blaisdell's last deep-water command. Few details survive of his life ashore in Kennebunk during the fourteen years that remained to him. However, it is hard to imagine that he relegated himself to the storefront existence described by Andrew Walker after a visit to Kennebunkport in 1851.

> As I had plenty of leisure I went into nearly all of the stores. The habits of the people who frequent the stores, appear to be about the same as they were twenty years ago. Still clustering around the stoves in the stores may be seen superannuated sea-captains, ex-sea-captains and sea-captains waiting to be employed. Some of the old familiar faces have disapeared and others have taken their places. But they all appear to have the same characteristics. Generally speaking old sea-captains do not feel so much interest in the affairs of the land as they do in the affairs of the sea and it is natural that it should be so. Whenever you see a cluster of these "old sea-dogs" you may be nearly sure they are conversing of something relating directly or indirectly to the ocean. Some of these men retain for many years after they have left the sea a reserved manner, which was acquired while having a ships crew under their command. In fact it is a rare occurrance that we meet with a sea-captain who has that ease and suavity of manner that we often see in landsmen.[12]

Initially upon his return, the captain's energies would have been taken up with shipping and the vessels in which he held shares. Records show that he later tried his hand at small scale land investment. As demands on his time became fewer, he turned to fishing. It was not a commercial venture for him. Was it the ocean that he missed, or the solitude? Perhaps both, for he continued to fish to the end of his life. Listed in the inventory of his estate was a fishing boat and tackle valued at $30.00.

There was a great difference between the brigs, barks, and ships that Captain Blaisdell had once commanded and the small boat he sailed along the shoreline in his later years. That transition in his personal life mirrored in many respects the evolution in the maritime life of his community, his state, and the entire New England region. The ascendancy of the American square-rigger in foreign trade was over; the "Golden Age" had been eclipsed.

The luster of that "Golden Age" had already begun to tarnish when Captain Blaisdell left the *Mount Washington* in 1852. Shipbuilding in Maine went on to reach a peak in 1855. The 215,904 tons launched from her yards that year represented one-third of the national total. But supply had out-stripped demand, and by 1859 the aggregate figure for vessels constructed in the state had dwindled to 40,905 tons. There had been prophecies of doom as early as 1853. In the boom year of 1855 there were already real signs of impending trouble. The selling price that Maine-built ships commanded in that year was one-quarter less than what it had been during the previous twelve months.[13] With the Panic of 1857 and the ensuing economic slump, the shipping decline began in earnest. Hard on the heels of depression came the Civil War. The closing of the cotton ports had an immediate and disastrous effect on Northern shipping. Before long Confederate raiders were at sea preying on Northern commerce. More damaging than the physical losses they inflicted were the far reaching reactions their activities caused in shipping circles. Northern shipowners saw their insurance rates skyrocket. Northern shipmasters found themselves cut out of the transatlantic trade because foreign shippers were reluctant to expose their goods to the dangers of capture and destruction.

With the return of peace there was no revival in foreign shipping. During the war years the British had made great inroads into the shipping routes once dominated by Yankees. Many American vessels had been either sold to foreign interests or transferred to foreign registry in order to escape the Confederate threat. After the war, increased building costs discouraged their replacement. Adding to the overall negative climate was the increasingly poor quality of both the crews and the officers serving in the American merchant marine.[14]

While New England's transatlantic trade had fallen on hard times, the coasting trade, closed to foreign competiton, flourished. Steamers and sailing vessels plied the coastal routes carrying passengers, mail, and heavy cargo. Preeminent among the coastwise carriers was the schooner, its fore-and-aft rig making it ideal for sailing the coast in the face of the prevailing winds.[15]

Maine had a long-standing reputation for building serviceable and relatively inexpensive vessels. As construction costs climbed in the postwar years, Maine became the shipbuilding center of New England. From her shipyards came the Down Easters, the last square-rigged survivors of foreign commerce, which were employed largely in transporting West Coast wheat. Like American cotton freighters of the 1850s, they had the advantage over foreign vessels of protected coastal freights from the East Coast to California in this trade. For East Coast trade, schooners of ever increasing size were launched from Maine shipyards as coal became the leading waterborne commodity on the coast.[16]

The ship *Vigilant* and bark *Hiram Emery*
under construction at Kennebunk in 1877.
(Courtesy Brick Store Museum)

Shipbuilding continued long after Kennebunk men
retired from the sea. At the site of the D. & S.
Ward yard at Kennebunkport, the four-masted
schooner *Savannah* nears completion in 1901.
(Courtesy Brick Store Museum,
Charles S. Morgan Collection)

In Kennebunk during the sixties and seventies, square-riggers continued to slide down the ways. In fact 1874 saw the launching of the 2,546 ton four-masted bark *Ocean King*. But it was the schooner that allowed the tradition of building large craft on the Kennebunk to survive in a modest way until the turn of the century.[17]

The rise and fall of American sail in foreign commerce—Captain Blaisdell had witnessed it all. First as a cabin boy, then as an able seaman, and later as first mate he had participated in the traditional trade between the coast of Maine and the islands of the Caribbean. From trader to freighter, he and his vessels had been part of the American expansion into transatlantic trade in the 1820s and '30s. Then, for more years than he probably cared to remember, he had puzzled over the complexities of the cotton trade. Finally, the end of his active career and his anticipated retirement to modest comfort in Kennebunk coincided with the economic and political events that brought ruin to the way of life he had known.

Much was different. Though vessels were still built on the river, few were locally owned. The men and boys who went to sea from Kennebunk were more likely to be fishermen than the crews and masters of merchant vessels. Captain Blaisdell's own son left his hometown for Boston and a land-based trade as a painting contractor. Even the shipmaster's job had changed by the 1870s. With transatlantic and transcontinental telegraph, he was no longer required to be a self-reliant business agent far removed from his owners. Masters of the "Chronometer age" still had to be consumate seamen, but much of the business responsibility, which had tormented Blaisdell, was removed from their shoulders.

At home both the captain and his wife Elizabeth were outwardly changed from the young couple who had exchanged vows in 1825. Each in their turn, the Blaisdell children had left to start homes and families of their own. Elizabeth had married Captain Curtis in 1853, and other marriages followed: Sarah to carpenter Charles C. Wells, Maria to Jacob Clark, Eunice to Joseph S. Brown, and William to Emma S. Emery. Outside the family, the circle of familiar faces grew smaller with each passing year. In 1873 the captain's great, good friend William Lord died.

In 1874, in the spring of the year, Captain Blaisdell died at the age of eighty-one. He was buried alongside his mother and infant son at the Kennebunk Landing. Season followed season, year followed year, and one by one the vestiges of his world slipped away. Family, friends, and neighbors were laid to rest in the rolling field around him. The day came when the last large wooden vessel slid down the ways, and an era ended.

It had been an era that asked much of sailing vessels and the men who sailed them; an era whose maritime pursuits have, with the passage of time, become wrapped in a romantic mist that often obscures reality. Undeniably, sailing vessels could be objects of great beauty, and the men who sailed them often faced daunting situations, but there is little evidence to support the romantic image of life at sea that has become fixed in the modern imagination. Captain Blaisdell's experiences bear out the fact that the command of a vessel was a difficult and demanding job and often little else. Tedious, or in his own unique orthography "teagous," was the word the captain invariably chose at the end of a voyage to describe his time at sea. And when it was not tedious it was often dangerous, with sinking ships, collisions at sea, and hurricanes being but a few of the diversions that might break the monotony. Whether tedious or dangerous, the command of a vessel remained an arduous task.

Taking into consideration the conditions they worked under and against, it is amazing how well Captain Blaisdell and countless men like him, often with scant formal education, filled their roles of navigator, disciplinarian, financier, and market analyst. Though a man might command a vessel and her crew, he still had to suffer the vagaries of wind and weather; and the fluctuations of distant markets, the outcome of foreign wars, and the threat of disease and pestilence could all conspire to to wreak havoc on the most carefully made plans.

Throughout all the vicissitudes of his long career, one line from Captain Blaisdell's earliest surviving letter echoes, sometimes stated, always implied, "I done of course what I thought for the best." A man can do no more.

Accounts of the Ship
Mount Washington
1848–1849

Cost of Ship *Mount Washington*, including outfit and cargo for first
  voyage $31,128.52
¹/₈ share charged to Jotham Blaisdell $3,891.06

New Orleans, 1848

Disbursements and		Sale of hay cargo	$678.88
port charges	$4,036.46		

Cronstadt & St. Petersburg, 1848

Disbursements and		Freight on 2,250	
port charges,		bales of cotton	
Cronstadt	$1,086.10	983,105 lbs. @	
St. Petersburg	776.12	1⁵/₃₂ cts.	$15,914.13

Vybourg, 1848

Disbursements and	
port charges	$372.76

Elsinore, 1848

Disbursements and port charges	$651.66

Bordeaux, 1848

Disbursements and port charges	$2,765.81	Freight and primage on deals	$4,212.74
Commission on deal freight	$450.76	3 days demurrage @ fr. 150	$84.11
		passage money—cabin passengers	$439.25
		passage money—steerage passengers	$329.72

New Orleans, 1849

Disbursements and port charges	$5,820.49	Net on freight from Bordeaux	$1,871.74
		passage money	$315.00

Liverpool, 1849

Disbursements and port charges	$2,930.40	Freight and primage from New Orleans	$11,501.42

Captain Blaisdell's Primage and Wages
1 December 1847–6 July 1849

On freight from New Orleans to St. Petersburg	$ 568.40
On freight from Vybourg to Bordeaux	241.22
On freight from Bordeaux to New Orleans	109.30
On freight from New Orleans to Liverpool	547.30
On freight from Liverpool to Boston	299.99
Wages @ $20.00 per month	384.00
	$2,150.21

Notes

CHAPTER ONE
Beginnings

1 Diary of Andrew Walker, vol. 6, p. 375, Kennebunk Free Library, Kennebunk, Maine.

2 Ralph Waldo Emerson, "History," in *Essays* (first series, 1841).

3 William H. Rowe, *The Maritime History of Maine* (New York: W.W. Norton, 1948), p. 97. Blaisdell's year of birth and introduction to the sea are inferred from records of seamen's protections. In December 1805, at what must have been the beginning of his career as a deep water sailor, he was described as "about 13 years of age." He was 4'7" tall and had a light complexion, greyish eyes, and brown hair. Seamen's Oaths, 1804–1806, Port Records of Kennebunkport, Collection 1389, Harvard University, Cambridge, Massachusetts. In July 1819 he was described as being twenty-five years old and 5'11" tall. By then, life at sea had turned his light complexion dark. Abstract of Seamen's Protection Certificates, 3rd Quarter of 1819, Records of the Collector of Customs, Boston, Massachusetts, Bureau of Customs, Record Group 36, National Archives, Washington, D.C., hereafter cited as NA.

4 Edward E. Bourne, *The History of Wells and Kennebunk* (Portland: Thurston & Co., 1875), p. 575.

5 Daniel Remick, *History of Kennebunk From Its Earliest Settlement to 1890* (Kennebunk: Carrie S. Remick, 1911) p. 17.

6 *Ibid.*, p. 174.

7 Impost Book, 1800 to 1867, Records of the Collector of Customs, Kennebunk, Maine, Maine Historical Society, Portland, Maine, hereafter cited as MHS.

8 Robert G. Albion, et. al. *New England and the Sea* (Mystic: Mystic Seaport Museum, 1972), pp. 80-81.

9 Charles Bradbury, *History of Kennebunk Port From Its First Discovery by Bartholomew Gosnold, May 14, 1602 to A.D. 1837* (1837; reprint ed. Kennebunkport: Kennebunkport Historical Society, 1967), p. 188.

10 Albion, *New England and the Sea*, p. 81.

11 Bourne, *History of Wells and Kennebunk*, p. 597.

12 Seth E. Bryant, *A List of Vessels Built, From 1800 to 1878, District of Kennebunk* (Kennebunk: Brick Store Museum, 1950).

13 Bourne, *History of Wells and Kennebunk*, p. 603.

14 Remick, *History of Kennebunk*, p. 260.

15 *Ibid.*, p. 259.

16 Bourne, *History of Wells and Kennebunk*, pp. 605-06.

17 Bryant, *A List of Vessels Built.*

18 Bradbury, *History of Kennebunk Port*, p. 191.

19 Rowe, *Maritime History of Maine*, pp. 108-09.

20 George R. Taylor, *The Transportation Revolution, 1815-1860* (New York: Rinehart & Co., 1951), p. 190.

21 Remick, *History of Kennebunk*, p. 383.

22 Albion, *New England and the Sea*, p. 85.

23 Joseph Blunt, *The Shipmaster's Assistant and Commercial Digest* (New York: Harper & Brothers, 1853), pp. 31-32.

24 Brig *Augustus*, Crew List, 30 June 1821, Records of the Collector of Customs, New Orleans, Louisiana, Bureau of Customs, Record Group 36, NA.

25 Bryant, *A List of Vessels Built.*

26 Bourne, *History of Wells and Kennebunk*, pp. 763-64.

27 William E. Barry, *Sketch of an Old River* (Boston: Alfred Mudge & Son, 1888), pp. 6,9. The *Augustus* typified the vessels constructed at the time for trading with the Caribbean. The two-masted, square-rigged brig was especially popular for overseas, rather than coastal, trade. Later, as vessel size increased, three-masted ships and barks would supplant brigs, except in small ports. Brigs for Caribbean trade were often built with shallow draft, enabling them to sail into shoal coves and bays in search of cargo. The government tonnage formula of the day calculated a double-decked vessel's depth of hold to be one half its breadth. This encouraged the construction of short, full-ended, deep vessels that could carry much more cargo than indicated by their registered tonnage, thus saving on tonnage duties. As built in Kennebunk, these vessels were framed and planked with oak, and decked with pine. For protection, their bottoms were smeared with tar rather than sheathed with more expensive copper. They had open rails forward to aid in fishing their anchors. Their decks were clear, except for a movable galley or "camboose" lashed in place. Accommodations were below: staterooms and a cabin with stern windows aft for officers and passengers, and a dark, cramped, and often wet forecastle in the very bow for the crew. While somewhat awkward and slow, these brigs were considered reliable sea boats. John G.B. Hutchins, *American Maritime Industries and Public Policy, 1789-1914* (Cambridge: Harvard University Press, 1941), pp. 216–17.

28 Brig *Augustus*, Crew List, 30 June 1821, Records of the Collector of Customs, New Orleans, Louisiana, Bureau of Customs, Record Group 36, NA.

29 Impost Book, 1800-1867, Records of the Collector of Customs, Kennebunk, Maine, MHS.

30 Bryant, *A List of Vessels Built.*

31 Bourne, *History of Wells and Kennebunk*, p. 770.

32 *Ibid.*, p. 580.

33 Bryant, *A List of Vessels Built*.

34 *Ibid.*

35 Brig *Florida*, Crew List, 8 November 1821, Records of the Collector of Customs, New Orleans, Louisiana, Bureau of Customs, Record Group 36, NA.

36 Rowe, *Maritime History of Maine*, p. 151.

37 *Ibid.*, pp. 153-54.

38 John A. Garraty, *The American Nation to 1877, A History of the American Nation* (New York: American Heritage Publishing Co., Inc., 1966), p. 220.

39 *Kennebunk Gazette*, 30 November 1822.

40 *Ibid.*, 30 October 1824.

41 Bryant, *A List of Vessels Built*.

42 *Kennebunk Gazette*, 11 June 1825.

43 *Ibid.*, September 1825.

44 Records of the Second Congregational Church, Kennebunk, Maine.

45 *Kennebunk Gazette*, 26 November 1825.

46 *Ibid.*, 10 February 1827; *New York Shipping & Commercial List*, 30 August 1826.

CHAPTER TWO
The Captain Takes Command

1 George R. Taylor, *The Transportation Revolution, 1815-1860* (New York: Rinehart & Co., Inc., 1951), pp. 104-06.

2 *Ibid.*, p. 198.

3 *Kennebunk Gazette*, 10 February, 21 July, 4 August, 11 August 1827.

4 *Ibid.*, 3 May, 28 June, 1826.

5 Blunt, Joseph, *The Shipmaster's Assistant and Commercial Digest* (New York: Harper & Brothers, 1853), pp. 655-56.

6 *Ibid.*, pp. 654-55.

7 Impost Book 1800-1867, Records of the Collector of Customs, Kennebunk, Maine Historical Society, Portland, Maine, hereafter cited as MHS.

8 *Kennebunk Gazette*, 25 October 1828.

9 *Ibid.*, 14 March, 26 September, 29 November 1829.

10 *Ibid.*, 23 April 1832.

11 Impost Book 1800-1867, Records of the Collector of Customs, Kennebunk, Maine, MHS.

12 *Kennebunk Gazette*, 23 February, 2, 23, 30 March, 13 April, 1, 15 June, 6, 20 July 1833; 1 February, 1, 8, 15, 29 March, 12, 19 April, 3, 17 May, 21, 28 June, 12 July, 1 November, 6, 13 December 1834.

13 William E. Barry, *Sketch of an Old River* (Boston, Alfred Mudge & Son, 1888), p. 23.

14 York Deeds,

15 Charles Bradbury, *History of Kennebunk Port From Its First Discovery by Bartholomew Gosnold, May 14, 1602 to A.D. 1837* (1837; reprint ed., Kennebunkport: Kennebunkport Historical Society, 1967), p. 216.

16 Seth E. Bryant, *A List of Vessels Built, From 1800 to 1878, District of Kennebunk* (Kennebunk: Brick Store Museum, 1950).

17 *Kennebunk Gazette*, 15 February, 4, 26 April, 19 May 1835.

18 *Ibid.*, 7 June, 15, 22 August 1835; *New York Shipping & Commercial List*, 22 August 1835.

19 Bryant, *A List of Vessels Built*.

20 *Kennebunk Gazette*, 14 January, February, July 1837.

21 Blunt, *Shipmaster's Assistant*, pp. 578-79.

22 *Kennebunk Gazette*, 2 September 1837.

23 *Ibid.*

24 *Ibid.*

25 Bonita A. Coro, "William Lord: Merchant and Shipowner of Kennebunk, Maine" (research paper, Munson Institute of American Maritime Studies, 1969, G.W. Blunt White Library, Mystic Seaport Museum, Mystic, Conn.), pp. 7, 9, 24, 26, 49, 63, 142.

26 Bryant, *A List of Vessels Built*.

CHAPTER THREE
The Brig *Swiss Boy*

1 William E. Barry, *Sketch of an Old River* (Boston: Alfred Mudge & Son, 1888), p. 6.

2 Cleaves to Lord, 1857, William Lord Collection, Brick Store Museum, Kennebunk, Maine , hereafter cited as LPBSM.

3 *Kennebunk Gazette*, 6 January 1838.

4 Barry, *Sketch of an Old River*, p. 6.

5 *Kennebunk Gazette*, 3 February 1838.

6 *Ibid.*, 13 May 1838.

7 George R. Taylor, *The Transportation Revolution, 1815-1860* (New York: Rinehart & Co., 1951), p. 185.

8 Joseph Blunt, *The Shipmaster's Assistant and Commercial Digest* (New York: Harper & Brothers, 1853), pp. 797-803.

9 William H. Rowe, *The Maritime History of Maine* (New York: W.W. Norton, 1948), p. 115.

10 Taylor, *Transportation Revolution*, p. 184.

11 *Ibid.*, p. 184.

12 Rowe, *Maritime History of Maine*, p. 117.

13 Blunt, *Shipmaster's Assistant*, p. 801.

14 *Ibid.*, pp. 806-07.

15 *Ibid.*, p. 801.

16 *Kennebunk Gazette*, September 1838.

17 Blaisdell to McCulloch, 12 September 1838, LPBSM.

18 Blunt, *Shipmaster's Assistant*, pp. 556-64.

19 Blaisdell to McCulloch, 7 November 1838, LPBSM.

20 *Kennebunk Gazette*, 16 March 1839; *New York Shipping & Commercial List*, 13 February 1839; J. R. McCulloch, *A Dictionary, Practical, Theoretical, and Historical, of Commerce and Commercial Navigation*, 2 vols., (Philadelphia: Grey and Hart, 1847), 1:174.

21 Bonita A. Coro, "William Lord: Merchant and Shipowner of Kennebunk, Maine" (research paper, Munson Insittute of American Maritime Studies, 1969, G.W. Blunt White Library, Mystic Seaport Museum, Mystic, Conn.), pp. 7, 9, 24, 26, 49, 63, 142.

22 Tobias Lord to William Lord, 8 March 1839, LPBSM.

23 *Ibid.*

24 *Kennebunk Gazette*, 3 August 1839.

25 Brig *Swiss Boy*, Crew List, 7 March 1839, Records of the Collector of Customs, New York, Bureau of Customs, Record Group 36, National Archives, Washington, D.C.

26 *New York Shipping & Commercial List*, 18 September 1839; Tobias Lord to William Lord, 17 September 1839, LPBSM.

27 Tobias Lord to William Lord, 11 December 1839, LPBSM.

28 *Ibid.*

29 Callender to Lord, 25 December 1839, LPBSM.

CHAPTER FOUR
An Unfortunate and Troublesome Business

1 Joseph Blunt, *The Shipmaster's Assistant and Commercial Digest* (New York: Harper & Brothers, 1853), p. 221.

2 *Ibid.*, p. 212.

3 *Ibid.*, pp. 214-23.
4 *Kennebunk Gazette*, 25 January 1840.
5 *Ibid.*, 1 February 1840.
6 Wainwright to Lord, January 1840, Lord Papers, Brick Store Museum, Kennebunk, Maine, hereafter cited as LPBSM.
7 Francis Dixon, *The Law of Shipping* (New York: 1859), p. 544.
8 Blunt, *Shipmaster's Assistant*, pp. 234-37.
9 Dixon, *Law of Shipping*, pp. 604-05.
10 Callender to Lord, 6 February 1840, LPBSM.
11 Callender to Lord, 17 February 1840, LPBSM.
12 Cotting to Callender, 29 July 1840, LPBSM.
13 *Ibid.*
14 Blunt, *Shipmaster's Assistant*, p. 262.
15 Cotting to Callender, 29 July 1840, LPBSM.
16 *Kennebunk Gazette*, 28 March 1840.
17 *Ibid.*, 25 April 1840.
18 Callender to Lord, 28 April 1840, LPBSM.
19 *Kennebunk Gazette*, 23 May 1840.
20 McCulloch to Lord, 25 May 1840, LPBSM.
21 Callender to Lord, 28 April 1840, LPBSM.
22 *Kennebunk Gazette*, 1 August 1840.
23 Callender to Lord, 20 January 1841, LPBSM.
24 Callender to Lord, 25 January 1841, LPBSM.
25 *Kennebunk Gazette*, 30 January, 27 February 1841.
26 *Ibid.*, 27 March 1841.
27 *Ibid.*, 10 April 1841.
28 Callender to Lord, 11 May 1841, LPBSM.
29 Brig *Swiss Boy*, Papers, 1841, LPBSM.
30 *Kennebunk Gazette*, 25 July 1841.
31 John W. Crackly to Lord, 21 July 1841, LPBSM.
32 *Kennebunk Gazette*, 25 September 1841.
33 Blunt, *Shipmaster's Assistant*, pp. 606-07.
34 *Ibid.*, pp. 734-35.
35 *Ibid.*, p. 735.
36 *Kennebunk Gazette*, 27 November, 18 December 1841; 19 February 1842.
37 Callender to Lord, 17 September 1842, LPBSM; *New York Shipping & Commercial List*, September 1842.
38 *New York Shipping & Commercial List*, 16 September 1843; Brig *Swiss Boy*, Papers, 1843, LPBSM.
39 Blunt, *Shipmaster's Assistant*, pp. 674-76.
40 Dixon, *Law of Shipping*, p. 226.

41 Blunt, *Shipmaster's Assistant*, p. 279.

42 Blaisdell to Lord, 12 August 1844, LPBSM.

43 *New York Shipping & Commercial List*, 16 October 1844; Brig *Swiss Boy*, Business Papers, 1844, LPBSM.

44 *New York Shipping & Commercial List*, 18 June 1845; Callender to Lord, 24 April 1845, LPBSM.

45 Blaisdell to Adam McCulloch & Co., 15 June 1845, LPBSM.

46 Callender to Lord, 24 April 1845, LPBSM.

47 Callender to Lord, 21 June 1845, LPBSM.

48 McCulloch to Lord, 24 June 1845, LPBSM.

CHAPTER FIVE
Another Venture

1 Bark *Abbot Lord*, Registration, abstracts from the collection of the Peabody Museum, Salem, Massachusetts.

2 C.C. Lord, *A History of the Descendants of Nathan Lord of Ancient Kittery, Maine* (Concord: Rumford Press, 1912), p. 137.

3 Bark *Abbot Lord*, Registration.

4 Bark *Abbot Lord*, Freight List, New Orleans, 25 November 1845, Coll. 140, Lord Collection, G.W. Blunt Library, Mystic Seaport Museum, Mystic, Connecticut, hereafter cited as Coll. 140, MSM.

5 Blaisdell to Daniel W. Lord, 26 November 1845, Coll. 140, MSM.

6 Blaisdell to Daniel W. Lord, 13 April 1846, Coll. 140, MSM.

7 William H. Rowe, *The Maritime History of Maine* (New York: W.W. Norton, 1948), p. 117.

8 Blaisdell to Daniel W. Lord, 19 April 1846, Coll. 140, MSM.

9 Joseph Blunt, *The Shipmaster's Assistant and Commercial Digest* (New York: Harper & Brothers, 1853), p. 403.

10 Blaisdell to Daniel W. Lord, 25 April 1846, Coll. 140, MSM.

11 Blaisdell to Daniel W. Lord, 9 May 1846, Coll. 140, MSM.

12 Blunt, *Shipmaster's Assistant*, p. 19.

13 *Ibid*.

14 Blaisdell to Daniel W. Lord, 2 June 1846, Coll. 140, MSM.

15 Blunt, *Shipmaster's Assistant*, pp. 17, 142.

16 Robert Towne to Daniel W. Lord, 3 June 1846, Coll. 140, MSM.

17 Acter P. Patterson to Daniel W. Lord, 11 June 1846, Coll. 140, MSM.

18 Patterson to Daniel W. Lord, 11 July 1846, Coll 140, MSM.

19 Patterson to Daniel W. Lord, 13 July 1846, Coll 140, MSM.

20 Thomas R. Jones to Daniel W. Lord, 12 August 1846, Coll. 140, MSM.

21 Patterson to Daniel W. Lord, 17 August 1846, Coll. 140, MSM.

22 Callender to William Lord, 24 June 1846, Lord Papers, Brick Store Museum, Kennebunk, Maine, hereafter cited as LPBSM.

23 Callender to William Lord, 6 July 1846, LPBSM.

24 Seth E. Bryant, *A List of Vessels Built, From 1800 to 1878, District of Kennebunk* (Kennebunk: Brick Store Museum, 1950); Bark *Francis Watts*, Construction Invoices, LPBSM.

25 Margaret J. Thompson, *Captain Nathaniel Lord Thompson of Kennebunk, Maine and The Ships He Built, 1811-1889* (Boston: Charles E. Lauriat Co., 1937), pp. 15-16.

26 Bark *Francis Watts*, Construction Invoices, LPBSM; the names of the men read like a Kennebunk directory: William Stevens, Benjamin Sandborn, Philip Brown, Thomas Low, Jacob Towne, Israel Rhodes, Nahum Brown, Jason Brown, Andrew Robinson, Joseph Durrell, Nathan Boston, Cyrus Boston, Edmund Wells, William Mitchell, Eben Mitchell, Ivory Wormwood, Charles Stevens, and Hugh Towne.

27 *Ibid.*

28 Bryant, *A List of Vessels*.

29 Thomas R. Jones to Daniel W. Lord, 22 August 1846, Coll. 140, MSM.

30 Daniel W. Lord to Blaisdell, 31 August 1846, Coll. 140, MSM.

31 Blaisdell to William Lord, 12 October 1846, LPBSM.

32 Perkins to William Lord, October 1846, LPBSM.

33 Blaisdell to Daniel W. Lord, 3 November 1846, Coll. 140, MSM.

34 Hajo Holborn, *A History of Modern Germany, 1840-1945* (New York: Alfred A. Knopf, 1969), pp. 14, 123.

35 Blaisdell to Daniel W. Lord, 27 December 1846, Coll. 140, MSM.

36 Blunt, *Shipmaster's Assistant*, p. 42.

37 Bark *Francis Watts*, Papers and Accounts, LPBSM.

38 Blaisdell to Daniel W. Lord, 22 February 1847, Coll. 140, MSM.

39 John A. Garraty, *The American Nation to 1877, A History of the United States* (New York: Harper & Row, 1966), p. 339.

40 Blaisdell to Daniel W. Lord, 23 April 1847, Coll. 140, MSM.

41 Blunt, *Shipmaster's Assistant*, pp. 453-55.

42 Blaisdell to Daniel W. Lord, 11 May 1847, Coll. 140, MSM.

43 Blunt, *Shipmaster's Assistant*, p. 453.

44 Blaisdell to Daniel W. Lord, 20 June 1847, Coll. 140, MSM.

45 Justin Winsor, *The Memorial History of Boston*, 4 vols., (Boston: James R. Osgood & Co., 1881),4:232-33.

46 Blunt, *Shipmaster's Assistant*, pp. 456-57.

47 Blaisdell to Daniel W. Lord, 21 June 1847, Coll. 140, MSM.

48 Herndon & Company to Daniel W. Lord, 26 June 1847, Coll. 140, MSM.

49 N.& C.B. Dana to Daniel W. Lord, 28 June 1847, Coll. 140, MSM; *Boston Shipping List*, 30 June 1847.

50 Blaisdell to Daniel W. Lord, 2 July 1847, Coll. 140, MSM.

CHAPTER SIX
The Ship *Mount Washington*

1 Ship *Mount Washington*, Construction Invoices, William Lord Papers, Brick Store Museum, Kennebunk, Maine, hereafter cited as LPBSM.

2 Barry to Lord, 1846, LPBSM.

3 *Old Ship Portraits of Kennebunk* (Kennebunk: Brick Store Museum, 1943).

4 Ship *Mount Washington*, Construction Invoices, LPBSM.

5 Ship *Mount Washington*, Certificate of Registry, 1847, Records of the Collector of Customs, Kennebunk, Maine, Bureau of Customs, Record Group 36, National Archives, Washington, D.C., hereafter cited as NA.

6 *Ibid.*

7 John G. B. Hutchins, *The American Maritime Industries and Public Policy, 1789-1914* (Cambridge: Harvard University Press, 1941), pp. 264-65.

8 *Ibid.* p. 239.

9 Ship *Mount Washington*, Construction Invoices, LPBSM.

10 Blaisdell to Lord, 22 January 1848, LPBSM.

11 Ship *Mount Washington*, Papers and Accounts, 1848, LPBSM.

12 Blaisdell to Lord, 12 February 1848, LPBSM.

13 Blaisdell to Lord, 24 February 1848, LPBSM.

14 Barry to Lord, 1848, LPBSM.

15 Joseph Blunt, *The Shipmaster's Assistant and Commercial Digest* (New York: Harper & Brothers, 1853), pp. 201-02.

16 Ship *Mount Washington*, Papers and Accounts, 1848, LPBSM.

17 Blaisdell to Lord, 27 March 1848, LPBSM.

18 Hartley Lord to William Lord, 23 March 1848, LPBSM.

19 Hartley Lord to William Lord, 28 March 1848, LPBSM.

20 Blaisdell to Lord, 29 March 1848, LPBSM.

21 Blunt, *Shipmaster's Assistant*, pp. 41, 47.

22 Blaisdell to Lord, 20 May 1848, LPBSM.

23 Shepard B. Clough, et. al., *A History of the Western World*, 2nd ed., 2 vols. (Lexington: D.C. Heath & Company, 1969), 2:1028, 1043.

24 Blunt, *Shipmaster's Assistant*, pp. 734-48.

25 Blaisdell to Lord, 21 June 1848, LPBSM.

26 American Consul at Belfast, Ireland, to William Lord, 12 July 1847, LPBSM.

27 Ship *Mount Washington*, Papers and Accounts, 1848, LPBSM.

28 Blaisdell to Lord, 5 July 1848, LPBSM.

29 Francis Dixon, *The Law of Shipping* (New York: 1859), p. 226.

30 Callender to Lord, 31 July 1848, LPBSM.

31 Barry to Lord, 8 October 1848, LPBSM.

32 Ship *Mount Washington*, Papers and Accounts, 1848, LPBSM.

33 See U.S. Coast Survey, "Reconnoissance of the Passes of the Delta of the Mississippi, Louisiana, Showing the Changes Since 1839, 1852," in *Report of the Superintendant of the Coast Survey Showing the Progress of the Survey During the Year 1852* (Washington, D.C.: Robert Armstrong, 1853).

34 Blaisdell to Lord, 27 December 1848, LPBSM.

CHAPTER SEVEN
Home the Hard Way

1 Joseph Blunt, *The Shipmaster's Assistant and Commercial Digest* (New York: Harper & Brothers, 1853), pp. 159-60.

2 Blaisdell to Lord, 3 January 1849, Lord Papers, Brick Store Museum, Kennebunk, Maine, hereafter cited as LPBSM.

3 Mitchell to Mitchell, 3 January 1849, courtesy of Joyce Butler.

4 Blaisdell to Lord, 5 January 1849, LPBSM.

5 Blunt, *Shipmaster's Assistant*, p. 11.

6 Blaisdell to Lord, 24 February 1849, LPBSM.

7 *Ibid.*

8 *Ibid.*

9 Hartley Lord to William Lord, 26 March 1849, LPBSM.

10 Ship *Mount Washington*, Papers and Accounts, 1849, LPBSM.

11 Stan Hugill, *Sailortown* (New York: E.P. Dutton & Co., Inc., 1967), p. 96.

12 Blunt, *Shipmaster's Assistant*, pp. 615, 670.

13 Ship *Mount Washington*, Papers and Accounts, 1849, LPBSM.

14 Ship *Mount Washington*, Passenger List, 2 July 1849, National Archives, Washington, D.C.

15 Blaisdell to Lord, 5 May 1849, LPBSM.

16 Blaisdell to Lord, 2 July 1849, LPBSM.

17 Callender to Lord, 2 July 1849, LPBSM.

18 Hartley Lord to William Lord, 4 July 1849, LPBSM.

19 Hartley Lord to William Lord, 13 July 1849, LPBSM.

20 Callender to Lord, 21 July 1849, LPBSM.

21 Hartley Lord to William Lord, 27 July 1849, LPBSM.

22 Ship *Mount Washington*, Papers and Accounts, 1849, LPBSM.

23 Callender to Lord, 23 August 1849, LPBSM.

24 Callender to Lord, 24 August 1849, LPBSM.

25 Hartley Lord to William Lord, 30 August 1849, LPBSM.

26 Callender to Lord, 31 August 1849, LPBSM.

27 C.B. Williams to Lord, 21 September 1849, LPBSM.

28 Blaisdell to Lord, 26 October 1849, LPBSM.

29 Blunt, *Shipmaster's Assistant*, p. 12.
30 Callender to Lord, 20 November 1849, LPBSM.
31 Ship *Mount Washington*, Classification of Averages, 1850, LPBSM.
32 Blaisdell to Lord, 29 November 1849, LPBSM.
33 Ship *Mount Washington*, Papers and Accounts, 1849, LPBSM.
34 Stone to Lord, 2 December 1849, LPBSM.
35 Blaisdell to Lord, 4 December 1849, LPBSM.

CHAPTER EIGHT
A Duty to Take Charge

1 Blaisdell to Lord, 28 June 1850, Lord Papers, Brick Store Museum, Kennebunk, Maine, hereafter cited as LPBSM.
2 Callender to Lord, 2 July 1850, LPBSM.
3 William E. Barry, *Sketch of an Old River* (Boston: Alfred Mudge & Son, 1888), p. 6.
4 Correspondence with Richard E. Wells of Sooke, British Columbia, March 1980. In January 1859, while carrying lumber from Oregon, she sprang a severe leak, causing her master to seek shelter in an inlet on the west coast of Vancouver Island. The captain intended to beach the brig in an attempt to make repairs, but he never got the chance. The day after coming to anchor the *Swiss Boy* fell prey to local Indians, who boarded and pillaged her. The crew escaped uninjured, and made their way to San Francisco. The old brig eventually sank at her anchor.
5 Seth E. Bryant, *A List of Vessels Built, From 1800 to 1878, District of Kennebunk* (reprint, Kennebunk: Brick Store Museum, 1950).
6 Lord to Stone, 22 November 1850, LPBSM.
7 Bryant, *A List of Vessels.*
8 Blaisdell to Lord, 31 December 1850, LPBSM.
9 Hartley Lord to William Lord, 13 January 1851, LPBSM.
10 Blaisdell to Lord, 2 January 1851, LPBSM.
11 Joseph Blunt, *The Shipmaster's Assistant and Commercial Digest* (New York: Harper & Brothers, 1853), p. 11.
12 Bryant, *A List of Vessels.*
13 Blaisdell to Lord, 15 January 1851, LPBSM.
14 Blaisdell to Lord, 24 January 1851, LPBSM.
15 Hartley Lord to William Lord, 29 March 1851, LPBSM.
16 Blunt, *Shipmaster's Assistant*, pp. 663-64.
17 Lord to Blaisdell, 10 February 1851, LPBSM.
18 Ship *Mount Washington*, Papers and Accounts, 1851, LPBSM.
19 *Ibid.*

20 Callender to Lord, 11 April 1851, LPBSM.
21 Ship *Mount Washington*, Papers and Accounts, 1851, LPBSM.
22 Margaret Jefferds Thompson, *Captain Nathaniel Lord Thompson of Kennebunk, Maine and the Ships He Built 1811-1889*, (Boston: Charles E. Lauriat Co., 1937), pp. 31-34.
23 Blaisdell to Lord, 10 April 1851, LPBSM.
24 Blaisdell to Lord, 30 June 1851, LPBSM.
25 Ship *Mount Washington*, Papers and Accounts, 1851, LPBSM.
26 Blaisdell to Lord, 9 July 1851, LPBSM.
27 Blunt, *Shipmaster's Assistant*, p. 271.
28 Blaisdell to Lord, 21 July 1851, LPBSM.
29 Blaisdell to Lord, 23 July 1851, LPBSM.
30 Blaisdell to Lord, 25 July 1851, LPBSM.
31 Blaisdell to Lord, 29 July 1851, LPBSM.
32 Blaisdell to Lord, 6 August 1851, LPBSM.

CHAPTER NINE
An Unfortunate Business

1 Blaisdell to Lord, 27 August 1851, Lord Papers, Brick Store Museum, Kennebunk, Maine, hereafter cited as LPBSM.
2 Hartley Lord to William Lord, 13 September 1851, LPBSM.
3 Margaret Jefferds Thompson, *Captain Nathaniel Lord Thompson of Kennebunk, Maine and the Ships He Built 1811-1889* (Boston: Charles E. Lauriat Co., 1937), p. 30.
4 Callender to Lord, 17 September 1851, LPBSM.
5 Blaisdell to Lord, 17 September 1851, LPBSM.
6 Blaisdell to Lord, 19 September 1851, LPBSM.
7 Blaisdell to Lord, 20 September 1851, LPBSM.
8 Callender to Lord, 23 September 1851, LPBSM.
9 Tobias Lord to William Lord, 25 September 1851, LPBSM.
10 Blaisdell to Lord, September 1851, LPBSM.
11 Blaisdell to Callender, 26 September 1851, LPBSM.
12 Blaisdell to Lord, 27 September 1851, LPBSM.
13 Joseph Blunt, *The Shipmaster's Assistant and Commercial Digest* (New York: Harper & Brothers, 1853), p. 21.
14 "Wrecks, Wrecking, Wreckers, and Wreckees, On Florida Reef," *The Merchants' Magazine and Commercial Review*, conducted by Freeman Hunt, 6 (1842):349-54.
15 *Ibid.*, 18 (1848):553.

16 Blaisdell to Lord, 8 October 1851, LPBSM.

17 Blaisdell to Lord, 11 October 1851, LPBSM.

18 Blaisdell to Lord, 24 October 1851, LPBSM.

19 Blaisdell to Lord, 26 October 1851, LPBSM.

20 Ship *Mount Washington*, abstract of salvage trial, made from original documents in the Federal Archives and Records Center, East Point, Georgia; Joseph T. Durkin, *Stephen R. Mallory: Confederate Navy Chief* (Chapel Hill: University of North Carolina, 1954), pp. 9, 19, 31-32.

21 Blaisdell to Lord, 6 November 1851, LPBSM.

22 Callender to Lord, 24 November 1851, LPBSM.

CHAPTER TEN
Bordeaux

1 "Commercial Cities of Europe—Bordeaux," *The Merchants' Magazine and Commercial Review*, conducted by Freeman Hunt, 18 (April 1848):376-81.

2 Blaisdell to Lord, 30 December 1851, Lord Papers, Brick Store Museum, Kennebunk, Maine, hereafter cited as LPBSM.

3 Joseph Blunt, *The Shipmaster's Assistant and Commercial Digest* (New York: Harper & Brothers, 1853), p. 255.

4 *Ibid.*

5 Blaisdell to Lord, 5 January 1852, LPBSM.

6 Blunt, *Shipmaster's Assistant*, p. 259.

7 Blaisdell to Lord, 14 January 1852, LPBSM.

8 Blaisdell to Lord, 26 January 1852, LPBSM.

9 Blaisdell to Lord, 10 February 1852, LPBSM.

10 Blaisdell to Lord, 16 February 1852, LPBSM.

11 Blunt, *Shipmaster's Assistant*, pp. 258-59.

12 *Ibid.*, pp. 260-61.

13 Blaisdell to Lord, 24 February 1852, LPBSM.

14 Shepard B. Clough et. al., *A History of the Western World*, 2nd. ed., 2 vols. (Lexington, Mass.: D. C. Heath & Company, 1969), 2:1020-21.

15 Ship *Mount Washington*, Papers and Accounts, 1852, LPBSM.

16 Constantine to Lord, 6 April 1852, LPBSM.

17 Blaisdell to Lord, 31 March 1852, LPBSM.

CHAPTER ELEVEN
A Change for Luck's Sake

1 Blaisdell to Lord, 6 June 1852, Lord Papers, Brick Store Museum, Kennebunk, Maine, hereafter cited as LPBSM.

2 Norman E. Borden, Jr., *Dear Sarah: New England Ice to the Orient and Other Incidents from the Journals of Captain Charles Edward Barry to His Wife* (Freeport: The Bond Wheelwright Co., 1966), pp. 167, 181-83.

3 Daniel Remick, *History of Kennebunk From Its Earliest Settlement to 1890* (Kennebunk: Carrie E. Remick, 1911.), p. 507.

4 Diary of Andrew Walker, vol. 1, p. 27, Kennebunk Free Library, Kennebunk, Maine.

5 Blaisdell to Lord, 23 June 1852, LPBSM.

6 "The Cotton Trade," *The Merchants' Magazine and Commercial Review*, conducted by Freeman Hunt, 37 (November 1857):558, 560.

7 "The Cotton Trade," *The Merchants' Magazine and Commercial Review* 25 (December 1851):661, 664.

8 Diary of Andrew Walker, 1:27.

9 "Commercial Statistics," *The Merchants' Magazine and Commercial Review* 23 (December 1850):539; 29 (November 1853):627.

10 Blaisdell to Lord, 25 June 1852, LPBSM.

11 Hartley Lord to William Lord, 3 July 1852, LPBSM.

12 Blaisdell to Lord, 12 July 1852, LPBSM.

13 John G. B. Hutchins, *American Maritime Industries and Public Policy, 1789-1914* (Cambridge: Harvard University Press, 1941), p. 264.

14 Thomas W. Murphy, Jr., *The Landing—A Remembrance of Her People and Shipyards* (Kennebunk: Thomas Murphy, 1977), pp. 49-50.

15 Diary of Andrew Walker, 1:112.

16 *Ibid.*, 1:9.

17 *Ibid.*, 1:27.

18 Blaisdell to Lord, 18 July 1852, LPBSM.

19 Goodwin to Lord, 20 July 1852, LPBSM.

20 Blaisdell to Lord, 22 July 1852, LPBSM.

21 Lord to Goodwin, 17 August 1852, LPBSM.

22 "The Cotton Trade," *The Merchants' Magazine and Commercial Review* 25 (December 1851):667; 37 (November 1857):558.

23 *Ibid.*, 37 (November 1857):558.

24 *Ibid.*, 25 (December 1851):667.

25 *Ibid.*, 26 (October 1852):433.

CHAPTER TWELVE
The Master at Home

1 Seth E. Bryant, *A List of Vessels Built, From 1800 to 1878, District of Kennebunk* (reprint, Kennebunk: Brick Store Museum, 1950).

2 "The Cotton Trade," *The Merchants' Magazine and Commercial Review*, conducted by Freeman Hunt, 37 (November 1857):558.

3 Diary of Andrew Walker, vol. 2, p. 166, Kennebunk Free Library, Kennebunk, Maine.

4 Lord to Goodwin, 17 January 1853, Lord Papers, Brick Store Museum, Kennebunk, Maine, hereafter cited as LPBSM.

5 Goodwin to Lord, 11, 18 March 1853, LPBSM.

6 Goodwin to Lord, 29 March 1853, LPBSM.

7 Lord to Goodwin, 11 May 1853, LPBSM.

8 Blaisdell to Lord, 22 August 1853, LPBSM.

9 Goodwin to Lord, 30 May 1853, LPBSM.

10 Lord to Goodwin, 17 May 1853, LPBSM.

11 Goodwin to Lord, 9 June 1853, LPBSM.

12 Lord to Goodwin, 31 May 1853, LPBSM.

13 Diary of Andrew Walker, 2:166.

14 Blaisdell to Lord, 6 October 1853, LPBSM.

15 Blaisdell to Lord, 4 November 1853, LPBSM.

16 Blaisdell to Lord, 27 November 1853, LPBSM.

17 Bryant, A List of Vessels Built.

18 Blaisdell to Lord, 16 January 1854, LPBSM.

19 Charles W. Morgan, *Shipbuilding on the Kennebunk: The Closing Chapter* (Kennebunkport: Kennebunkport Historical Society, 1970), p. 12.

20 Ship *Abby Brown*, abstract of Certificate of Registry, 1854, Records of the Collector of Customs, Kennebunk, Maine, Bureau of Customs, Record Group 36, National Archives, Washington, D. C., hereafter cited as NA.

21 Davis to Lord, 4 October 1853, LPBSM.

22 Ship *Mount Washington*, Certificate of Registry, Records of the Collector of Customs, Kennebunk, Maine, Record Group 36, NA.

23 Blaisdell to Lord, 15 February 1854, LPBSM.

24 Maling to Callender, January 1854, LPBSM.

25 Blaisdell to Lord, 18 March 1854, LPBSM.

26 Callender to Lord, 12 August 1854, LPBSM.

27 Morrill to Callender, various dates, 1854-55, LPBSM.

28 Blaisdell to Lord, 6 June 1855, LPBSM.

29 Diary of Andrew Walker, 3:113, 153.

30 "The Cotton Trade," *The Merchants' Magazine and Commercial Review* 37 (November 1857):558, 629.

31 Bryant, *A List of Vessels Built*.
32 Blaisdell to Lord, 9 August 1856, LPBSM.
33 Diary of Andrew Walker, 3:194.
34 *Ibid.*, 3:227.
35 Blaisdell to Lord, 4 March 1857, LPBSM.
36 Blaisdell to Lord, 21 March 1857, LPBSM.
37 John A. Garraty, *The American Nation to 1877, A History of the United States* (New York: Harper & Row, 1966), p. 350.
38 Blaisdell to Lord, 22 February 1858, LPBSM.
39 Blaisdell to Lord, 19 March 1858, LPBSM.

CHAPTER THIRTEEN
The Final Years

1 Bark *Jacob Merrill*, abstract of Certificate of Registry, 1858, Records of the Collector of Customs, Kennebunk, Maine, Bureau of Customs, Record Group 36, National Archives, Washington, D. C.
2 Vital Records, town of Kennebunkport, Maine.
3 *Ibid*.
4 Carl Cutler, vessel registration file, G. W. Blunt White Library, Mystic Seaport Museum, Mystic, Connecticut.
5 Diary of Andrew Walker, vol. 4, pp. 89, 115, Kennebunk Free Library, Kennebunk, Maine.
6 Hartley Lord to William Lord, January 1859, Lord Papers, Brick Store Museum, Kennebunk, Maine, hereafter cited as LPBSM.
7 Lord to Blaisdell, 3 February 1859, LPBSM.
8 Blaisdell to Lord, 5 February 1859, LPBSM.
9 Blaisdell to Lord, 20 December 1859, LPBSM.
10 Blaisdell to Lord, 7 January 1860, LPBSM.
11 *Boston Shipping List* and *New York Shipping & Commercial List*, 1860-62.
12 Diary of Andrew Walker, 1:16-17.
13 William H. Rowe, *The Maritime History of Maine* (New York: W.W. Norton, 1948), pp. 188-89.
14 Robert G. Albion, et. al., *New England and the Sea* (Mystic: Mystic Seaport Museum, 1972), pp. 161-63.
15 Charles S. Morgan, *Shipbuilding on the Kennebunk: The Final Chapter* (Kennebunkport: Kennebunkport Historical Society, 1970), p. 7.
16 Rowe, *Maritime History of Maine*, pp. 208, 240.
17 Morgan, *Shipbuilding on the Kennebunk*, pp. 5-6.

Index

From W.H. Rosser & J.F. Imray, *North Atlantic Directory*
(London, 1869)

NORTH ATLA[N]

HUDSON'S BAY

DAVIS STRAIT

NEW SOUTH WALES

Hudson Strait

Ungava B.

EAST MAIN

LABRADOR

Str. of Belle Isle

BRITISH POSSESSIONS

James B.

L. Superior

Anticosti

G. of St Lawrence

NEWFOUNL[AND]

St. John

L. Michigan

L. Huron

L. Ontario

R. St Lawrence

Quebec

St. Johns

Breton I.

C. Race

G. of St. [...]
Newfoundl[and]

L. Erie

Portland

Halifax

Sable I.

New York

Boston

C. Sable

C. Cod

Long I.

Philadelphia

UNITED

WASHINGTON

Delaware R.

From the Gulf of Mexico

STATES

Richmond

Chesapeake B.

From the Wes[t]

From U[...]
New

C. Hatteras

C. Lookout

From the Antilles

Bermudas

Savannah

Charleston H.

Mobile

Isths. of the Mississippi

Galveston

Tampa B.

G. of Florida

WEST

To United States

Bahamas

Southern route from Engla[nd]

G. of MEXICO

Tampico

INDIAN

To the West Indian Isla[nds]

Vera Cruz

Bay of Honduras

Haiti

Porto Rico

Belize

CENTRAL

Jamaica

To the Antilles

ISLANDS

C. Gracias a Dios

CARIBBEAN SEA

AMERICA

Leeward Is

Tobago

Guatemala

Leon

G. of Darien

Trinidad

Quibo

Gulf of Panama

NEW GRANADA

Maracaybo

R. Orinoco

R. Surinam

VENEZUELA

Essequibo

Cayenne

PACIFIC

GUYANA

OCEAN

SOUTH

Galapagos Is.

AMERICA

Guayaquil

R. Am[...]